Copyright @2021 by Arthur Richter

All rights reserved. No part of this book may be reproduced in any form or by any electronic or mechanical means, including information storage and retrieval systems, without permission in writing from the publisher, except by reviewers, who may quote brief passages in a review.

This publication contains the opinions and ideas of its author. It is intended to provide helpful and informative material on the subjects addressed in the publication. The author and publisher specifically disclaim all responsibility for any liability, loss or risk, personal or otherwise, which is incurred as a consequence, directly or indirectly, of the use and application of any of the contents of this book.

WORKBOOK PRESS LLC
187 E Warm Springs Rd,
Suite B285, Las Vegas, NV 89119, USA

Website: https://workbookpress.com/
Hotline: 1-888-818-4856
Email: admin@workbookpress.com

Ordering Information:
Quantity sales. Special discounts are available on quantity purchases by corporations, associations, and others.
For details, contact the publisher at the address above.

ISBN-13:   978-1-954753-85-3 (Paperback Version)
            978-1-954753-86-0 (Digital Version)

REV. DATE: 08/04/2021

ARTHUR RICHTER

Chapter 1

My name is Daryl Henderson otherwise known as Dice. I'm a 30-year-old struggling private detective living in California, managing to get to my office late as usual to do what I do best, prying into the other people's lives.

* * * *

"Well good morning Miss Miners." I greeted her saying entering my office. Seeing her sitting in her usual spot behind the reception desk, looking busy putting on her face.

"Yeah, good morning . . ." Doris replied without stopping applying her makeup replying back saying." Coffee's on if you want some."

"I'll take it in my office." I walked by her saying. Stopping before opening the closed door to my office to get a photogenic gander at her side profile.

Noticing that she was looking extremely gorgeous in the morning but, that's what I hired her for. She's what every successful private eye need greeting him and any potential clients in the morning. If nothing as a status symbol for potential clients to say.

"This guy is good at what he's doing." And she surely provided all that insensitive, and more.

Not only adding to what my dingy office needed but, what better way to brighten not only me but, the place up. Than having a gorgeous secretary greeting one with more than a smile.

Giving the place a status symbol that she was working for the best money can afford, right? Where she not only illuminated the place but, also got my adrenaline all hyped up.

With me knowing of her potential to be able too, keep any potential clients occupied for hours.

Just fantasizing about her.

The way I figure it. It pays to cover all the bases where making money was concerned, and that's what I was in business to do.

I no sooner walked in, and sat behind my desk and reached for the file I left on top of my desk. Than Doris came in with my coffee.

I was in the process of going over the file of one Mrs. Sandy Peterson to update her going about living her daily life.

"Not bad . . ." Doris admired my work saying. Standing behind me looking over my shoulder." So this is what you do all day long. Taking pictures of women sunbathing . . . You must really enjoy your work immensely?

"It's a hard burdensome job but, someone has to do it. Besides if the pay is good that makes it even more bearable. You know how it is. If you see one, you saw them all but, only shaped differently.

Her husband wants me to catch her fooling around on him. If she is, she's being very discreet about it where her husband isn't.

I'm glad that it isn't his wife paying me to investigate him. I wouldn't be able to afford to pay you this week, and we would both be out on the street."

"Isn't that the way it always is? "

"Not always but, in this case it is but, you know. Maybe I've been in the business to long. I've this gut feeling that she isn't all that virtuously loyal, and she's just being a lot sneaker about it but, I'm in no rush. If I'm lucky, I might even break even this month. "

"Are you quite sure it's stemming from there, as well as from your greed?"

"Yes, I'm sure. Well, greed might have something to do with it. How else could I afford the privilege of paying you that elaborate salary I'm paying you?

Beside I'm sort of establishing a resentment toward her husband. For subjecting me to the abuse of having to just spy on her.

That woman has a lot going for her. That's she's hiding from me, under those scanty bathing suits she keeps exposing me to.

I'm telling you that one is, up to no good, and it's getting frustrating as hell. I mean a guy can only stand so much . . .

Besides I'm beginning to believe that her husband is ling through his teeth about her cheating on him, or he's telling the truth, and he's paying me to keep away from her.

Need I say more? I mean I'm a man of very little moral character. Having very immoral thoughts. That seems that's all that woman wants to wear, and as you can see she wears very little of them to cover herself up.

"You know boss there's an old saying. It takes a woman to get close to another woman. Men don't usually think the way women due. Maybe this need another women touch? "

"Yes, I know, and I've been seriously thinking about it but, that would ruin my chances of finding out for myself, now wouldn't it?

If she's fooling around I don't want to miss out on the benefits I might be able to gain if I approach her right . . .

"You men are all alike . . ."

"Yeah, aren't we though? But, it pays in my racket to maintain good public relations. Advertising costs, so why should I pay when I can get it free of charge?

She's not about to forget who it was that got the goods on her. Catching her is only going to be half the adventure.

The rest is going to fall on her as too how she's going to convince me not to tell . . . And I do have a loyalty to my client, and that hypocrite thought that I must abide by. I just can't allow myself to be compromised by dishonoring my moral character.

If you hang around long enough. Who knows you might wind up even having some of me rubbing off on you.

I don't have as much going for me as you do, and I'm always looking to lean new ways to learn the business from the bottom up and if I play my cards right. I just might get lucky enough to learn a great deal from you.

I can't always keep up maintaining this high standard of work ethics. I've to live up to the long standard that's been establish about being a private detective, and their indisputable reputation of being underhanded, and contemptible that's been earning me my impeccable reputation. That's been getting me the exuberant fee I get paid. Now don't I?

Look at me. I'm handsome, yet rough in appearance, along with being as sneaky and underhanded as they come. I'm perfect for this job wouldn't you say?

My only benefit that gives me the up upper hand is that she doesn't think like me. Where if she finds out the way I think. She'll discover that I have a one track mine, and use it against me.

So that's why I'm not getting up close and personnel where I could possibly lose out on the good thing that's been going, by keeping my distance.

Lucky for us that I've strong willpower where thinking the job comes first, or I would be in serious trouble with both you and her.

So I've been hearing from Janet. Don't think you're going to pull on me what you did with her. She brought me up to date on where your antics are concern.

She simply put that you don't have any character, and not to trust you, and to especially fall for any of your sneaky underhand tricks where women are concern.

You see what I mean? I've an outstanding reputation . . . It pays to keep up appearances. By the way you look gorgeous this morning.

Seeing how I could come up with the time, and I've saved some extra film in my camera, and the sun is shining, and as for a suit I'm sure we could up with an alternative to suffice. Where all you need her to do is to pose and the camera will do the rest.

I'm sure you can come up with something to improvise for a suit. Underneath that ever so accentuating an outfit that you are already wearing that would bring out your ravishing beauty on film . . .? I suggestively inferred hoping that she would model for me.

"Forget it! I'm not on your benefit plan. She walked out of the office saying. Swaying her hips compressed within that extra tight short skirt she was wearing.

Making me dream that I could explore the possibility of improvising a benefit plan that would be negotiable to her to change her mind.

Feeling confident that my irresistible charm will eventually wear her down, or she'll just up, and quit because she'll find my good nature intolerable.

✳ ✳ ✳ ✳

I left the office at 9:00 A.M., and arrived at the Peterson estate at 9:30 sharp. Too, take up my position in the boathouse as always. To be able too, observe her going about her daily activities.

I set up my observation base in the storage area of the boat house. Where I could see all the vital windows on the side, and the back of the main house, plus the pool area.

Where I've already previously managed bugged her phone, as well as certain other places in, and about the house.

I even had a high power telescope set up with a camera that had a telescopic lens. Too where I could see into her bedroom balcony glass doors, and downstairs into the living room. Then down at the pool site.

Mr. Norman Peterson was an accredited broker. A man in his early fifties. Where is wife Sandy, was in her middle twenty?

I couldn't see what he could see in cheating on her with another woman. Where the one he was married to was twice the woman than the one I saw him with but, who was I to judge on what's going on in that senile mind of his.

As far as I was concern I personally couldn't see ever ruining the great thing he was having going for himself where that wife of his was concern.

That women had it all, and then a lot extra. In ways I was having trouble trying not to imagine. That's how stunningly suburbs she was in appearance anyway.

In the three weeks that I've been observing his wife. There wasn't very much I didn't see, or didn't want to do more than see.

That women had the world by the ass every time she showed it. Where the entire male population was, captivate by it, every time she went out to show it off.

It didn't make sense that she would risk what she had for an affair with her husband being worth multimillions but, my client Mr. Peterson kept insisting that she was having one.

He also kept saying that she wasn't the same women he married. What women is after marrying into millions?

I guess it was even beginning to affect me as well. That I too was finding myself harboring those same feelings, and was actually trying to notice the slightest difference in her appearance, as well as her activities.

Where the only thing I had to good bye was my camera, and the pictures I been taking knowing that pictures don't lie.

Feeling subconsciously that there was something about them that weren't telling me that something that I have been missing catching but, for the damn of me. I couldn't figure out what it was.

I had her checked out by associates of mine. Nothing was abnormal about her life. Where that I wasn't already aware of.

Learning that she was a top -A-student in high school, and as I figured one of the most popular.

That she came from a middle class family environment, and was their only daughter.

That after high school she pursed a movie career but, wound up in modeling because she didn't mind exposing herself naked before a camera but, didn't want to have any parts of having personal interviews with agents, or directors.

Who would promise everything but, deliver nothing while would be expecting a lot more than she wanted to give in return.

Who eventually ended up going to work for Mr. Peterson as his private secretary. Where she finally married him a year later. Where they've been married for two, years before I became involved in their life.

Just by looking at his wife. One could tell she was one of those hard to please sex-pot. However, that did not exclude her from being on the fidget side either, where I seriously doubted that was the case.

That's where my indifference started to erupt where the two, of them was concern.

Where if that was the case where one, or the other did have some sort of sexual hang-up, and it was sex that was the problem in their marriage.

I was sure it wasn't she. Just by the way she fraternized herself when she was sunbathing, or admiring herself before her full length mirror in her bedroom. I couldn't see it being on her part.

Even though I never saw the two, of them together.

Which I thought was very strange not to at least catch him with her at home, or elsewhere while I was following, and monitoring her.

However then again if it was she that was having the problem with sex. That would explain what he was doing going out cheating on her.

What drew my attention to them having sexual problems at home? Was the fact that he was never being around at home with her, and the fact that the few times' I ran into him he was always out getting it on with women not as attractive woman than his wife?

Now that were ringing bells in my head that I was having trouble explaining to myself that would sound logical.

To which I didn't want to kill the golden goose who was handing me the golden bucks by asking him. So I just kept on focusing my attention of the wife and kept my nose pretty much out of getting too involved.

In my line of work, it didn't pay to get caught up in the middle between both the client, and the reason behind being paid to follow the one they are paying for me to you get the goods on. Especially when there's a fabulously attractive woman involved.

In my opinion Mr. Peterson couldn't have done better for himself. His wife only draw backs could have been money where he was harboring doubts about that's why she married him.

She spent it frivolously. Spending impulsively paying $1,000 for nighties. That was as thin as tissue paper. That didn't appear to be keeping her warn even on calm uncomfortably warm night. When she would stand out on her balcony modeling it for the noon on that night.

What I did discover that I consider very strange was that she wasn't one for wearing jewelry.

She wore only her wedding ring. That was a copy of the original five, karat diamond ring her husband gave her on her wedding day.

Nor was she one for the night life. Or social clam-bate. Where she loved taking long drives in her Curvet, convertible. Letting her long blond hair to flap failingly about in the breeze about her head.

I felt certain I knew where her passion did lie. She loved Art, scuba diving, even water skiing, and for that matter even football. I came to discover that she was a real football fanatic.

She also loved to tease but, doesn't every woman? The outfits she wore would enchant the devil himself.

They were so provocatively risqué but, accentuating ravishing that raveled everything but, yet not enough. She was a beautiful woman who didn't mind flaunting herself. By fragrantly putting herself on display, purposely drawing attention to her exquisiteness.

She had this beach front cottage she goes to, just to be by herself. She paid for security to preserve her privacy, and she got it.

I had to pose as one of the security officers in order too even to get close to her place. Where I did manage to bug her telephone, and plant a few more bugs throughout the place.

Just so I could monitor that she was all right when she was all alone. Wanting her confidant that her privacy was intact, you understand.

Following her around was nothing less than an ordeal. Especially having to watch she constantly changing from one, outfits into another, and then into those damn confounded bathing suits.

You have no idea how mind challenging madding that woman was on me. It was as if she was purposely trying to torment me, by turning me into some sort of pervert.

The way she appeared to be posing for every shot of the camera took. As if knowing the camera was capturing every exquisite feature of her expressionism.

Exposing just so much. To insatiably want me to capture more causing me to becoming irate as hell. When she altered her position. Infuriating the hell out of me!

I was scheduled to meet Mr. Peterson that evening at 8:00 P.M. At his office as I did the previous weeks before. To give him my report.

Where his secretary would be present to note down all that was being said, as she did the previous times previously.

"Mr. Peterson if you want my opinion you're wasting your money. I don't mind taking it but, I've to be blunt with you. She's not involved with anyone." I spoke out openly as I sat before his desk watching him reading my reports not looking very impressed by anything.

"She has to be!"

"It's none of my business but, I have to be openly honest with you in saying that I can't help but, to wonder. Why it is that you feel so positive that she is?

I have been monitoring her for over three weeks now, and I have yet to catch her even being alone with anyone else, and when she is. There's always a crowd of people somewhere close by, and she never ventures off with anyone alone.

I admit that she's one hell of a tease who loves to flirt, and gets enjoyment out of taunting any guy that takes an interest in her but, that goes for every guy who lays their eyes on her.

You already have one extremely beautiful woman. You do understand that?"

"You just do what I'm paying you to do, and I want results not your opinions! Just keep watching her.

Getting closer dammit! I want to know when she passes gas . . .! It's not your money I'm the wasting it! Just keep on with what you're doing, and get me the results I'm asking for dammit!"

"Mr. Peterson if there's something going on here that I'm totally ignorant of. By all rights I should be made aware of it.

You know what I'm doing comes very close to being construed as illegal as hell.   You only have money to loss where I've my career.

I don't like being place in a jeopardizing position. I gave you my report as far as I'm concerned I've gone as far as I could. I thank you for your business.

Do remember me when you need the services of a private detective but, I think it's time for me to call it quits . . ."

"You can't withdraw from this case!" He authoritatively rebutted.

Challenging my decision.

"But, I am." I rose up from the chair saying. Walking out of his office saying." I'll send you my final bill."

Arriving back at my office around 10 P.M. All detectives make it a point to be back at their office by 10:00 P.M., or later.

Believe it, or not. That's when they get most of their business. I've seen plenty of movies. I got the routine memorized . . . To make sure as just in the movies that I'm sitting behind my desk drinking scotch.

Going over in my mind the facts of the case I just quit, and was I going over it. Regretful hating myself for quitting. When I could have gotten at least a couple more weeks' worth out of it.

Where I finally had to admit to myself that I was becoming too involved. More so with her than with the case. I had to come to the grim realization that I reached my limit. As too just how much I could stand before making a move on her myself.

Where sure enough in walked this gorgeous mysterious voluptuous blond. Wearing a large rim hat, enshrouded in the tightest dress that personalized every inch of her luster.

To my astonishment the person in the dress was Mrs. Sandy Peterson herself. Walking up to my desk. Bringing herself into the light I'd lite on my desk. Where even in the dark I would recognize that figure of hers anywhere.

"I do believe that you're Mr. Henderson otherwise known as Dice . . .?" She asked posturing herself. Sitting on the corner edge of my desk beside me.

Positioning herself just enough so that she could cross her long legs to expose her captivating enticing thighs.

"I feel that it's time we meet person to person. You know so much about me, and I know so little about you . . ."

She politely said while so suggestively implying promiscuously leaning back slightly upon one of her bracing arms.

Making sure to get my mind as well as my eye's attention forcing them to ogle her splendor. All the way up to her beautiful face.

"I didn't think that I was fooling you one bit. Tell me how long have you known?" I cautiously spoke up. Still not answering her question, as to whom I was

"Not long. Tell me, how long have you been spying on me?"

"I can't do that but, I can tell you you've nothing to worry about."

"That's nothing unusual. I never had but, I would like to see what you've been reporting to my husband about me."

"Can't do that?"

"Sure you can. If I were to retain you for say . . . $5,000 dollars . . .? It would be your obligation to me to supply me with whatever I ask for."

She reached into her evening bag, pulling out a stack of bills. Placing them on the desk before me asking." Are you for hire Mr. Henderson . . .?"

I looked at her. Then down at the money. Then back up at her." What your asking is unethical . . .? Sure I'm for hire."

I opened my center desk drawer pulling out her file. Debating whether or not to show her what I complied on her." Here keep them I've copies."

"Thank you." She took the file from my hand say. Raising up from my disk walking over to stand before the window beside my chair looking briefly through the file, I handed her.

While I sat uncomfortably asking myself. 'Why do they always have to stand at the window . . .? Where those damn street lights, and flickering business signs should be outlawed!'

Because they never fall to entrap an investigator eyes too caught every glance hoping to spot some unseen danger, or evidence that could be hidden in some provocative places where a woman is concern making it imperative to concentrate on the most unlikely spots . . .

When she came back to reseat herself back upon the edge of my desk once again crossing those mesmerizing legs of hers.

Again speaking to myself. Asking myself about what sort of precarious situation I was placing myself in by patronizing her. Where I should be thinking about all the things, I should be considering.

' Like what in the hell she might be up too.' Then another such as. 'Now should I react to discover what her intentions are behind her coming to visit me, or How I could relate to her to obtain what I want to find out.'

Thinking of several difference scenarios. Such as acting irresponsibly immature. To give her the impression that I'm harboring more preconceive notions in my mind where she's concern.

Or should I take the aggressive approached. By questioning her about what exactly is going on between her and her husband?

Deciding to play it by ear, and to go with my charming good mature, if that was at all possible. Finally having her all up close, and getting personal with my manly instinct side of me.'

While following my manly disposition by visually searching her large full breasts for hidden weapons . . .

Then going to her narrow waist to see if she was concealing another hided weapons there that I had to be made aware of.

Where upon further investigation I happen to notice the contrast of her hips were the same as I remembered they blended into the curvature of her upper thighs ever so desirably.

Too regretfully having to move on too scanning my eyes across the flat of her stomach onto the most likely place where she might be concealing something hazardous to my health.

Knowing there was no way I could dare to overlook looking more closely with my X-ray vision up under her ever so enticing lee suggestible partially exposed thighs.

languish allowing my eyes to fantasize, as they anxiously but, very cautiously pursued to endeavor to venture further.

As the complexion of her thighs faded up under her skin tight skirt into darkness then discouragingly back up upon the flat stomach.

Where I knew I was hooked, and she visually caught sight of my lingering eye's obsession exposing to her where my weakness lied.

Causing her to have to distract my train of thought by speaking out to get my attention back the discussion she was wanting to have with me saying.

"Mr. Henderson." She slid her eyes off from the file catching me with mine blatantly locked in where the light didn't shine under her skirt.

Where she magnetically pulled them out of trouble by rising up to stand beside the desk.

Drawing my eye's attention onto her gorgeous face, and those ruby red glistening lips, then finally back onto her sparkling blue eyes saying

" How would you like to make $20,000 dollars? As if totally ignoring my immature display of making a fool out of myself."

"Sure." Enthusiastically answering her back. Covering myself form achieving my strategy of making a fool out of myself.

"Whom do I've to kill for it?" I snapped back attempting to recapture some of my manly pride.

"No one. Just be around when I need you." She released my eyes saying. Slowly sliding her eyes back onto the open file, she was holding. Looking at the photos, I took of her.

" I must say you don't miss much . . ."

"My client said close surveillance."

"If you got any closer, I most certainly would be in trouble. I take it that my house is also bugged as well?"

"Yes, my client was very interested in me observing your every move. Seeing how it wasn't possible for him to always be around. Still not wanting to divulge that it was her husband I was working for."

"I take it that you also have tapes. Those tapes where are those tapes?"

"My ex-client has them. I quite working for him before you hired me. That's why you are able to be looking at that file now"

"I see . . . and when did you last see my husband. It was my husband you were working for wasn't it?"

"I left him at his office around 9:30 this evening. It's my guess that he's still there"

"9:30, did you say.? But how could that be. When he was with me until 9:30 . . .? I just left him a while ago."

"That's impossible! He couldn't have been. He even had, is secretary with him taking notes of the conversation . . .?"

"My husband's secretary. Was it and he, or a she?"

"A she, naturally.

"No, not naturally. My husband doesn't have a female secretary. My husband appalls women. I'm only married to him in name only. My husband is a homosexual . . . It couldn't have been my husband you were with."

"It was your husband. I know my own clients! He's in his late 50's about 5 foot 10 inches tall, slightly porky around the middle, weighting about 200 pounds, or so"

"I don't mean to disagree with you but, that's not my husband you just described. My husband stands over 6 feet tall, he has light brown hair, and weighs a good 220 pounds, and just only turned 30 I was sure that something was wrong. That's why I came to see you."

"Mrs. Peterson I've been a detective too long to be made a fool out of. Even though it was obvious that I made myself out as one.

You got what you wanted! I can attest to what I uncovered as long as you're my client. This conversation could be considered as a case of conflict of interest.

Where I have impeded the credibility of the evidence. None of which I've obtained can be used against you where I'm concern if in fact I have been manipulated into believing it was your husband who hired me."

"Yes, I know that. Now I want you to find out who it was whom you were working for. That person invaded my privacy, and that's against the law! If that other file was ever expose. I am going to be holding you liable for the injustice you imposed upon me.

"Lady, if he wasn't your husband how, was it that I never saw your so call other husband you just described?"

"Because he just got back this very day. He's been in Europe for the past two, mouths. Tell me, this man you were working for. Did you ever see him with me?"

"The second she asked me that it instantly struck an accord where I could be found liable if she decided to sue me for infringing on her privacy.

Thereby having my license revoked. Leaving me, no choice but to figure a way out of the mess I could have gotten myself into, and fast. Before I say, or do anything more that would provoke her to pursue pressing charges against

"This has gone far enough!" I rose up saying." Come on let's go . . .!" I snapped at her walking towards the door.

"Go. Go where?!"

"We're going to my ex-client's office, and get this straightened Out right now!"

"Why of course, but I'm telling you my husband won't be there." She walked towards me saying as I held the door open.

We took my car to the Parker building. I parked in front of it. Thinking of taking her directly to where is office was located.

"What are we doing here? This isn't my husband's office building. His office is in the Peterson building he owns it."

That's when it alarmingly struck me that something was terribly wrong about what was taking place.

That I wasn't about to say anything to her that would place my licenses, or my business in jeopardy. As once again I found myself speaking to myself again saying.

'That it wasn't taking a genius to realize that I could have just been had, but by whom, and why.!? I distraughtly ask to myself'

" Come on . . .!" I climbed out of the car saying. Walking around the car opening the door for her impatiently waiting for her to exit my car before leading her into the building. Taking the elevator up to the eight, floor.

Then lead her up to the door I knew my client's office was behind. Only to discover that the plaque on the door was gone.

Upon trying the door. I came to the grim discovery that it was unlocked. Then when I entered I startlingly found myself entering into an empty utter office as I turned on the lights.

Angrily leading her into the inner office. Finding that it was also empty. dumbfounding I stood in the doorway. Feeling like a dope! Hating myself for being made a fool out of. Where someone sure as hell did a damn good job of doing just that!

"Now will you believe me?"

"Sure . . .! Sure I will lady . . .! When I find out why I'm being made out a stupid asshole! Why is it that your choice this particular night to come see me!?

Why the five, grand, and what's this about twenty grand, and how did you find out about me watching you to begin with . . .?!"

I aggressively verbally attacked her firing multiple questions at her.

Hoping that I could slip her up to where she would reveal what was going on.

"I could answer all your questions but, won't! Not until you find out the who, or why, then tell me! I've paid you a $5,000 dollar's retainer. Now get your ass busy and earn it!"

"Wait a minute . . .! Let me see that file." I yanked the file out of hand saying. Opening it up looking for the contract that was signed by my ex-client." Is that your husband's signature?"

"Why yes, it sure looks like it is but, it has to be a forgery. He couldn't have signed it he wasn't here."

"You know something?! I smell a set up, but who's going to take the heat, and for what? What did you mean by? Just be around for you?"

"I'm leaving for Spain. I wanted you to watch my husband. Several threats have been made against his life, and seeing you were already on my case. I was going to have you watch, and protect him if need be.

My husband wants an heir. Our marriage was consummated but, only once. Arrangements have been made for me to be artificially inseminated.

I'm going to Spain, to conceive his child. Once I become pregnant, my husband plans to join me there. I know $20,000 sounds like a lot of money, but it's not."

"You bet it's not! I'm not a bodyguard!"

"I know that, but at least you would have been nearby. I just can't leave just anyone looking out for him.

My husband is worth millions, and he has a great many enemies. Where I have no way of knowing if his own bodyguards can be trusted, or not. He just hired him before he came back home."

"The man I describe to you. Does he ring any bells?"

"No, and again yes, maybe. It could be a number of my husband colleague, or associate. What I can't understand is why he only had you watching me . . .? What do you think could be going on . . .?"

"I don't know, and I don't want to find out after it happens. Let's get out of here. I'll take you back to my office, and go to do some snooping around."

"If you wouldn't mind I would like to accompany you? Sitting around waiting isn't my way of doing things. I can handle myself.

If need be, I can put off my departure for a few more days so that we can get this settled before I leave."

"That I don't have any doubts that you might be able to protect yourself. I saw you in action working out. It's I I'm concerned about. You're far too distracting for my own good . . ." I lead her out the door saying.

I drove her back to my office to drop her off at her car, parked out in front of it. Her chauffeur was still standing waiting to open the door for her.

As I drove past them seeing him standing out front beside the car as I drove up and she got of mind and walked over to get into her own.

I headed to a friend of mine who was an artist. His name was Frank. Where I spent until 1:00 A.M. with him. Describing the man who claimed to be Mr. Peterson and his secretary while he drew their likeness.

From there I went and opened another friend of mine print shop, and made up hand fliers of my ex-client, and his secretary. If they were in the city, I was going to find them.

I then drove around hitting all the night spots. My friend Janet's card room place, and the hookers who patronized the place where my fastest source that I could think of to track those two down.

Finally getting back to my office around 4:00 A.M., and crashed on the sofa.

Chapter 2

Doris, woke me up when she came into the office. I sat drinking coffee watching her walking around making a fresh pot coffee.

Wearing a pair of skin tight slacks, and an eye opening infuriating almost transparent off the shoulder blouse.

That every time she walked by the window the sun's rays silhouetted through upon her braless breasts. That I would catch an aggravating glance of but, only the silhouetting shadow.

"Damn . . .! Shit . . .! "I blunted out from frustration getting so close to getting a full side view before she would move out of the light of the window.

"Is there something wrong boss? You see to be getting upset about something . . .?" She inquisitively asked. Flaunting herself in a sinuous seductive manner, bending over ever so picturesquely pouring my cup of coffee.

Letting her pendulous breasts draped before my ogling eyes. Only being held up by the material of her blouse. Exposing the cleavage between them nonchalantly asking.

"Would you like some cream in your coffee . . .?" As she rose up to go sashaying tauntingly off. Knowing I always drank my coffee black

'Damn . . .! That women had a body on her, and was she ever beating me to death with it . . .!' I said to myself watching her every teasing motion, as she walked out the door.

"Doris, come back in here." I yelled out moving from the sofa to sit behind my desk.

"Yes, what is it?' She came walking in up to my desk asking.

"Here." I held out the five grand." Deposit this in my account. If this thing goes well, there might even be a rise in it for you but, don't pay anyone until I tell you too. I don't want to ruin my outstanding reputation."

"Sure thing boss anything you say. By the way I've several messages for you. Some women called before I left yesterday.

She said for you to call her at this number." She placed the message slip down on my desk." Do you want me to dial it for you?"

She walked around to the back of my desk asking swaying hips back and forth, and sideways making sure to keep me noticing.

"What seems to be the problem?" I inquisitively asked Doris hoping that her tight red slacks would burst from the pressure of her hips action while struggling with anticipation over hoping, and praying that the seams would split wide open from where the most pressure was being applied.

"Nothing really boss. I just have this twitch that I can't seem to shake . . . I'd this frustrating evening not to mention one, hell of a stressful day.

There's not very much to do around here but, answer the phone, and feel abandoned. I don't know if I'm cut out for this type of work. There's nothing happening around here.

I only took this job because I thought that a detective life was exciting. I'm sure it is for you but, I'm missing out on so much just sitting around here doing nothing. If things don't change, you might have to find yourself another secretary"

"I just can't win. Alice left me because she couldn't handle all the running around she had to do, and now you want to leave because I'm not giving you any excitement.

"Well Miss. Miners if it's excitement you want . . ." I reached out grabbing her around her waist pulling her down upon my lap.

"Why Mr. Henderson?!" She startlingly gasped out." I'm not that kind of girl when I'm not working . . .

That kind of excitement I can always get at the card room. I need something far more thrilling and sensationally inspiring to get me inspirationally enthusiastic inspired.

That I can occupy myself with other than just playing hanky-panky because you became sexually attracted. Can't you come up with something more spectacular?

I'm not saying that I'm not interested but, what am I going to do with the rest of the day when you're not here for my amusement?"

Just as I was about to find out just what kind of girl she was by given spectacular my best shot. In walks Mrs. Peterson saying.

"Well, good morning Mr. Henderson . . . Please don't let me interrupt you . . ." She obnoxiously walked towards my desk, and sat down in the chair before me. Acting as if my demeanor was nothing less than what she expected from me.

Doris jumped up from off my lap. With a beat red facial expression from embarrassment on her face. Acting as if she was actually embarrassed by Mrs. Peterson's alarming intrusion by her just busting into my office the way she did but responsively thinking fast. To respond to why she was sitting upon my lap.

"Thank your boss . . . I do think whatever was in my eye is out now." Hastily walking out of my office saying. Closing the door behind her.

"I hope that I didn't disturb you . . .? But I didn't know that you were an early riser."

"You didn't, and what makes you think I went to sleep? What brings you here at this time in the morning?"

"I missed you . . . I've sort of became attached to you snooping. Seeing how you didn't show up his morning.

I came to find out why you missed out on your fantastic chance to get me in my new nighty but, judging from what I just saw. I see that you're not only a voyeur but, a man of action as well. She's very lovely."

"Now that you brought up the subject a question has just came to mind. How is it that you're able to refrain from not being affected from not having sex?

I'm finding it extremely hard too believed that your husband would leave you alone knowing your marital situation as I do"

"That's no concern of Yours!" He snapped back at me

"Touchy aren't we . . .? It's such a pity that money, and security are a poor substitute for such a great sacrifice. It makes me wonder why?"

"There's more than sex! I'll have you know!"

"Yes, and you most certainly have that."

"What are you implying?"

"Nothing, at the moment. I'm just thinking out loud. Here takes a look at these pictures."

I handed her the composite prints I had made up of my Mr. Peterson and his secretary.

" The man is the one who said he was your husband, and the woman was his secretary. Do they look familiar?"

"No, but I'll show these to my husband, he might know them." Sandy instantly recognized who it was but, thought it best not to divulge that she did for personal reasons.

"No, don't do that just yet. Not until I find out a few things. If these two, are still around I want them to think they don't have anything to worry about.

I not only want to find them but, follow them as well. The way I see it there can be only one motive behind what's going on. Revenge.

No one stands to gain anything by discrediting your husband but, you. I don't think that it's you yourself they're after."

"Me? Why me . . .?"

"I don't know yet but, I'm going to make sure that when something does happen we're going to have are butts covered.

I'm not easily fooled, and I have been giving them detailed reports on you, and not your husband so it's obvious to assume it's you all right."

I picked up the phone saying. Dialing another friend of mine number. One Sergeant Randy Thomas who was an extremely close cop associate of mine.

"Yeah, Randy this is Daryl. I've this sort of problem that hasn't happened yet.

No, there's no body I want you to look into for me but, keep the offer open I might be needing you too.

However, I am having one hell of a gut feeling that there might be a problem coming up. As to what it might entail, or how serious, that is yet to be determined. When can we get together?'

All rights see you at noon, and thanks again." I hung up the phone.

"Well how about some breakfast? I'm striving. I'll just put it on my expense account, and just bill the client, or you could keep my overhead down by paying for it. You name the place the sky is the limit."

"You're awfully liberal with my money."

"Hell, you can't take it with you." I rose up saying walking towards the door, opening it for her. Leading her out of my office.

Making sure to say good-bye to Doris. Telling her to keep the home fires burning until I got back. Closing the door behind me. Leading Mrs. Peterson down into the garage below my building and up to my car. Where I then drove off heading for Denny's.

We ate, and talked. The more she talked the more I felt positive she was holding something back on me where she kept avoiding certain issues, or subjects that were to be discussed.

She was not only evasive, but also conducting herself very aristocratically I might add by. Answering questions with questions, always keeping me on the defensive with open end questions that were contrary to the subject at hand.

Nor would she let me get close to her where her affairs were concern, and she was very selective about her words answering indirectly.

Using words that were above my limited vocabulary. Making sure to let me know that I was out of my league, and for me to knew it.

That was when I first got to know her. Where now that I was getting to know her I was discovering some of her weaknesses, and that's what I'd to work on. If I was going to find out the why's about what's going on with her that would warrant someone being interested enough in her to hire me to spy on her

"Sandy I can call you Sandy now that we have gotten to know each other more intimately." I ask. Not waiting for her to answer me before continuing to finish what I was going to say.

"I still can't get over it. How could any man ignore anyone as beautiful as you? Homosexual, or not I know I couldn't."

"It's not him it's I. It cost him a million to marry me. That one, time was his last time he got what he wanted. A front, and I got what I wanted.

I admit it was hard at first but, it got easier. Believe me, the sight of seeing him making it with another man. Would turn any woman's stomach?

Besides there's no way I could have myself a fling. He made me sign a prenuptial agreement. I could lose everything if it could be proved that I was unfaithful.

I've invested too much to lose it all now. That's why when I found out you were spying on me I'd to find out what it was you were collecting on me.

Those pictures and your opinion hold very little merit where it's you and you alone can substantiate what was on those tapes that you give the person claiming to be my husband.

Until they're found, I'm going to keep you where I can see you. Anyone can doctor tapes . . . How many were there?"

"Four, that's all but, there was nothing on them that could harm you I can assure you of that."

"We know that but, tapes can be altered as if I was saying something else. Where seeing how you were able to take such revealing photographs of me?

I'm sure that they too could even be doctored as well but, I have your copies to disprove if any show up altered."

"Let them I still have the negatives. Sorry about those tapes. I have my reputation to protect, and I don't trust anyone to be honest with me but most of those tapes were so incoherent I couldn't even make out what, or whom you were speaking too.

I haven't been in this profession all that long but, I have been screwed over too many times not to learn to cover my ass."

"That might be true, but I don't have those tapes. You've to find the originals for me to be sure about your honesty.

I've been around for over 27 years 15 of them. Learning the hard way not to trust anyone myself. I need you to find the originals, and give them to me."

"I'll find them. There's only a few people who could alter them. If your suspicions are right. It also takes special equipment, and I know where to look but, you're right we're both involved. You best stick close to me. You don't want anything to happen to me, now do you?"

"I should have known better than to open my big mouth but, I guess I'll just have to take my chances.

You might look rough and resourceful but, I bet that you're nothing but a pussy cat? You bark too much to be ferocious . . ."

She slid out of the booth saying." Buy the way you invited me, you're paying." She walked away from the table stopping to speak to the waitress saying.

"Don't let him get away without paying. He's one of those cheap dead bets. Before heading towards the lady's bathroom."

I paid the bill, and stood waiting for her to come out of the lady's room. Pondering over in my mind all we discuss. Taking mental notes on the key issues but, not totally disavowing myself with the rest.

I was sure about one thing. That she was involved, and that's all I was sure about but, it was a place to start from where I could weed out all the bull crap I was attempting wiggling out of her.

My only concern was hoping that I had enough time before what I'm dealing with here would hit me where it hurts, and how bad.

As I stood thinking, my eyes began to take notice of my surroundings. It's surprising how one's attention is drawn on the simplest things. When one feels uncertain about their surroundings, and I was really feeling uncomfortable as hell.

I kept thinking that someone was going to pop up from out of nowhere, and start blasting away using real bullets, or something else was going to come tumbling down on me. That its intent was going to be on getting me out of the way. So that I can't attest to anything.

Call it a gut feeling but, things were to quiet, and when things get too quiet was also when everything becomes extremely more dangerous. Leastwise that always the way it happened in the movies I've seen.

If Sandy's suspicions where right I was the one, who set my own self up as the prime target. When I first accepted taking on the case.

Where I placed myself in the position of being the only one, who could discredit any accusations relating to those tapes, or those photos I took.

Which brought my attention to why I never heard the usual sounds coming for her bedroom. Even if the two, of them weren't getting it on together. There were still her alternative ways that I never heard any sounds of taking place?

The sounds . . . Why that's it . . .! There were no sounds. It wasn't her original bedroom . . . She just was using it to pose for me . . . That means that she most had known all along that I was spying on her?

Wait a minute . . . That asshole who hired me. He had to have known the layout of her house . . .

She had to had recognized one of them. When I show her those sketches . . . Why that sneaky conniving Bitch. . .? She's been stringing me along . . .!"

I ran towards the lady's room to go busting in through the door. Only to startlingly find it empty.

"Damn . . .!" I angrily grunted out." She must have snuck out though the kitchen . . .?!"

I went to ask around inside the kitchen. Sure enough she did sneak out the back door.

"She made a snap out of me . . . Damn it to hell . . .!" I irately shouted out, storming out of the restaurant going to my car. Fool played. Feeling certain that all, she was doing was sucking information out of me.

That I didn't even know I was supposedly giving her. That she obviously must have extracted from me, and that's why she snuck out to find out for herself.

I drove back to my office and went storming in past Doris into my office plunking my ass down in my chair behind my desk.

When Doris came walking in looking curiously inquisitive. To find out what just happened from her being subjected to my childish temper tantrum directly addressing the attitude that I was exhibiting.

"Boy, what in the world peeved you off. What in the hell happened in under the hour you've been gone?"

"That bitch! She gave me a royal shafting. That's what happened . . .! She's been stringing me alone from the second I met her!"

"Hey, all right . . . Calm down. Nothings worth getting a stroke over."

"She pissed me off! Not only thinking but, actually pulling it off. Proving just how literally stupid I am . . .?! She conned me good dammit! I hate being made out a gullible Ass-Hole! Any calls?!"

"You don't need to shout at me. I didn't do anything."

"I'm sorry . . . I'm just so passed off! I didn't mean to take it out on you."

"No, no calls. It's been quite as a tomb up until you came storming back in. What did she do anyway?"

"She extracted something I said from me, and what's worse I don't have any damn idea what it was I said!

Those pictures I had made up. She had to know who they were, and they also have some tapes that I had of her. That had practically nothing at all on them. Dammit . . . What in the hell is missing?!

Those tapes I took of her. She claims they could be altered to be used against her. She wanted me to find out who has them. Then just up and took off on her own.

Don't you understand?! She knew all the time, and was just preforming making up what she was saying, and those sounds purposely. I'm being set up dammit!"

"Come on you can't be serious. All you were doing was doing a job that you were being paid to do, and you got paid for doing it, and you got paid for it I might add, didn't you? So what's there to get so rattled up about?

You never knew anyone, so how could anyone be conspiring on setting you up. Think about it. Hell you couldn't possibly have anything worth their while.

To go through so much effort for the likes of you. You're a two-bit detective not some sort of international spy, or anything like that?"

"I guess you're right. My involvement is no longer required . . . Hell!

Let her do her own thing. I've the bucks I'm out of it. It just infuriates the hell of me when someone plays me and makes me out the fool."

I pulled out my bottle of scotch saying. Pouring myself a stiff self-persecuting drink. Gulping it down." Want to join me?"

"Sure why not." She replied walking over to the sofa to sit down." Come sit over here by me where it's more comfortable."

Just as I was about to join her, The phone rings.

"Relax boss I'll answer it. "Doris rose up from the sofa saying. Walking over to the desk picking up the receiver. Momentary stopping before speaking into the receiver, consoling speaking out to Daryl

"I guess it's just not your day boss." Then spoke into the receiver saying." Henderson's detective agency . . ." Doris spoke into the phone." Yes, he's here. Now just calm down."

"It's your missing bitch." She handed me the receiver saying." She seems very upset about something."

I took the receiver from Doris. Skeptically speaking. Annoyingly addressing her by her name. "Sandy where in the hell are you?!

What . . .?! Who's dead . . .?! Shit . . .! You couldn't wait for me could you . . .?! Sure you didn't do it . . . Where the hell are you?! Will you calm down and just give me the damn address!

Yes, all right got it . . ." I angrily yelled into the receiver, writing down the address she was at.

"All right, now stay there, and don't touch anything! I'm on my way." I slammed the receiver down saying. Rushing out of the office.

The address she gave me was that of a printing shop on El Cajun Blvd. I drove there and parked across the street facing it. When I spotted Sandy standing looking out the second story picture window above the shop.

I got out, and walked across the street. Exposing myself to, where she could spot me. Where she frantically startled waving for me to hurry.

Pointing to a door to the right side of the shop entrance.

The door leads into a hallway, and up a flight of steps that turned into an open door. As I skeptically entered. I was nervously greeted by Sandy frantically saying.

"I swear Daryl . . .! I didn't kill him . . . He was already dead when I got here, I swear . . .!"

"All right . . . Now just calm down. Where is he?"

"He's in the bedroom lying in front of the closet door. I opened it and he falls out.! He nearly gave me a heart attack . . .! Come on I'll show you." She leads me into the bedroom.

There was a body of a man lying face down on the floor. I walked over to it to examine the body. Looking at his face first. It was the same man who impersonated Sandy's husband all right.

He was stabbed several times in the chest and once in the right side but, whoever it was who stabbed him, took the knife with him.

That told me that his death wasn't caused by an argument but, that he was intentionally murdered. Whereas the room itself showed no signs of a struggle or a fight taking place.

Whoever it was. Was invited, and was familiar enough to him to be able to get in one good stab before he realized what was happening? His hand showed no signs of a struggle and only his left hand showed any signs of blood.

Telling me that whoever it was literally shocked him, and that he was stunned by being stabbed. Again telling me that the person was very close to him when he was stabbed.

The multiple stab wounds about his chest told me that the person wasn't frightened, but sure about the damage they were inflicting, but made it appear that they were uncertain by the depths of the wounds.

The first most obvious wound was deep and elongated between his ribs. The blade went straight into his heart. Then appeared to have been twisted, then slid sideways.

Where the three, other stab wounds were scattered randomly about his chest. Appeared to be mostly gouges. Made indecisive with short indecisive jabs

The one in his stomach was more on the scope of another gouge but, shallow. As if the blade was pulled upwards towards his rib-cage.

Where the one in his right side was deep and precise. Which told me that he was stabbed by two, different people. While he was either sitting down, or standing up being held bent backwards as if being held when the initial attack took place.

Even though it was only my personal preliminary deduction I concluded the following took place.

He was first stabbed in the heart while getting stabbed in his right side at the same time. Then was stabbed again by the one who stabbed him in the heart.

In his stomach as the other one who stabbed him in his right side continued to stab him about his chest. I however concluded that his death wasn't inflicted in his apartment but someplace else.

The lack of blood on the closet floor, and on the floor of the bedroom told me that he wasn't killed there but, somewhere else, and brought back to his place.

Where he was shoved into the closet purposely to give the impression that he was killed in his own place and whoever did it was attempting to hide the body.

I looked up at Sandy standing beside me. She was wearing the same clothes I last saw her in. The only sign of blood I could see that was on her, was on her shoes.

There was no way she could have killed him but, that doesn't mean she couldn't have had it done . . .?

'But why would she want to become linked to his death? She could have just left his place to avoid getting herself involved' I asked myself.

"He's dead all right . . ." I rose up from a squatting position beside the body saying. Taking special note to her hands to examine them. To see if I could notice any signs of blood on them, or damage to her expensive manicure, or finger nail polish.

"Daryl, I swear I didn't kill him . . .!"

"Calm down. I know you didn't but, we were both seem coming in here. We've to call the police. We both have alibies . . . By the looks of him he's been dead for several hours. Why did you come here again?"

"The tapes . . .! The door was unlocked when I came here. I admit I came in and looked around but, I couldn't find them. That's when I came upon him, when I went to look into his bedroom closet. You did say you gave them to him?!"

"This doesn't come as any surprise. The only one who could have been involved was his secretary. It's my guess that she now most likely has them, or maybe even dead herself. Meaning there's someone else after you.

You knew who he was, and that goes for that secretary of his as well. You also know who she is don't you?

Don't lie to me dammit! I'm tired of playing game with you. Why the hell didn't, you tell me that you knew who that guy was dammit?!"

"Yes, I know who she is but, she not his real secretary. She's his wife her name is Mary and, his name is Steven Morehouse. He once was a business associate of my husband.

They went their separate ways just before I marred my husband. Daryl I just can't get involved in this . . .!"

"Sorry sweetheart but, you're now. Right up to your ears." I walked to the phone to call Randy my friendly stepfather detective on the police force saying.

"Yeah, Randy this is Daryl. I've a cold one for you. I'm at 444 El

Cajun Blvd. Upstairs, the doors are open I'll be here." I hung up saying cutting my conversation with him short.

"Listen Sandy I'm going to have to clue Randy in on what was going on anyway but, as my client. You do have the right to confidentiality.

However, that was before when we were only dealing with a personal domestic matter where it's murder now."

"All rights, I get the drift but, keep to the facts only. Don't give any more information than you have to. If he doesn't ask don't volunteer any. Do you understand?

I don't want any notoriety if at all possible I want to avoid it so no discussing anything that's irrelevant to my calling you, and telling you what I found here.

I'll do all the rest of the talking. I don't want you disclosing any information relating to my case."

"Thanks a bunch. You sure leave me a lot to talk about."

"Sorry, but until we find those tapes. Their existence must go unknown. Nothing we've discussed can go beyond us."

"I hope you realize the position you're placing me in?"

"Yes, I do but, it's only temporary, and for $20,000 more I think you can afford to take the risk."

"Now you're making a lot of sense, but just to make my position clear. You best not be trying to make a fool out of me. I'm through being the stooge. We're in this together. If it becomes one-sided I'll call cop."

We waited for the police to arrive. Sandy, and I were questioned by Randy personally. Randy was no fool. He's been a cop for as long as I knew him even before he became like a stepfather to me he was a personal friend of mine.

Randy knew why I was evading answering his questions. All the information I gave him was are alibies, and my evaluation to the crime scene.

Along with what I thought happened leaving the rest up to Sandy who only substantiate what transpired when I arrived.

Referring back to my ought of confidentiality that anything I discussed prior to what happen here were confidential, and not associated.

Sandy, and I left a few hours after I arrived on the scene. Taking my car, we preceded to go to Mr. Morehouse's house to talk to Mary his wife.

Knowing the second she saw Sandy, and I together that she would know why we came to visit if in fact she would be there. Which I doubted she would be. While driving Sandy to Mr. Morehouse's house. I couldn't help to think to myself. 'Where was Sandy's chauffeur? And how did she get to the print shop without being driven or driving herself?' Suddenly she became my number one suspect.

We were greeted at the front door by the butler saying that Mrs. Morehouse wasn't home. He didn't mention anything about Mr. Morehouse's death, so I took it that the house hold wasn't notified as yet.

So I thought it best not to mention it not wanting to add still more despair to their hardship if the same fate happens to befall Mrs. Morehouse as well.

We left and stopped to have a liquid lunch. She told me that she was sorry for not telling me that she knew who it was that impersonated her husband.

She filled me in on Mr. Morehouse association with her husband, and as far as she knew they still were the best of friends with her husband.

Saying that she couldn't figure out why they would scheme against her. As far as she was aware of she was on a first name bases with them.

That was another reason why she went to visit Steven. Was because she wanted to hear why from his own lips?

She said that she knew that he separated from his wife, and he took up living in that apartment above that printing office.

He owned the building, and often used the place when he had to remain in the city instead of having to rent a hotel room.

That they were falling on hard times financially but, the way she heard it. They were still trying to hold things together between each other.

"I didn't want to bring the subject up but, I was having reservation about is wives' welfare. Thinking that he wasn't the only one that was going to wind up the same way that her husband did.

It's my guess that Mrs. Morehouse is, or was also going to turn up dead, or is being held prisoner somewhere for the time being before she too winds up dead.

Knowing that it's obvious that someone is out to discredit Sandy and was using them to accomplish doing it.

Coming upon a grin thought. 'Could it be one of her husband's lovers, or even her husband himself?'

Which left me no choice but, to bring up my suspicions?" Sandy I didn't want to bring this up mainly because the thought just now entered my mind but, do you think personally that your husband, or maybe one of his lovers could be involved in what's going on here?"

"You know I never thought about them . . .? But, there's so many. Norman never keeps an affair going for too long but, there are a few he does see somewhat regular.

Then there is Our chef Carl he's a fantastic chef. Then there's Jerry my husbands' hair stylist, now that's a real feminist number. Put a dress on him, and you would never know he is a guy underneath it."

"What role does your husband like to play?"

"He wants to be the women but, once in a while he gets the urge to feel manly."

"Is your husband physically impudent, or is it a biological disorder?"

"Not to my knowledge his not. The one time we did get together it was wonderful. So wonderful in fact. That it tore me up inside when he rejected me afterwards, and went to another man.

How I hated and despised him for that! As for him being able to deal with his gender. He carries himself very masculine.

As far as I know I'm the only one who knows that under that manly facade he presence himself to be he's all bitch, and I literally mean that.

Why do you think I'm always out buy expense nighties, and risqué underwear all the time? It's because he's always ruining the ones I buy wearing to turn on his lovers.

I should have known there was something wrong with him when I caught him wearing women's silk underwear under his swimming trucks.

Besides the other indicators that he was bisexual when I was working for him before I started dating him.

Since I married him the past two, years have been a living hell for me. I thought it would be easy but, you don't have any idea what it does to a woman emotionally."

"I know what it would do to me, and I wouldn't put myself through it for any amount of money."

"You say that because you never had the opportunity presented to you. He represents everything that I didn't have. Where I didn't have to do a damn thing but, be a status symbol for him.

That along with having to tolerate his rudeness. When he was out proving himself being envied amongst those, he associated with, and his business clients.

It's the loneliness that I was having the most difficultly handling. Knowing that he was in the next room making love to a man.

Not being able to go out to find satisfaction sexually as a woman was the most berating thought that besieged me. It got so I was detesting myself . . .

How I wanted to be held but, he wouldn't even do that. Unless he was trying to make an impression, or to boost about his status of being the most envied.

His money is mine because I can expose him for what he really is. It belongs to me . . .! I'll be dammed if I will have anyone deprive me of it!"

"It's your life. Let's say we go talk to a few of my friends about some equipment. However, before we do, answer me one question.

How would your husband know if you did cheat on him unless he's having you watched?"

"I was wondering when you would get around to that. Let's just say that he would, and leave it at that, and no, I'm not being watched.

If I was, you would have been caught long before I spotted you. Well, not you personally but, that lens too that telescope you had set up in the boat house.

The sun's rays made a reflection. I went down to investigate, and after I found it. I to set up an observation device myself.

It's called a video camera when I then waited observing the boathouse with binoculars. After I saw someone leave by a roll boat I went down, and retrieved the camera.

At first I thought that it was my husband paying you to watch me. Then after I thought about it. I began to think otherwise but, I had to make sure.

As well as find out all about you, and what you manage to obtain before I caught onto you spying on me.

Judging from the size of that telescope, and the pictures, you were able to take using that telescope. You really brought out my finer qualities a lot more than I expected you did."

"I have to admit I can't take all the credit but, that camera still left a lot to my insatiable imagination. Where you didn't help by knowing that I was spying on you. If you hadn't maybe, you would have been a little more liberal while posing for me. You're one incredibly beautiful woman if you don't me saying so."

"Why thank you? It's a pity that your flattery can't gain you more than my praise."

"Sandy you're driving me crazy with curiosity . . .! I watched you for weeks. I saw you in action flaunting yourself. There's nothing that could have stopped you."

"That's where you're wrong. Why do you think I'm going all the way to Pairs, to get pregnant? After are marriage was consummated I had an operation.

It's impossible for me to have intercourse. As for one-sided sex, forget it! That's all I'm going to tell you, now shall we be going?"

Chapter 3

We left the cocktail lounge, and went to visit a very close friend of mine. His name was Andy whose field was electronics. He was a specialist in hydroponics, sound was his thing.

We talked then he demonstrated how easy it was to doctor a tape. He gave me three, names of people whom he knew could doctor a tape.

He also gave me the names of two, people who peddled the equipment needed. If someone wanted something they couldn't obtain legally, they would go to them.

Some of the equipment could only be bought under strict glide lines, and only by licensed qualified people. Only specialized experts could obtain access to this type of advanced technology.

Andy is where I got most of my devices from. He also said the key to spicing tapes is modulation.

Voice vibrations that can be amplified to different megahertz duplicating, or pitching those megahertz with sensitive tone's definitions.

Takes highly technical equipment but, if it's done right. Detection would be virtually impossible but, it would take reel to reel computer banks to pin point where to spice in. Then there's the sonic filter tone that would have to be filtered out.

The cost to transpose a tape to such an extent would be at the very least five, grand and to buy the equipment needed that would run in the neighborhood of hundreds of dollars.

He said that inexpensive recorders are the worst to jury rig.

The tapes are cheap and full of static. They pick up every sound, and there's no toning, or filtering the sound out.

To spice them it would have to be done in three, stages. Sound, voice, and pitch before one could spice into it.

Computers run off electricity, and through phone lines. Someone using them has to be jamming sound frequencies.

He says, find the frequency. And you'll find the base. Contact the phone company, and ask if someone is outputting an excessive out put on their lines. That will cause them to investigate."

"Andy could you detect if someone was using excessive power?"

"Sure but, only with another jamming device detecting it, and finding the exact frequency. Then one could possibly pin point the exact location by jamming it with the same frequency. When the two, come together the frequency will automatically double on the meter.

The one with the most intensity would short circuits the other. Both bases would become seriously damaged when it would activate a powerful surge.

If the computer is equipped with a ground, or surge protector. The scanner could still short circuit it. That's why I used a frequency transformer. It puts the surge on hold by connecting to the other frequency actually locking into it."

"How can one pin point it? "I Ask

"A sonic range finder will pick up the frequency. One just has to check out the one producing the most power being generated one a particular frequency to establish a generalized location and follow it. To where the intensity doubles or even triples and you found what you were looking for.

A simple way however is to be in the area where you can create the most static. That's done by using a simple hand radio, or your car radio receiving station where you'll most like spot a tall tower somewhere nearby.

The closer you get to the interference the more static your reception will become but, that's like finding a needle in a hay stack.

I'll tell you what I'll do. I'll see what I can do from here, and if anything comes up I'll give you a call."

"Thanks, I know I could count on you, come on Sandy I've a few more places I want to go. Take care Andy."

I then drove to the police station, and caught Randy sitting behind his desk. I asked him what he found out. He said that Mr. Morehouse was killed around 2:00 A.M., down in the office of the print shop.

"Mrs. Peterson I'm glad you're here. It saved me a trip coming to see you." Randy opened his desk drawer saying. Pulling out some photographs.

" I do believe these are of you. I can recognize Daryl's work anyplace but, what I would like to know is how Mr. Morehouse came in possession of them?"

"That's a long story Randy." I spoke up answering for her." I gave them to Mr.

Morehouse. I was working for him. However, legally I can't say any more at this point. Seeing how I'm obligated to decline to answer right now due to the fact that she's became my client."

"I see..." Randy evasively replied. "Mrs. Peterson I hope you realize that these pictures do make you a suspect?"

"Yes, I'm quite aware of that but, aren't I already seeing how it was I who found him dead? So it shouldn't matter. Besides it's like I said before, I don't have anything to hide.

Mr. Henderson here took those pictures without my knowledge for reasons that were of personal nature for Mr. More house that isn't irrelevant to what transpired thus far.

Where I have now retained Mr. Henderson services, and I want it noted right here, and now. That I'd no part in Mr. Morehouse's death.

So the reason why those pictures came into Morehouse's hands are irrelevant to me. Those pictures are of me and I would like them returned back to me if you don't mind."

"Why of course as soon as Daryl here comes across with why Mr. Morehouse hired him to take them. With or without your knowledge."

He looked at me sternly as if expecting me to crack to tell him everything like I knew something relative to the case that he should know about right there and then.

"I don't suppose you would care to enlighten me if you knew anything that would be pertinent to Mr. Morehouse's death?"

"I can't. It involves my client here, Mrs. Peterson." I spoke up answering in her behalf.

"Daryl, every time you get involved with a client, bodies start popping up. You're skating on thin ice. That's very close to cracking out from under you.

I don't need to remind you that you've an obligation to the authorities. We could pull you license for failure to cooperate."

"I realize that but, it's not I that's doing the killing. I just happen to have the misfortune of finding the bodies after they're dead."

"I thought that you were working on that fraud case?"

"I was but, the police solved it without my help, and put me out of a job. One of which I almost had him and would have if he cops didn't get to him before I did.

To which I might add. If it wasn't for my help, they never would have gotten the jump on me in the first place.

"That's right it was Paul cracked that one. The way I heard it he nearly brought you up on charges of obstructing justice.

Daryl if you're withholding any pertinent evidence, or information regarding Mr. Morehouse's death." Randy abruptly stopped short of finishing what he was going to say. Deciding not to peruse intimidating Daryl any further.

"I'm not!" I defensively rebutted knowing what he was going to say. "I don't even know what's happening yet.

If I find out anything, you don't already know you can be assured that I'll tell you. By the way did you know that Mrs. Morehouse is missing?"

"Yes, but she's not missing. She took a plane to London, early this morning. Her flight left at 1:00 A.M. We're checking out the manifest to see if she got on the plane.

Now where were you two, at 2:00 A.M. this morning?"

"I was in my office sleeping."

"I was at home doing the same." Sandy spoke up speaking for herself

"You two, sure do have a lot in common? I'm warning the two, of you. Neither of you've convinced me that you didn't kill Mr. Morehouse, or have anything to do with his death. Need I remind you both that you both had an ulterior motive, and are still suspects until I decide otherwise."

"Come on Randy, you can't be serous?"

"I am Daryl. The two, of you are stuck together like glue. You're both withholding evidence that could be vital in apprehending the person, or persons who could have killed

Mr. Morehouse.

Then there's these pictures of you Mrs. Peterson. You could have killed him to prevent a scandal.

You are married to a very rich and influential man.

Like I said, I am very familiar with Daryl's expertise with a camera, and to be totally honest with you. It sure looks to me that you were actually posed for them.

Mr. Morehouse could have been blackmailing you. Threatening to show your husband. You most of all have a very connected alternative motive.

As for you Daryl. You could have found out what he was doing with these pictures. You could have put the bite on him for some of the action for more money for your services.

The two, of could have been on it together.

Where he could have attempted to fight to save his life. Where you both wound up killing not in his apartment but, downstairs in the print shop.

The weapon that killed him was a letter opener from off the desk at his house where either one of you, or both of you could have gone to comfort him on what he was attempting to do with these pictures.

We spotted the letter opener that resembled the murder weapon possibly that was used to cut him up and to stab him.

When we went to his house to speak to his wife, and did some snooping around on our own as detectives searched the house looking for her.

Where I personally came upon the bloody letter opener laying in the middle of his personal desk myself while in his office.

When I had it bagged up for it to be examined by forensic to find out whose blood, it was on it that I also spotted.

Too where I just now got back the report that it was Mr. Morehouse's blood on it. Just before the two, of you arrived. Which I thought was to confess.

As for Mrs. More house the way we found out where she was. Was by her chauffeur calling up. When he heard the new about Mr. Morehouse, and informed us that he just left watching her board the plane. Heading for London earlier today around 1:00 A.M.

We're monitoring the situation, and that's all I'm going to tell either of you right now. Seeing how the two of you are being so tight mouthed about supplying me with anything that might help solve this case.

'Where again neither of you can prove your whereabouts around the time of Mr. Morehouse's death. Where I might add the two, of you are involved up to your necks with him.

Both of you best realize right here, and now. That it wouldn't take any effort for me to build a case against one, or both of you."

Mrs. Peterson you're a very attractive woman, and it wouldn't be the first time that a detective became involved with the one, he was investigation. Where I also might add, Daryl here was seeing a lot of you.

Where accordingly seeing how up close he seemed to have gotten. I'm sure you are finding very offensive. I know it would me if it was I he was getting that familiar with."

"Detective I'm beginning to realize my position more clearly now, and now that I do let me make my position known. I'm fully aware of your tactics and they are not working on me!

Theorize all you want but, you better have substantiating facts to base your deductions on! I know a little bit about the law, and what I don't know my attorney does!

Now if you'll excuse me. I think I'll wait for Mr. Henderson here out in his car!" Sandy rose saying. Leaving Daryl sitting before Randy's desk.

"That's some lady Daryl."

"Yes, I know, and this is beginning to get to be some case. Stop by my office around 11 tonight, and I'll fill you in on all I know. Which isn't much but, it's beginning to become very interesting?"

"Daryl be careful. This could get nasty. I'm serious you know as well as I do when cases involving beautiful women, and a lot of money usually lead. Now with murder becoming involved I don't know if it's wise for you to keep her as a client. There's nothing she can say or do to force you to keep her on as your client."

"Randy I know why you are talking to me like this. All I can say is. Don't worry I got it handled and I'll be careful."

I rose answering him walking away from his desk. Leaving the building to join Sandy sitting in my car.

Looking at her gorgeous angrily self. Just waiting for me, to give me a piece of her mind over my stupid idea of going to see my friend Randy.

While having to listen to her ragging on me while I drove to National City to see another friend of mine by the name of Carl.

Figuring to start at those I already know and work my way up the list of names Andy gave me Seeing how my idea of starting from the bottom and working my way up wasn't working were Sandy was concern.

Annoyingly unable to figure out. How it was humanly possible for her to go on depriving herself. From relieving all that boiled up sexual pressure that she obviously had to have bottled up inside her without exploring from the pressure.

Feeling certain that she was as human as I was but, wasn't showing any anxieties over being denied sexually. I know that I would be climbing the wall or have gone stark raving mad if I didn't follow my natural instincts.

There was something diffidently wrong with her, or she was some sort of superhuman with a mental disorder which made her extremely dangerous to be around. If and when she did pop her cork.

I was heading for my friend Carl's place. Who also ran an electrical repair service along with selling very high technical equipment that could be obtained illegally to anyone who could afford paying from it through him.

He was a man in his 40's, who was well built, and rugged looking. For being an ex-boxer. He was one hell of a boxer with one vise. He had a glass jaw, and a sensitive nose. That neither one could tolerate being hit on.

He greeted us by saying that Andy called, and said that I might be dropping by. He told me straight out that no one has approached him wanting to by the equipment I was interested in.

I didn't believe him but, who was I to call a 6-foot ex-boxer a lair. Besides he was a very close friend of mine even though I only met him once or twice maybe?

✶ ✶ ✶ ✶

We left his shop. Along with my gut feeling certain that he knew more than he was telling me, which was nothing according to him.

Seeing how I wasn't connecting with his hand gestures. Suggesting that he wanted something for the nothing he was neglectfully not giving me.

"Well Daryl, or is it Dice that you want to be referred to by!" She annoyingly blurted out wanting to know how to refer to me. As we walked back to my car

"Anyone will due. I'll answer to either so don't let it get you upset. I keep telling you that I'm not hard to get along with, maybe that will convince you that I'm not"

I stood holding the car door open for her impatiently waiting for her to get in. Then finally being able to get in myself. To head for the next name of Andy's list.

"Listening to her replying to my last comment saying. "I'm not amused or faltered by any of them. Mr. Henderson." She barked back at me.

"What do you think where your friend we just left is concerned?" She inquisitively asked me my opinion to what I thought about his credibility, as I pulled away from the curb.

"He's lying."

"Yes, I know that! I just wanted to see if you were worth what I'm paying you. So now what?"

"Now we wait, and listen." I pulled the car around the corner and parked. Reaching over to open the glove compartment to turn on a miniature receiving base.

Looking up into those beautiful blue eyes of hers saying, or was it I was trying to, and was able to get by those lumpish breasts of her as I set it up on the set between us.

Finally, being able to become distracted long enough to tell her what I was up too." I stuck a bug to one of the TV, sets. Don't worry it's not legal so we have nothing to worry about.

I just want to hear what he might say behind my back that's all." I tuned it in to remove all the static so that I could hear if he says anything and what it was he was saying. Picking up Carl's voice speaking to someone.

"Yeah I know." Carl's voice came somewhat statically over the small speaker as he talked to someone on the phone.

"Dammit! Whom is he talking too?! Sandy frustratingly whispered out as if he could hear what she was saying.

"You don't need to whisper he can't hear us. Now hush up so way can hear him dammit! There's a lot of static coming in from somewhere. I'm having trouble hearing what he is saying."

"But you didn't mention, or include murder in the deal. "

" Come on dammit say a name!" Sandy once again anxiously blurted out. Wanting to hear a name being mentioned.

"No way! Forget it! I haven't killed anyone, and I'm not going too! Do it yourself!"

"Yes, it will be arriving this evening. I'll bring it to you when it gets here. You best have the bucks. It's C.O.D.!"

"Yes, he's agreed to meet you at the prescribed place but, he's going to cost. It seems to me that you're going through a hell of a lot of trouble, and expense for nothing. When you can just rid yourself of her swiftly, and save all, this hassle.

That Daryl character is no fool. He might look, and act like a moron but, the longer that guy keeps snooping around, the more he's going to get hold of.

I hope you can handle him when the time comes. He's no push over. It would be a mistake on your part to think him as one.

He was practically raised by his cop stepfather and he's by no means could be considered a slouch. That guy really knows his stuff when it comes to getting up close and personal.

If you know what I mean, so just leave me out of it if, and when the shit comes down.

"Yes, I know. How can I forget when you keep telling me to Relax . . .? Even if he was listening in. It wouldn't do him any good. Yes, again dammit! I'm checking now."

"Well it was worth a try." Well at least I started the ball rolling." Shutting off and replacing the receiver back into the clove compartment then closing it.

Pulling away from the curb discouragingly say." Well there went another idea that didn't work." I frustratingly said out loud

"You're not just going to ignore what he just said are you?"

"Sure I am. He only said what he said to keep us occupied while was looking for the bug I planted but, he hasn't out smarted us yet. He only out smarted himself.

Now at least I know that there's someone else involved in all this including him. Which tells me you could be right about your suspicions that someone could be attempting to duplicate something that I already gave to Mr. Morehouse.

He also knew about a murder taking place, and there's only one that took place associated with us.

What I can't figure out is. If Mr. Morehouse was a stockbroker what was he doing running a print shop, or what else would he be doing downstairs but, obviously printing something, if it wasn't his place.

Where Randy said that he was actually murdered, and why from a letter opener from out of his own office desk, at his own home.

When he was supposedly living upstairs from the printing shop down below. Now that's not making very much sense what-so-ever?

Then there's you. Where you didn't actual tell the truth about being at home sleeping. If I recall you were with your chauffeur around that time.

I saw you getting into your car out in front of my office building around that time with that chauffeur of yours holding the car door open for you to get in.

I don't think that I'll be eliminating you as a suspect just yet either. I can see now where I can wind up getting myself in a hell of a lot of trouble if I'm not extremely careful from here on out."

"Think what you want. All I'm interested in is in finding those tapes."

"Listen Sandy the more I think about those tapes. The more I feel trying to doctor them is ridiculous.

Too many people would have to be involved, and now that the killings started. Anyone that would have been, would be backing out, or trying to cover up having any involvement in whatever it is going on.

Mr. Morehouse's death won't remain a secret for long. Whoever killed him would also have to kill anyone connected with him in order to be sure not to get caught.

I don't think it's the tapes at all, or what you said on them. I think that there's something larking behind what's going on. That started the ling so early on since you showed up.

I never heard anything on them, or you say anything that could be used against you. However, you sure did a lot of talking on the phone?"

'The phone…?!' I shockingly said to myself. 'What if what she said was in code…? But, about what, and too who…? Could she be playing me for a sap?'

"All right Daryl just what's going on in that suspicious mind of yours? Your thinking about something, so what is it?"

"I'm just trying to make sense out of all that's been happening. Sandy you said your husband has been in Spain, on business. How do you know for certain he was where he said he was?"

"I don't. He called me every day, or night. I never had any reason to question is whereabouts, or did I care to want too"

"Why is it that I never heard you talking to him over the phone?"

"Because we talked on his private phone line in his study. Every day at 2:30 in the afternoon, he would call me.

If he didn't, he would make it a point to call me by 11:00 P.M. every night. He told me to be waiting for his call when he left at those time."

"What did he talk about?"

"Nothing in particular. He just wanted to see how I was getting on. You know now that I think about it.

After he hung up, a buzzing sound came into the receiver just before I hung up. I took it for the dial tone."

"Who were all those people you were talking too over the phone?"

"Just friends. I am allowed to have friends you know/"

"Friends of whom. Yours, or your husband?"

"Both. Why do you ask?"

"I don't know...? I guess I'm just searching for something that might make some sense. I need a drink! Want to join me?"

I pulled over to the curb asking. In front of a cocktail lounge waiting to shut the engine off. Until after hearing her answer.

"Sure why not." She said excepting my invitation.

We went inside and sat in a corner booth. We sat drinking martinis' going over everything that happened since I first took her case on.

Figuring out what it all boiled down to was a bunch of nothing but, yet a man was killed. There was a giant chunk missing along with a lot of incriminating circumstantial evidence involving me in whatever it was.

Which amounted to me, pictures, tapes, a print shop, and them More house's... With Mrs. Morehouse now over in London. How did they all fit together? There had to be someone missing...?

Sandy and her phone conversations. Her life style, and her husband being a homosexual.

Then her supposedly spotting my lens? How could she when I had a photo sensitive lens. Then there was I. With me being a two, bite detective. Being handed thousands of dollars, from both parties involved. One of which was just murdered

My guts were telling me cover up. No women could go as long as she said sustaining from having sex. In my estimation that just wasn't humanly possible?'

I looked over at her sitting beside me.

Trying to figure out where she was coming from. Not knowing how to put the squeeze on her to find out.

Mainly because I didn't have any idea of the sort of question to ask, or what sort of answers. That wouldn't confuse me even more than I already was.

"Sandy where's your husband now?"

"I don't know. He comes and goes when he wants too."

"Did you ever stop to consider that it could be your husband like I suggested before, and that he could want out of the marriage?"

"You bet I've but, then I would make him regret it, and he knows it, and that if I ever found out he would pay dearly!"

"How?"

"I've my ways. He would be a fool to think I would let him get away with cutting me off but, then again. I wouldn't put anything past him.

He knows that I could destroy him with what I've on him. I was his private secretary before I married him."

"Tell me. Why wouldn't your husband have a male secretary when he's gay?"

"Appearance that's why. If it was ever known that he's gay, it would ruin him. Besides he had Jim, and most likely still has for all I know, as his personal bodyguard. Those two, really had a thing for each other.

When he told me that they had a falling out, and he left him. It didn't make any sense seeing how the way those tow felt towards each other. Now if anyone would want me out of the picture where Norman is concern it would be him."

"What about those he's sleeping with. What's stopping them from exposing him?"

"Besides his cook I don't know. After we got married, he would never talk to me about any of those he was seeing, nor would he never talk to any of them about me, or would they talk to me.

When Norman would bring one of his lovers home I would confine myself to my room, or tried not to be there.

Like I said we were only married in name only, and put on appearances that we were a happily married couple. Then only when it was only absolutely necessary.

Hell he lived in one side of the house. Where I lived in the another, where I only saw him occasionally sometimes for breakfast, or when I was to appear for social occasions"

"Have you ever seen him making love to another man?"

"Yes, several times. They were men's all right."

"Were they strangers, or did they do business with you husband?"

"I really don't know for certain. I never gotten involved in his business affairs, after we got married. Why all those question about my husband?!"

"Sandy you might slap my face for this but, I've to find out." I reached over giving her breasts a firm examining squeeze.

"What in the hell...?! She startlingly jerked back out of my hands frantically looking around hoping that no one saw what I just did. "You can't be serous?!"

She repulsively slid out of reach of my hands so that I couldn't embarrass her again in such an appalling manner.

"Sorry, but I had to find out."

"Well, did you! Don't you ever do such an outrageous thing like that again. Damn you!"

"They are real all right but, in this day and age nothing is impossible."

"Are you suggesting that I'm a transvestite?"

"It's possible, and it would explain you being able to hinder yourself for as long as you have. You're as human as the rest of us."

I lowered my hand down below the table attempting to place it upon one of her knees.

"Forget it!" She irately grabbed hold of my hand. Pressing it firmly down against her naked kneecap making it impossible for Daryl to move his hand.

"I'm not opening up for your personal evaluation. I'm all women. You're just going to have to take my word for that! Don't even think of finding out for yourself!" She defensively became very aggressive for the first time as her tone of voice became threatening

"Amazing...?"

"What is?!"

"You. Seeing how no man has touched you for so long, and you don't ever quiver in the slightest.

Why you're not even breathing heavily. You're too unreal to be believed. Are you sure you're alive?" I asked giving her kneecap a firm squeeze.

"Stop that! I mean it!" She angrily whispered out, not wanting to create a sense. "Just what are you trying to prove?!"

She irately attempted to yank my hand off her kneecap. Startlingly finding herself unable to do so without drawing attention to herself. By creating a disturbance that she was hoping to avoid.

"Amazing . . . You've such self-control, how can you do it?"

"It's called willpower!" She annoyingly replied finally being able to yank my hand off her knee.

"You sure didn't exercise it when I was taking pictures of you. Now can someone so sinuously provocative become so unemotionally responsive?"

"I know what you're trying to get at! That's how! It might be curiosity on your part but, I'm not about to let you indulge yourself at me expense! I know if I let you I wouldn't want you to stop. So knock it, to hell off!

Money dictates to me more than your amorous hand does! You're really trying the hell out of my patients with you. If you don't want all hell to break loose in here, I advise you to keep your revolting hands to yourself!"

"Whom are you trying to kid? It's not the money it's you! It's not your husband who's gaining from the marriage, it's you."

"That's a lie!" She rebelliously snapped back at me defending her femininity. "You're not going to prey on my femininity so you can do your manly thing!"

Bells, went off in my head. It was the love of a man that she hated. She hated men...! Some giant pieces just fall into the picture of the puzzle. Her denial was towards men . . . There could only be one explanation. Another woman.

"Go to hell damn you . . .! I know what you're thinking, and you're wrong!" She irately rebutted my train of thought.

"If I am. You can always fire me but, I don't think I am. It's amazing how both are minds came upon the same thought simultaneously?"

"Damn you Mr. Henderson! This is a public place . . . Shit . . .!" She whispered out apprehensively looking around nervously.

"All-right damn you! Go ahead . . ." She replaced my hand upon her knee. Nervously picking up her drink gulping it down.

"No thanks." I slid my hand off her knee and slide out of the booth saying. Leaving her sitting at the table, and I went back out to the car. To wait for her to join me.

Slamming the door shout as she got in. Furiously yelling out." All right so now you know! Just what was I supposed to do?! You tell me?!"

"I'll tell you what you can do." I started the car, and pulled out into traffic. You better start telling me the truth, or I quit!"

"All right dammit! Let go someplace where we can talk."

"We are, now start talking."

"What I told you is true. I just couldn't handle it anymore. The only one I could trust was those thinking they held something over on me.

Norman been wanting out of the marriage for some time now. I found out from Mary that Steven hired you to get something on me as a favor for Norman.

Mary's been using me to gain back the fortune Steven lost because of what Norman did to him. That printing shop was all they had left.

Norman paid him to get something on me but, Steven was planning on double crossing Norman where something went wrong.

Mary wouldn't tell me at first that the reason Steven hired you was because you were cheap, and that he felt certain he could by you off if he needed too.

You had to have given him something on Norman, or it was something

I said in those tapes. I need to find out what it was.

I've every reason to believe that Norman killed, or had Steven killed. Someone has those tapes and it isn't Mary.

I talked to her before I came to see you. She said Steven had them, and that he was going to mail them to Norman.

That she was getting scared that something was going to go wrong but, wouldn't tell me what Steven was up too.

Then she told me that she was going to leave, and get away as far as she could from the situation until everything settled down when she would come back.

I've been looking for Steven since I left you. When I decided to go check out that printing shop, he owned. I haven't even been home yet. I stopped and bought the clothes I'm wearing.

Mr. Henderson I'm going to need you to cover for me. If that detective friend of yours checks out my alibi. For the time I can't account for until the time I called you, and you joined me at the printing shop.

All you've to say is that I slept on your sofa at your office, and that you were trying to protect me

honor.

Doing so would establish an alibi for the both of us, and hopefully his investigation will stop where we're concern."

"Damn you Sandy! Why didn't you come out, and tell me all this from the beginning? You been having me chase my own ass! Leaving loopholes that I might not be able to get out of if I start ling for you now."

"I know! but, I was hoping you would lead me to those tapes. I've read your reports. Whatever it is, has to be on those tapes, and I had to have said it.

I made every effort to keep my secret but, I've to had said something that drew attention to it that Steven caught."

"Not necessary. I'd the house wired. I only listened to your conversations I scanned over the rest.

It could have been something someone else said, in fact it had to be. Nothing you said amounted to anything.

Those were four hour tapes that I only left run when I wasn't watching you. When the tape's time limit ran out no one has any way of knowing what transpired. Until I inserted a new tape, and started listening in on your conversations again.

There was no way that the Morehouse's could have known that, or anything you could have said to your husband when you were talking to him on his private telephone line.

Maybe, now mind you I'm only saying maybe now. But, maybe I wasn't the only one listening in, and Steven was having someone else along with me watching you. That I didn't even know about?"

"Daryl that can't be it. I know personally that my husband already has listened to them and that he knows about More house, and you.

Because he was the one, who help him set it all up. He wasn't interested in what was going on between More house, and you. He was looking for something else, and I guess he found it.

You have to get me through this, and there's $25,000 more in it for you. Plus, what I've already promised you, and once I get Norman where I want him maybe more."

She slid over close to me saying placing her hand upon my knee. Suggestively smiling at me saying.

"Yes, I know but, we are all alone right now. Relaxing the tense muscles of her legs allowing him to do likewise not resisting is endeavoring impulsive fingers nudging their way up her inner thigh while submissively responding likewise as he drove attempting to keep his eyes on the road.

"You're making it hard for me to refuse."

"Then don't but, just keep driving, and don't even think of stopping, and don't let my pervious outburst brother you.

It's been one hell of a long time but, if you accept my proposition. I will assure you that rescinding my present sexual preference won't present any problems what so ever. Not when it's compare to me standing to loss everything!

You must believe me. The only thing I'm guilty of, is being neglected, and now that's it's going to be out in the open I need to have your insurance that it will only stay between us two."

"You're talking a lot of money. More money than I ever had. People are being killed where even I could wind up behind bars.

I'll be sticking out my neck if Randy catches wind of what you've been suppressing. I stand to lose my license, and the one person who's been more of a father to me than my own father?

Where this sudden change of sexual preference makes me wonder if you're still holding something back on me?

Where I'm working for you not against you, and I'm having to pry everything out of you where I have you talking now but, can I believe in what you're telling me?"

"Daryl there was nothing to tell you before. Steven got himself killed over something else. Those tapes were all I wanted.

I realize the position I'm placing you in that's why I'm compensating you for your risk with cash. I've given you plenty of cause to be skeptical of me but, I did so to protect myself. You have to realize that just one mistake could cost me everything.

I have to be absolutely sure that you weren't still collaborating against me, and by doing what I am without really knowing is even placing me at even a much greater risk.

You're easily bought. Money means everything to you, as it also does to me. After all I've put myself through with him to keep it from getting away from me.

I put myself through hardships that you couldn't even begin to comprehend! To get where I am I'm not going to open myself up to you unless I know I can honestly confide in you."

"Are you sure about me now?"

"No! But, I've no choice but to confide in you. If money is what it is going to take to earn your loyalty. I'm going to make it extremely difficult for you to betray me.

You've $5,000, you don't have the rest I promised you, and it might continue to keep going up. It's yours. All $50,000, of it plus more. You've my word on that but, if I loss so due you! We're both involved in murder. We both want the same thing. Money, and lots of it! My question is. What's it going to cost for someone else to get you to betray me.

Not to mention what it might cost us both personally where we're concerned...?" She slid her hand down the inside of my thighs and upwards. Stopping to taunt me.

"Is the risk worth the rewards...?" She leaned towards me asking." It's for you to decide...? From here on out I'll be placing all I've painstakingly suffered for on your shoulders..." She slid her submissive hand upwards.

Chapter 4

Now at least I'd some idea what was going on but, what I also did was obligate myself in the process. I stood to make 50,000 grands plus benefits, and was she ever that.

Stopping now would be the hardest thing I could do, and she didn't make it any easier by smoothing the savage beast that emerged from me.

It was the first time I ever saw her budge on compromising her stringent position in regards to letting anyone gets very close to her. Least of all actually loving every moment of answering the call of the wild beast in me.

Which was only enough to resurrect the suppressed women that needed so desperately to be freed.

To excel uninhibitedly as the woman, she truly was without being apprehensive over exhibiting the freedom to express herself.

Only to startlingly withdraw back into her protective shell. Denying herself of experiencing the ultimate revelation that made all that intense stimulation to become worthwhile for the both of us by panicky gasping out." No, I can't, not yet! Please Mr. Henderson kindly take me home now, please."

I returned to my office after 5 P.M. Doris was just locking up when I caught her at the door saying." Hi, love, what's been cooking?" I greeted her saying.

"Me!" She snapped back annoyingly saying." And I've been steaming for hours. Where have you been?!"

She opened the door letting me enter asking. Following me inside then into my office where he plunked down in his chair behind his desk. Discouragingly speaking out.

"Out! Wasn't that obvious by not having me chasing you around the office?" I answered opening the desk drawer to get my bottle, and my dirty special glass.

"Don't you ever wash that glass?"

"Hell on. Water ruins the favor, and drinking out of a dirty glass puts hair on one's chest. Want some hair?" I offered her my glass half full of scotch.

"No thanks I don't need any hair." She sat on the desk top beside my chair saying. Leaning back on one of her hands making sure to elaborate on her overlarge bulbous breasts.

" Would you want hair on a chest like mine? So tell me all about what's been going on between you, and your new lady client, or has if gone beyond that point of confidentiality already?"

"Any calls?" I asked, avoiding answering her question. Not wanting to brag about just how far things went between the two, of us.

Thinking it best to keep my mouth shut, not wanting to ruin any changes I might have with Doris now that she was warming up to me.

Not wanting to miss out on two, golden rings in one day.

I hate setting records that I don't have any chance of overcoming in the near future. Wondering just how hot Doris was going to allow herself to get.

Getting the impression that my luck was on the verge of changing recalling where the two, of us where interrupted.

Taking special notice of the way, she was posturing herself sitting on the edge of my desk beside me. Making a point to empathize on taking in deep breathes, and slowly exhaling.

"Sure your messages are on your desk right in front of you." She repositioned herself sitting sideways, using one leg to brace herself from sliding off. Leaning slightly sideways using her other hand to brace herself up on top of my desk.

Pointing that the small stack with the only means, she had left to point with. Taking those inflating breathes that empathized on her breasts capacity to inflate without bursting using them to point to the small stack.

"It looks like you're going to be awful busy now thanks to your successful relationship with your new client. I take it that she's the reason behind your sudden popularity?

You haven't been holding back on by not telling me something that I should have been told about before Janet sent me here, are you?

Like maybe there was something special about you that would make this boring job more interesting to get through the long drawn out monotonous days I'm having to spend here all alone."

I reached out picking up the slips to glance through the messages while actually concentrating my eye's attention more so on watching her breasts expanding, and collapsing out of the corner of my eye. Before turning my head to speak directly to them, cockily replying back.

"Can I help it that I'm a roll. You wouldn't want to be here on one of my moral days getting even more bored, or upset by not waiting to get rid of me. I can become very nerve-racking on people, especially gorgeous women.

It happens at times but, then again it you couldn't have picked a worst time to be asking me that question.

When I can't accept any of these cases, not while I'm still on the one, I'm presently on right now. That is more than I can handle right now, as it is."

"Now really boss. She doesn't look to be all that much to handle but, then again I could have overestimated you being able to handle yourself on certain up close situations."

She suggestively implied that I was getting myself in over my head where she was concern. That she might be more than I could handle.

"By the way Janet called. She told me to tell you that she has to see you as soon as possible. What should I tell her when I go to work?"

"Tell her I'll get to her around 1 A.M."

"By the way boss I told her about the five, grand."

"I figured you would. You do work for her. Where I'm only renting you. That's her way of keeping track of me."

"Well you can't blame her now can you? She does have a great deal invested in you. Besides being crazy about you but, aren't we all. All meaning excluding me where I haven't even gotten to know you as well as all the other lady that come here that work for her?

Especially when you're the only man we know that we can always count on. When the need arises for your services where we would have allowed you to take advantage of the services that we could provide. In the way of compensating yourself in return for all you do for us.

By receiving practically all accentual services free, not to mention all the extra benefits we also have been providing without telling Janet.

Where luckily for all concern things have been working out quite amicably I might add, or so I've been hearing but, haven't yet been receiving any accredited firsthand knowledge for myself. For all the time I have spent diddle-dallying taking notes.

Your being in hock too Janet. Is the best thing that could have ever happened to you, and that's why you're staying in hock to her?

Which reminds me. You best be taking good care of yourself by keeping yourself out of trouble while I'm in charge of having to tend too by also the one having to be looking out for you for Janet.

I'll not have Janet getting mad at me, because you can't keep yourself out of trouble, or because you are getting yourself into situations you don't know how to get yourself out of.

Don't forget I know I might not know you personally but, I do know the way men think they can handle himself. Especially when it comes to women, and how easily they're manipulated by them.

Even if you don't care I'll have to account for your screwing up, and you've no ideal just how irate Janet can get because of you.

Especially with this obsession of yours to prove yourself at being good at this private detective nonsense. Maybe you can bullshit the others but, you can't me.

I know that you only care about the fast money, and your secret desire to latch onto some rich women. Who will give you the life style you always wanted but, could never be able to have.

You would think that you would have leant by now. Just how dangerous it is to be going off on your own sticking your nose in other people's business.

That you've no business sticking your nose into to begin with. From your past experiences with doing so.

You're not the only one who's constantly hearing Janet harping about you saying all the damn time."

I'm going to be holding you accountable if anything happens to him. If you knew what's good for you…"

"Does she really say that?"

"Oh, yes, and lots more but, that only goes for saying just how much she cares about you, and I'm not one for saying anything. As long as it works for my benefit that is.

Speaking of benefits seeing how you have never let any of us down when we needed your help, and Janet is paying me for my being here.

I can't see why I can't indulge myself in some free enterprising compensations as well. To which I promise not to tell if you don't. If you know what's good for you."

She grabbed hold of my hand. Sliding off my desk, pulling me up from my chair to stand before her. As she stood hesitating before speaking.

"Before I say anything more I first have to make sure that I can trust you not to betray my trust that I'm entrusting in you.

I want your assurance that this is going to stay just between me and you, and believe me I'll know if you dare to mention a single word of any of this.

Because I promised Janet that I wouldn't treat you any differently than the other girls have, and I have been hearing a lot of controversy things about you."

She leads me over to the sofa. Nervously appearing to try to be discretely uncomfortable. As if not wanting anyone to overhear what she was going to say, or do softly speaking out. As we sat down together upon the sofa where she whispered privately into my ear.

Any good detective would have known right there and then that something was peculiar but, as usual never gave it a thought anxiously allowing her to tell me what she wasn't going to tell me hoping that she would show me.

✶ ✶ ✶ ✶

"Alright Sandy I want to know where you've been for nearly two days." Sandy's husband Norman argumentatively shouted at her.

Demanding to know her whereabouts as he paced back, and forth in front of her sitting in the chair before his desk in his study.

"If you really must know I was at the cottage alone. Doing some serious thinking about us and are deplorable situation.

Then I went to see Mary, and found her not to be home, and thought her to be at Stevens place above the print shop.

Where when I went there I found him dead. In his apartment above his print shop! And still couldn't found Mary nowhere to be found in the apartment.

From there I hastily got my ass the hell back to the cottage. Why is nothing I just said failed to seem to have made any sort of an impact on you, when I said it. "

She infuriatedly asked noticing that nothing she was saying was having impact on him. Causing her to annoyingly get his attention speaking louder asking. "I take it that you did hear everything I just said...?"

Sandy continued to sit in silence waiting for some sort of a response to come from him. Shocking, or otherwise startlingly become uneasy about where Norman's mind was really at.

Nervously thinking that she might have placed herself in a very dangerous position where Norman was concern. Knowing all too well the position she had placed herself in with him knowing how high strung Norman was.

Also not wanting to complicate her position any worse than she already has. Deciding to continue on with her way in which she was answering him. Too see where things were going to progress from there.

"So that's where I've been hiding. Nervously hoping that no one spotted me going into too see Steven! The last thing I want was to get myself involved in murder, or with whoever killed him." She skeptically continued to answer his question as to where she was.

Norman broke his silence by annoyingly replying back. "So that's where you've be holding up and not even bothering to at least call me?!" Norman startlingly shouted back asking.

"Yes, dammit that's where! I see that you finally heard what I was telling you. Someone stabbed him.

I've been looking all over for Mary constantly attempting to reach her at home. The last think I excepted was to come upon finding Steven dead!

I don't need to get involved in any of that kind of crap. Not with having to deal with you, and your crap as well.

I'm worried about Mary that something could have happened to her as well! That's why I kept on calling here, because there again.

Like I said before I'm not going to get myself involved in something that's none of my business.

I have enough trouble with my own life, and this ungodly marriage. I don't need to get involved with what's going in her personal matters as well.

Something horrible has to be going on, and I'm becoming very concerned about her but, how can I do anything without becoming involved in what happened too Steven."

Sandy bewilderingly rattled on. Attempting to express how worried she was about Mary's welfare not being able to locate her in order to find out what was going on.

Thinking that with the way Norman was act that he himself could be involved. Due to his lack of concern over what happen to him. Along with his despise for him for embezzling million from him. She wasn't about to exclude him from not being involved.

While hoping to cover up what she's really been up to behind Norman back with Daryl. Contemplating on drawing his attention on what happen to Steven and away from her.

"Alright Sandy now just calm down." He calmly said. "Just tell me all you know about what happened from the beginning."

"What's there to tell?! Steven is dead, and Mary is missing. Mary told me last night that you were supposed to meet him. I when I last talked to her on the phone last night.

Not once did she ever give me any cause for concern for Steven welfare, and now he's not just dead. He's been murdered! Norman, you didn't kill him, did you?!

" No, I didn't kill him! Nor did I even see him last night. Mary was lying to you. I never spoke to her too begin with about wanting to speak to Steven about anything." He defensively attempted to protect himself from being involved in his death.

I told you long before I got rid of him to stay clear of those two. Now look what you have gone and gotten yourself involved in?

He was worth killing I didn't want my family or myself involved in with why someone killed him! Shit...! I've to think about this....".

"Why would she lie to me? I never known her to lie to me about anything. Norman if you had anything to do with Steven death I've to know now.

Norman I wasn't going to tell you because I didn't want to have to account for why I went to Steven place. Because I knew it would upset you if you found out that I was associating with them. Yes, them...

Mary is my closest friend, and regardless of whatever was going on between you, and Steven. I didn't want it to come between Mary and I.

I'm not going to stop seeing her, nor can you prevent me from doing so. The last thing I'm going to allow you to do to me. Is to dictate to me anymore than you already have.

With that being said. I have to also tell you that I already have been questioned by the police.

I couldn't just leave him just lying there dead without worrying about Mary, and the fact that she was missing. I called the police.

A detective named Randy Collins who questioned me. I told him nothing but, what I'm telling you now.

That's another reason why I didn't come back home. I wanted to think about the repercussions. As to where I would be concerned, if in fact you were involved.

I've been wanting to talk to you before but, was afraid to. Over not knowing if that detective wanted to question me further.

I had no choice but to give him the address of the cottage where he could reach me. For the reason that I had to make sure that you weren't involved somehow.

I was seriously contemplating just calling you but I wanted to see your reaction for myself when I told you.

I had no idea what was going on with you and him, or how you would react once you found out that I was defying your wishes by seeing Mary behind your back.

That detective hasn't approached me since I last talked to him, and I've to know where you stand, where his death was concern.

Are marriage might be as good as over but, I don't want to say anything that might incriminate, or implicate you in being involved in murdering him. I still have been family name to think about."

"You did the right thing. I don't want anything divulged that doesn't need to be. What else did you find out?"

"Nothing that's why I was looking for Mary. I was hoping she could tell me what could have happened."

"Sandy I want you to stay out of it. I don't need you meddling into affairs that don't concern you.

Now just stay out of it, and don't answer any questions unless I'm there to rebuttal them. I'll contact the detective Randy Collins, and handle this myself."

"Norman this is one thing you won't be able to handle by yourself. Even with all your influence you're not above the law."

"Hell! I am the law! What I don't want is any publicity. For the time being you're not to be disturbed."

"Forget you! I'm not going to hide for you, or from anyone! I don't have anything to hide!"

"You're going to do what I tell you!"

"Like hell I am! You don't dictate to me, nor do you frighten me! I'll come, and go as I damn well please, and speak to whoever I want too! and say what I want to. To who I want too!!"

"I'm not going to argue with you. Like it, or not you will do what I tell you! Let's not make are situation any more difficult than it already is.

It was a mistake from the very beginning but, I'm still your husband, and you will do what I ask of you to do."

"That's all you're! In name only! Alright it was a mistake! Just end it now, and give me my divorce."

"No! You will not bring shame, or disgrace upon my name. Try it, and I'll make you regret it to your dying day! No one walks out on me. No one!

I'll make your life a living hell. I'll cut you off without a dime.! I mean it. I'll have you living in the gutter...! Don't ever think I can't do it!

There's only one way to dissolve this marriage, and that's my way, a million for you to violate are agreement, and not a cent more! Plus, what you've already absconded with!

Should keep you living comfortably for the rest of your life, and a million more for bearing me a son. Girls are at your own expense."

"No, that's alright I'll hold out for the lump sum just as agreed upon. While I spend twice that million over.

I've learned to do without, and you're stuck with it! Make it twenty million, and no child, and I might consider it?"

"It's a deal! It will be worth it to get you out of my life once and for all. Then it's agreed?!"

"Yes, and no... I also want this house, plus my cottage, and you out as soon as possible. Like right now. Isn't soon enough!

I also want a contract stipulating my demands, and you agreeing to them. As well as to you admitting to having no knowledge of me ever breaking are original agreement.

That it was under you directing me too sign that damn agreement. You're too damn contemptibly under handed to be trusted."

"You shall have it first thing in the morning with the exception of me admitting to anything.

I'll not have you bringing disgrace upon my family name, or you will be the one to get the hell out! I'll leave tonight."

"That's a damn sight better than I already have now! Go right ahead get the hell out! no one is making you stay!"

"Tell me Sandy. Why is it that you suddenly decided to settle now? When you wouldn't before?"

Norman suspiciously asked as if he felt she hiding something from him. Knowing it wasn't Sandy to give up anything without a fight and that it was her greed to get at it all that convinced her to marry him.

"By any chance could you have weaken? Maybe I should have Phillip have a look at you? Just to make sure that you haven't already violated the terms of the agreement. That you signed so that you could get at my money!"

"Go right ahead! He'll find nothing as he always does. The inserted snub is still in tacked. Damn, will I be glad to finally get that atrocity out of me...!

As for weakening, forget it! The agreement stipulated once only to consummate the marriage. It said nothing about women, or self-satisfaction, or how to derive it."

"So that's how you've been able to hold out? I was right all along?! It's been Mary, and you haven't it?"

"You'll never know for sure but, after you sign on the dotted line. I won't have to hinder myself either from making up for all the years I lost denying myself because of you, now will I?!

Whereas always you get off cheap! Even though it really kills me not to drag you, and your revolting name through the mud. So you best not disappoint me by trying to back out!

You might have influence, and power but, I've determination, and wanting to start living again. Now get the hell out! After tomorrow I never want to see your revolting face again!"

****

After Norman left. Sandy walked around the house disconnecting the listening devices Daryl planted, thinking to herself.

'My plan was working perfectly. It's only a matter of time now before I will be a free person.' However still finding herself pondering over Norman giving in so easily.

'I can't get over Norman submitting to my demands so easily...?' Skeptically becoming unnerved about him following through with what he agreed too.

'It's not like Norman to give up with him losing out... I mustn't become impatient now that I'm finally rid of him.

I have to be more cautious, and maintain total control if I'm going to make it through this.' She went upstairs to change and go for a swim.

****

Sandy changed and went out for a refreshing swim. However, she uncomfortable kept looking over in the direction of the boathouse. Getting the uneasy feeling as if someone was watching her. Instinctively thinking of Daryl.

She thought to go investigate. Just to make sure that she was just imagining the unsettling apprehensiveness.

Getting the impression that it might be too dangerous to go venturing off on her own, and the thought that she could be right about it being her imagination. Where the thought of encountering someone other than Daryl became frightening to her.

As her mind flashed back on the grin fact of seeing Stevens body falling out of that closet not wanting the same fate to befall her.

She just couldn't afford to risk all she worked for. For something drastic to happen to her now. Especially when she had so much to live for now that she was free of Norman once and for all.

After actually getting the jump on all the others, and latching onto the financing that will set him up for life.

Where he could use automation, and robots to operate things without having to be there to maintain. and manage others. Who he'll just have to have the burden of having to get rid of eventually.

Where he'll have the means along with the capability to even surpass even the achievements he's already accomplished up to now, and into the future as well. Just by concentrating on obtaining the highly intelligent geniuses like myself.

Startlingly realizing that whoever killed Steven was still lurking around loose, and might be seeking him out as well to kill him, and isn't able to find him because he was no longer the person that he was.

Known only onto the once was Sandy Peterson that she was now harboring a secret that she couldn't let become known.

Knowing that her every action must be inequitably the responses of a hesitating women dealing with uncertainties.

Norman might be gone but, his staff wasn't. To everyone around her, she must appear as if she was facing a family crisis, as a woman in crisis.

One, that she had to appear unapprehensive about. So that she can gain the support of all those who would choose to take Norman's side.

Sandy became so engrossed in her own thoughts. That she never notices anyone approaching her while swimming. As she dove under the water to swim the length of the pool before surfacing.

Only to become startlingly shocked by spotting a dark figure coming out of the darkness into the lights of the pool lights.

"Well, well you really did it this time Sandy." Doctor Phillip Powell approached her saying. As she hastily climbed out of the water wrapping herself in a towel.

Then preceded to hastily go to sit down in one of the lounge chair.

Hearing Phillips congratulating voice congratulating her.

"Good evening Phillip. What bring you out here?"

"Your weekly checkup of course. I've my orders Sandy."

"Yes, of course." She reluctantly replied. Rising up from the lounge chair walking back

towards the house, with him following behind her.

Chapter 5

"Well lover I must be getting to work. I'll see you later won't I?"

Doris reluctantly asked. Walking back towards his desk hand pressing her extra tight skirt so that it would go back to clinging to that voluptuous body of hers.

"Yeah, sure." I answered her back. Rising up from the sofa. Making myself look respectable before going back to sit behind my desk. Pouring myself another drink.

Leaning back in my chair propping my legs up on the top of my desk. Nostalgically reliving the events of my glorious days' events feeling arrogantly proud of myself. Wanting to boost about my accredited accomplishments with two, gorgeous women.

" You can count on it sweetheart." I complimentary praise her. Regretfully disenchanted over the fact that our private office interlude was over.

"You're one hell of a secretary. Your professional mannerism is one of a kind. To say the least unprecedented as well as staggeringly reprehensible. If you aren't careful, I might put you on permanently."

"No thanks love. I couldn't afford the loss for all the effort I have to put in. It's far more pleasurable when I get rewarded twice for the price of one. The pleasure was commendable but, you don't pay enough to make it worth my while.

However, for the life of me I can't see why Janet doesn't land you for herself? At least she can afford you. Where I can't put my services on my expense account for her to reimburse me for."

"Don't let her fool you she's not the least bit naive where the services she's providing are concern.

Don't kid yourself you're not getting off cheap. She's not going to overlook the cost she's had to apply into keeping you out of trouble.

Believe me she's got all of us girls right where she wants us, and you right along with us. She's not about to let you put anything past her, so there's no need for you to concern yourself who's going to foot the bill for the overtime I just put in."

"Forget her I can cover you spending as much time as you want with me. After all this is a place of business, even though I don't pay overtime it's still a business expenses.

Which are taxable, and far be it for me not to appreciate your dictation to doing the best job possible.

As for Janet I wouldn't concern yourself too much. We go back a long way. We even tried the other way. It doesn't work for us. Neither one of us are ready to make a commitment as yet.

She says that I'm too unstable, and immaturely too presumptuous. That I jump to conclusions too prematurely.

I get her meaning but, not to what she might be referring too. I know I shouldn't take it personally. Therefore, it has been due to something with my business ethics, I guess.

Besides I wouldn't want to ruin the good things I've going. I couldn't afford to pay a secretary to be just sitting around here all day. By the way just how much did your service cost me?"

"Well you know how the old saying goes. Double the pleasure double the price. I'll see you later at the cardroom. By the way you should pay heed to what Janet says. You are unstable." She walked out the door saying.

I went back to going through my phone messages. Noticing that a woman by the name of Miss Jenny Perking called six, times in the past two, days.

Saying that it was important that I get in contact with her. I have to admit that her perseverance did arouse my curiosity, so I called.

"Miss. Jenny Perking?" I asked as a woman answered the phone, saying.

"Yes, hello this is she."

"Miss. Perking, my name is Daryl Henderson."

"Well! It's about time I must say! I've been trying to get a hold of you sense yesterday."

"Yes, I know. I just now got back in my office. What seems to be the problem?"

"I don't have the problem, you do! I was a very close friend to the late Mr. Morehouse. I just recently heard about his death over the radio. Which could have been avoided if you would have contacted me before this.

I knew all about his hiring you. I was his personal secretary. We've to talk but, not over the phone. I'm sure I know who killed Steven, and why. When can we meet?"

Not knowing whom I was speaking too. Lead me too wanting to find out who she was, and not being able to get her to tell me over the phone.

Whom she thought it was who killed Steven Morehouse made it imperative that I speak with her. Seeing how I was still a suspect to his death where Randy was concerned.

"Miss. Perking. Why don't you go to the police?"

"I can't! Not without placing my life in jeopardy. Whether you realize it, or not you've gotten yourself involved with some very bad, and very determined people who don't want to be recognized as such.

The only reason you're provable still alive is because they don't know how much you know.

I indiscreetly read a few of your reports, and believe me you know plenty but, of course you could choose not to believe me.

In that case just forget I called. If you want to hear what I've to say I'll meet you on Stevens yachts."

"All right I'll meet you on his yacht if you would be so kind as to tell me now to find it."

"It's anchored at Harbor Island; it's call the Mirabelle I'll see you there around 8:30."

She hung up saying.

I re-dialed the number. Only to get an interrupted message saying." This number is no longer in service."

The number she gave me had to have been a direct number that went straight to an operator at the telephone company in order for it to be disconnected so fast.

I had no choice but, to find out what was going on. It appeared that everyone knew but, me, and that was pissing me off! Even though it appears that I knew plenty but, about what?

'I asked myself. While going through still another copy of the files, I generated on Mrs. Peterson. Making a point to read all my notes.

Nothing seemed to be out of the ordinary, or incorrect to what I stated in any of those reports, and that only aggravated me more. Not being able to connect with that Miss Perking's said to me which only infuriated the hell out of me more.

Seeing how I wrote the reports myself.... Not knowing what, I could have been saying in the damn reports that I wasn't aware of?!'

I left the office around 7:00 P.M., and drove to Harbor Island arriving around 7:30 and went about finding out the location of the Mirabelle.

Which took all of about five, minutes. Seeing how it was one of the biggest yachts anchored off the back side of the peer.

From there I went back to the club house, and found myself a place to sit. Where I could see the yacht, and anyone, who might head for it.

Ordering myself a rum, and coke while I impatiently waited until it was time to make it to my appointment.

I was sitting having myself another before dinner drink looking at my watch saying 8:15.

When and young, not so attractive brunette joined me at my table.

Wearing the ugliest glasses, I ever seem. Where just by looking at her I could see that she was attempting to disguise her appearance.

"Hello Mr. Henderson, or should I call you Daryl? I'm Miss. Perking's as I'm certain you're aware of." She sat down saying. Hiding her facial appearance under the collar of her long black top coat.

"Listen to me. I haven't much time, nor do I want to be spotted talking to you. That's why I didn't wait for you to meet me on the yacht.

I was watching you when you were looking for Stevens yacht, and decided to approach you here instead.

I meant what I said about you being in extreme danger. Whether you realize it, or not. You saw, as well as also heard too much, that you obviously overlooked in your reports?"

"What are you talking about?"

"I can't tell you all of it but, what you've gotten yourself involved in, Ha...!" She frantically gasped out. Grabbing her temple.

Instantly collapsing her head down on top of the table sitting across from me. Catching me totally off my guard.

Panicky staring bewilderingly. As blood came seeping through her fingers. Causing me to instinctively drop down onto the floor pulling my revolver.

Taking cover below, and then behind the table cloth, using it for a shield to conceal myself behind.

Panicky peering out from the corner of the table cloth to look around to see large groups of people panicky running about. While other just sitting too petrified, or oblivious to move with shocked expressions on their faces.

I grudgingly walked on my knees under the table across to where she was sitting in the chair.

Reaching up I removed her hand from her right temple checking on if she was still alive. Spotting a long needle dart that was deeply lodged in her temple.

That someone to the right of her had to have used to murder her. Before she could finish telling me what it was I was supposed to already know.

I defensively pocked my head up above the table top to look towards her right. Realizing that I was protecting myself out in the open.

Where I was making myself an easy target to get at with my head sticking up above the top of the table.

Where once again total chaos broke out again. Where the people who were previously just sitting now started to panicky yell, shout, and scream. Stampeding for the nearest exits all about me at the same time.

That when it suddenly dawned on me that the attacker had to using the state of panic to make his, or hers escape amongst the crowd pushing and shoving their way, frantically attempting to escape before they were attacked to safety.

As I was left with her dead body and no damn answers, and no one too shoot at. Rising up very cautiously. Pointing my revolver aimlessly protecting myself. Creating even more panic. Finding myself standing alone in the middle of a disrupted dining room with distraught people nervously rising up about me staring at me. Apprehensively uncertain about what was going on seeing me holding a gun waving it about.

When who should arrive but, Randy himself with his gun drawn along with several other officers all pointing their guns at me, saying.

"Damn it! I just knew I would find you here! All right, let's hear it!

And it better be damn good if you have any hopes of getting out of this! Now start talking"

While I stood there. Not being able to comprehend Randy's timing, and how within what only seemed to be a matter of minutes after Miss. Perking's was killed he suddenly showed up.

With me still bewilderingly standing beside the table.

Exposing myself as the target of the night beside the table. Still, holding my gun drawn nervously scanning the area around me.

After everyone lowered their guns. Randy lead me outside of the dining room out onto the peer.

Where I filled him in on the details of the case I was on, and in on what little bit I knew about how Miss. Perking's got herself killed. Off the recorder of course.

Randy was a confused as I was. Where the only thing we could both agree on was that her death was connected to Mr. Morehouse's murder.

Where he filled me in on what, he found out about Mr. Morehouse death. Only to confuse things even more.

Now that I could associate that Miss. Perking's was his original secretary, and not the one that I remembered seeing him with. When I went to visit him to give him my reports.

The only thing we were sure of is that whatever it was had to be connected to both Mrs. Peterson, and Mr. Morehouse himself, and one allusive secretary. That could also be dead as well.

Ending up with me agreeing to give Randy a copy of all my reports that I gave to Mr. Steven Morehouse on Sandy Peterson excluding the tapes that seem to be one of the main articles that have something in common with the two deceased victims.

I asked Randy. How it was that he got to the scene so quickly. He said he was responding to a call that someone was murdered.

That appeared the call apparently came in some ten, minutes earlier before he arrived on the scene, of someone actually being murdered.

Meaning that someone knew that Miss. Perking's was going to meet me. Also meaning two, killings without me having a single code, to who could be responsible for them, and only knowing somewhat about why, or at lease could have been associated with the victims.

Two, people dead with the killer obviously being one step ahead of me. Knowing where I was going to be.

Even before I did as if making it a point to place me at the scene to become and implicated in what happened. While leaving me totally in the dark as to why

The only thing I felt certain about was. Whoever it was, were right on my ass. Meaning again, that I was the one, leading them to certain people that were connected with the late Mr. Morehouse as well as the Peterson's family.

Whatever it was they were involved in. It wasn't preventing them from not committing murder to keep why unknown.

It was past 11:00 P.M., when Randy told me to get lost. Where I headed to Janet's place.

Janet was nothing less than a thirty, year-old flaming gorgeous red head.

Who was her own free spirited person? Who inherited a card room located in the suburbs of the city?

I knew Janet since we were twelve. Meeting her in junior high school. She was exceptionally brilliant, and twice that in being gorgeously ravishing then, and even more so now.

Where I once made the mistake of taking her for granted, to which she never lets me forget. That she allowed me to get away with. The last thing anyone would dare attempt to do is underestimate her, and that ferocious temper of hers including even me.

As for her being vindictive, she never forgets a damn thing, and always finds a way to resolve her in differences with anyone who darned to cross her, or got in her way from doing what she had to do to achieve her purpose.

* * * *

Janet greeted me as she always did. With her hand-held out saying." You're late again! Now hand it over." As I enter her place of business approaching her.

As she sat overlooking a card game being played in her observation chair. Back against the wall behind the card table.

Making sure that everyone was playing on the up, and up, and there was no underhanded dealing going on.

Looking her gorgeous self-starring those intimidating beady blue eyes at me disgustingly shaking her head at me.

"Yeah, sure. Take a check?" I replied back as I stood beside her watching the card game being played.

"Cash lover. Your checks are as good as your word. Worthless." She snapped back. Sliding out of her chair positioning herself to stand before me. Still, holding her hand out wanting to be paid.

"For using my girls for your personal secretaries, and whatever else you can get away with, doesn't come cheap. Leastwise not at my expense."

"Well, I'll have to owe you than. I don't have the cash on me right now. I'll sign an IOU. My signature is still good for something. That's all I've left. You already got me body and soul."

"Damn you Daryl! You owe me! I can't keep carrying you like this. You'll ruin my reputation. I can't be showing favorites you know that."

"Hey . . . All right I promise I'll have something for you tomorrow. Better yet I know. Let me try my luck?"

"Forget you! Every time you feel lucky I wind up paying for it! And don't think your credit is good anyplace else. Where you want to shoot craps either.

Your lucky streak there has also long past. How you ever earned that name Dice I'll never know. When was the last time you had any damn luck at all?

I put the word out on you, but good. You couldn't play a penny slot machine on credit, let alone having any hopes of buying you way into playing poker.

Which I might add you don't know a damn thing about, or can afford to learn. Least of all at my expense.

You more than worn out that lucky name you got shooting craps. For the one called Dice, there's no Dice at all.

Until you pay me what you owe me first, and that includes for everything. Meaning no freer rides at my expense."

"You do look lovely tonight Janet my dearest... Let's say I let you take me out too show the world how lucky I am?"

"Your damn right you are lucky but, don't push it too far!" She took my hand saying leading me into her office.

With me closing the door behind us as I followed her in. Too amorously taking her into my arms. Suggestively saying.

"Hi, love. Have I told you that I've missed you..." Kissing her warmly. Showing her how much. Sneaky pulling down the zipper of her shoulder less dress.

Getting as far as down too her waist. When she grabbed my hand, and forced my hand to zip her dress back up.

Then stepped back from me, to hold me arm's length away. Giving me one of her annoying expressions, that meant she was really upset with me.

"Damn you Daryl not again...!? What's this I've been hearing about you getting yourself into trouble again?

Why is it that every case you get on people are dying all the time…? One of these times it could be you, and with my luck I'll be the one footing the bill to bury you.

You promised me after the last time, that it was going to be the last time… Yet you continue to keep getting yourself involved in things you don't have any idea of how to get yourself out of. You are making a nervous-rack out of me.

I want you to stop this nonsense of yours before you get yourself killed. Your no damn good at this private detective crap, and we both know it."

"Hey, lighten up will you! and at least give me a chance to explain before getting down on me. I didn't have any control over the way things turn out. It wasn't supposed to happen. Why blame me for what was someone else's doing?

All it was to be was a simple surveillance job, and I needed the money to pay you off. So that you will stop badgering me for it all the time.

I'm having a streak of bad luck that's all. I'll get through it I always do, now don't I? So just give me some room to handle things. So I can give you your damn money.

As for me not knowing what I'm doing. It's you who doesn't know what you are talking about. I'm better than any damn cop out there, and you damn well know it."

"Yeah, I know it!" She argumentatively snapped back. Challenging my last comment. Like you were the last time you were on one of your bad streaks. By nearly getting yourself nearly beaten to death.

What about the time before that? Where you nearly got yourself killed. I still have the hospital bill that telling my how skilled you are at taking care of yourself.

Dammit Daryl! You were shot twice on your last case, and once on the case before that. Not to mention getting the hell beat out of you more than once, and you've only been in business for just going on three, years.

After going through the police academy, and quitting the police force, even after all the training Randy has given you, your still not coming out on top.

I don't mean to put you down but, if you want my opinion. You couldn't fight your way out of a paper bag even if it was soaking wet.

Your luck can't last forever. You should have stayed on the police force instead of trying to go off on your own.

At least there you had the entire police department behind you, and saved yourself all this damn pain and suffering you are subjecting yourself too.

Just so you can do things your way, and getting yourself involved in all those dangerous cases you're taking on.

Daryl I'm always going to be here for you but, seriously. When is enough going to be enough. Go back to being just a cop at least there I wouldn't have to be constantly worrying myself sick about you."

"Forget it I'm not quitting! You aren't giving me a chance to prove myself. I'm not stupid. I've a college degree in criminal science, and an investigative license to practice.

As for getting myself shot twice. I ran the same risks while I was on the force. Where you were always on my case about how dangerous it was.

As for getting the hell beat out of me. You only saw me, and not those who didn't secede at convincing me that they were better than me.

Regardless how you feel about me, and the job I'm doing. I do know what I'm doing, and when I'm in over my head.

Besides I don't hear you, or anyone else offering me anything else to try. That will let me the buck this racket can net me.

If you can think of one that will meet all your requirements about being safe and protected, that well also satisfying me as well. That I haven't figured out just what it is I want to achieve.

Tell me, and I'll try out for it.

Otherwise bug out, and let me live my life the way I want to live it. That I don't mind saying I'm doing relatively good at.

Right now this is the only thing I have going for myself. I'm 30 years' old who's being drawn between you, and Randy. Who's been like a father to me.

Where there's been nothing I've taken an interest in that has been good enough for you, or would make you feel comfortable about the way you want me to live my life.

I have only been my own person for barely over a two, and a half now. Sure it gets rough at times but, I'm still here. Where I'm earning my own way, and establishing my own credibility.

As for you footing the bills for me. Don't! I never ask you too. You did what you did on your own, and I'm going to pay you back every cent.

I have to admit. I'm not doing great as of yet but, it's going to happen for me. As for the cases I take on.

I take on the risky ones for the sole purpose of establishing a reputation of being the most sought after. It's the ones I take on too make you and Randy happy that are the ones that got to me I might add.

As I recall it was either you, or Randy himself who recommended that I take them on because you both felt it was safe for me to do so.

As for the one I'm on known. Isn't hurting me any, and isn't bond too. If you just let me handle things my way.

Money, fame, and recognition, and a sense of accomplishment. Along with putting some excitement in my life is what I need to make my being here mean something to me. If it's not for your liking, or anyone else's that's just too damn bad!

I thought that you knew me better than anyone else. I don't need a nurse maid. I need you along with living my life the way I want to live it."

"Just who do you think you are trying to dump that load of crap on? This is Janet you are talking to, don't forget that. I know all too well who you are, and why you're doing what you're doing.

You're doing it for your own personal pleasure. That you're obtaining from exploiting those paying you to get evidence on.

To get something on them, mostly so that you can negotiate a settlement from one, or both without their knowledge of who they're paying for your silence.

It's always been that way with you, and nothing more. Besides away for you to get over on the system that won't come back and bite you in the ass.

While getting your kicks at thrill seeking. Just the way it has always been where you are concern.

While not wanting to miss out on anything that life might have to offer you.

Daring it to besiege you with the unexpected. Because of you wanting to take it to its limit of your endurance level.

As if you are riding on a fast moving train. Wanting to ride it to the end but, wanting to jump off but, not wanting to miss out on the thrill of the ride not wanting to miss out on the unknown that could be waiting for you if you continue to ride it all the way to the end.

Yes, Daryl my dearest we both know what is going on with you. I know that you will never really be satisfied with the mediocre way of life at playing cop.

You have to do better than just being an average cop. You had to take it to the next level of becoming a private detective to face the unknown dangers that gets your adrenalin all accelerated.

To show Randy, and all those who you were thinking were holding you from doing you thing. Just how much better you were while getting all the fringe benefits that they weren't.

Along with getting that adrenalin rush you weren't getting by not having to play by someone else's rules.

Daryl I'm not denying you anything. Like I said before that I'll always have been there for you, and hopefully always will be.

I just want you to be more conscientious about your surroundings, and the dangerous elements that you are totally ignoring.

To take into account before jumping in head first the uncertainty of the outcome of what you're getting yourself into. Not even thinking about your own safety.

You said it yourself. If I could think of something that would make us both feel comfortable. Too tell you, and you would look into it. Will that's why I wanted to speak to you about. "

She hesitantly lingered before continuing to tell him what she was thinking about. Before skeptically venturing to speak up.

"Daryl I just acquired a used car lot? Now hear me out before jumping to conclusions." She hastily spoke up hoping to sway his first impressions over what she was suggesting.

"Forget it! I'm not ready for retirement yet, nor do I need a mother hem. I might love, and owe you more than my gratitude but, that's as far as it goes. Forget it! I'm not interested...

For Pete-sakes! stop worrying about me so damn much. I can't believe that you would even think of trying to turn me into a car salesman. Just so you can have peace of mind for your sake only, and not even giving me, or my feeling a second thought.

Jesus Janet I'm 30 years old. At least give me credit for knowing how I got to be this old. I'm not about to go selling cars just to please you, and make my life more miserable than it was before I left the police office."

"Who's worrying about you? I just don't want to get the short end of the deal... Do you've any idea just how much I stand to lose if you get yourself hurt. Where you can't pay me...?

I'm trying to respect your ability to do for yourself but, dammit! You don't have to be proving yourself capable of taking care of yourself to me.

Your right Daryl I should know you better than anyone else, and I do, and you know I do. That's why I know why it is you are out trying to prove something. Even if it means risking your life to accomplish doing so.

Honey I love you just as you are, and if I'm in the position to make life easier on you until you do find your calling. I can't see any harm in doing so when it can make both are lives a lot easier.

What's wrong with me wanting you here for you to take advantage of me? When all I'm expecting from you. Is to start taking better care of yourself for my sake as well as yours.

You have to admit it.

Trouble seems to plague you like a bad curse, and you can't blame me from being concern about you the way I am."

"Now is a bit late to start reprimanding me for my short comings…" I wasn't sure at first, and I'm not totally now but, it's beginning to dawn on me. That you're getting the impression that I'm taking advantage of you.

Where you are beginning to feel infringed upon by me, where money isn't the only cause behind what's stressing you out."

"Daryl I wasn't referring to that but, seeing how you brought it up. You've been sticking it to me good. Where I have been attempting to accommodate you by patronizing you.

Because of certain shortcoming of my own.

That's obviously transpired in my life since them. Not only between us but, others as well. Like how it was I came to inherit this card room.

That we ourselves have become accustomed to obliging each other since we were kids together.

When we both swore too each other that we wouldn't let anything, or one hinder us from achieving the ultimate lifestyle, we both always have been striving for regardless what we had to do.

Honey I for one want nothing more than for you to have the finer things in life but, we both had to come to learn to live with each other indiscretions.

As well as our own, and what we both had to do during that time. Where we both vowed not to accept the uncertainty of neither one of us not making even if the other might not."

"Janet I don't have any idea of what you are trying to tell me but if I'm getting the jest of it right. The way I see it. I'm the one who's lagging behind where you're well on your way of achieving everything that will make you happy."

"Daryl I really need for you to listen to me. It wasn't all that long ago when life turned me a bad deal, and you were there for me when everything was stacked against me.

You not only extended yourself for me.

Where you have become everything, and everyone to me since junior high school, and we always relied, and confided in each other.

First when my father deserted my mother, and me. Then when my mother upped, and split on me. Leaving me alone and destitute. When you came to my aid asking, or expecting nothing for helping and protect me.

It was you who kept me from being put into an orphanage, and it was you who worked to put me through school, and you who found me a place for me to live by talking Randy into taking me in.

You were the one who was always there supporting me while Randy found one of my relatives to take me in.

Then continued to stay with me. Encouraging me to never give up but, to keep on going, or I wouldn't be where I am now.

I never once regretted extending myself forth for you, nor will I ever deny you anything. From the time you first came upon me.

Sleeping in the park under that picnic bench. I never stopped caring for anyone as much as I have for you.

Where I'm now forced to accept the fact that my past, and present comes with consequences, and I don't want you to be one of them.

Honey what I'm trying to say is that you know me better than anyone, and what it's taken for me to get where I am now, and it would hurt me terribly if you started to think harshly of me for doing what I had to do.

I know the type of person I became, and if it wasn't for you I know that I would have done a lot worse to get where I am now. Where thanks to you preventing me from doing worse what I did can't be ignored.

Honey, we've both done and cared for each other ever since junior high school. There's not only no need but, I personally don't want you to continue doing what you're doing.

Not when I'm here, and in the position to where I can finally do for you, and where we can both afford to take life somewhat easy now..."

"Janet I know what you're attempting to say, and I have every intention of doing what it takes for both of us to finally achieve that which we both richly deserve.

Not just for your sake but, for myself as well. If it's in my power to get us there I will, because it's you who I want to find waiting for me. Once I reach where my destiny is going to lead me.

We both have went to extremes to assure are future together. That which we shared or had to do most assuredly is looked back upon by both of us but, I'm not going to live regretting anything I did, and I don't want you regretting anything you did.

Janet all this arguing and bickering going on between us is justified by the feelings we do share for each other, and believe it or not I love you for all the affection you bestow upon me.

However, what I'm not going to let you do me is. I'm not going to let you turn me into a womanizer too. Where I will have to depend on you to get me what I want out of my life.

That's not me, There's no way I could ever let you make me dependent on you. Besides I like what I'm doing.

What kind of person would that make me if I allowed you to degrade me like that? As for your past, and present.

I wouldn't have you any other way than the way you're right now. As you well know I'm far from being an angle myself.

It was you who wanted an education I didn't, and yet I let you and Randy talk me into getting one. Where you never got the one you wanted for yourself because of me. When you could have gone all the way, and possibly avoid choosing the way you decided to go.

Where I thought that I could use my influence against you to get you to do what I wanted for you to do. Where I came to find out.

That you were the one who had your way with me, and got me to do whatever you wanted me to do.

By manipulating me into thinking that I was deciding for myself all along, and here I am the one with the college education with nothing to show for it but, your love for me.

Feeling that I was the one who's been letting you down because of my obsessions to be someone I'm not.

Your mistake was thinking of me as a fool, where I wasn't. I know all along that it's been you, collaborating along with Randy.

Who's always been manipulating me into doing thing that I didn't really want to do but, I did them because I love the both of you, and would do anything for either you.

Where now that I'm out there on my own. Where neither of you can have any control over me.

It's the both of you who are the ones that want me to fail because you both have your own opinions about why I'm doing what I'm doing trying to second guess me.

Janet we're the way we're because we're what we're. This is me, and this is the way I'm going to be until I get tired of being me.

If you want me to deny the way you're making me describe the person you want me to be I can't, because I'm honestly seeing myself becoming him knowing how easily it would for me to become that sort of derelict you want me to become.

But, doing so would only make me lesser the person than I an already until eventually you wouldn't be able to tolerate me any longer.

I might not have a lot of money, or a fancy pad, or office but, what I do have is you with Randy supporting you fraternizing me.

Telling me that you were right in saying. That you did tell me that you knew me all along.

Which you would be totally right to say it.

So why try to change me now especially when you are so bonded and determined to prove me wrong about myself? Seeing how I'm having the time of my life loving being the want to be me. Living off your success and my failures.

All you did by meddling into what was going on with me. You did on your own for yourself. I didn't try to manipulate the way you went about living your life, nor did I judge you for the way you lived it.

I conformed to accessibility that were being handed me, and became complacent and undependable.

The more you patronized my actions while not appreciating me as a person only made me become more unceasingly reckless.

Knowing what you do now. Kindly continue on with placating me, because what I'm now doing I'm now doing on my own in defiance of not becoming the jerk you what me to become.

Regardless what you, or Randy think or feel about it. You're not going to change my mind, or my determination to be my own person.

I'm not going to even being to want to understand what went on between you, and Randy because of me, or what could have caused the both of you to go your separate ways. If in fact that ever was the case but, to me you're both still all I have as a family."

"Honey, you're slowly killing yourself! You can't expect me to not care, or not worry about you?

You damn well better think of me as far more than family! If we were regardless how I felt about you them as well as now.

You would never have gotten as close to me as you have. So let's keep family out of this and stick to us..."

"I'm not asking you to even think as me as family. All I'm saying is I don't want to be anything but, as close to you as I am right now, as well as you do me as what, and who I am.   "Janet come what may I'll always continue to play the part of the fool, and spend your money, while continuing to do all I can to be a nerve-racking pain in your ass out of myself.

All I'm asking is too be given the chance to find out for myself whether, or not I'm any good at taking care of myself my way...

I'm thirty, years old I'm not a twelve, year old kid anymore that you have to keep looking out after me. Having that being said hopefully for the last time.

I don't want to be anything else that a very desirous guy you happen to knew and maybe somewhat love, maybe."

I walked up to her wrapping my arms around her slender waist. "You can nag, gripe, and bagger me all you want. It's not going to get me to succumb to you. When it's going to denounce me as a person.

However, if you were as smart as you are trying to make yourself out to be. You would know that if you want your money back.

That a shrewd business woman would try to receive some equitable compensation for her temporary setback, and give me the opportunity to show her how capable I really am too convincing her. That she could depend on me to honor my debt.

Believe it, or not I'm really here offering a proposal that I'm sure we both can come to a mutual agreement on.

Sliding my hand back up her side grabbing hold of the zipper clasp looking her directly into her eyes."

"You're are you? Let me guess what it is you're here offering. There's only one thing you've left to offer, and you're hoping that I'll jump on it. Is this it?"

She slides her hands around my neck hugging herself up against me." If it is I must say. You're sure gambling a lot on so little..."

"No, I'm not. I'm just keeping you interested like you always say." It doesn't take a lot if one knows how to use it, and I do know all your vital buzz spots. So it appears that I've the deck stacked against you...?"

"That you do, and you wouldn't know what you know unless I let you find out but, seeing how I now have your full attention. There's something I want you to do for me. So hold on tight and hear me out."

"I should have known that you were up to something...?"

"Well, I was only trying to be business minded. You want more time, and I might be willing to extend it to you." I started to sneakily nudge the zipper down suggestively saying

"I see what you are attempting to elaborate upon. You are asking me to put are personal feeling aside.

Knowing that I should know that it's not like me not to take the utmost advantage of the opportunity to apply any and all means possible to benefit myself is that it?

Whereas all you've left that could do me any good is your adventurousness, and your abstinence to prove yourself to me just how undependable as well unreliable you are.

Not to mention you can't be trusted to honor what you commit yourself too. Too which I might add hasn't been doing you any damn good except for at my expense.

Especially from what I heard, and how it is. I also have all your thoughts concentrated on one thing where I'm concerned.

That you are obviously attempting to make a very obvious impression on me while not giving any consideration to any of my concerns.

I must say lover your intelligence level has never ceases to amaze me. You've the potential to be an overwhelming success.

If you would divert only half of your obsessions to other objectives other than applying it on your adventurous attempts to surpass Romano's record of being a scalawag.

The two, of you must be related in some way. When all you are accomplishing is extending a lot of energy, and getting nothing substantial from it but, a reputation of not being able to think beyond your shortsighted limitations.

Naively relying on corrupted information. That you think you managed to obtain do too you obtaining it under duress circumstances.

For as long as I have known you I have been attempting to show you. Just how wrong you are about your tactics of extracting competent information is seriously flawed.

You still persist to continue to pursue the same methods. That has never worked on anyone else other than to inflate your own manly ego. When it comes to applying it where a woman is concern.

You need to change your technique, and ways of thinking, and start using that brain of yours.

You need to realize that you're the one being used, and not them. Even though you continue to deceive yourself otherwise.

Thinking that flirtatious attempts to manipulate isn't going unnoticed as well as your reasons why you become sexually attracted. It makes a women wonder where your motivations really lie.

Hopefully you will start to smarten up and pay heed to what I'm trying to tell you. To change your methods, and start taking what you're doing seriously. Not just trying to use it to gain personalized information that you still know very little about."

Little did I know that Janet was manipulating me into doing for her what she couldn't trust anyone else to do for her, and would still be able to orchestrate everything she wanted too knowing how loyally dictated he was to her.

"Alright Daryl have it your way. She once again stopped his hand from unzipping her dress.

"I'm through patronizing you, and even willing to pay you. Because I actually believing in you to be competent enough to complete this simple task for me. I had my doubts but, I thought better not to coddle you any longer.

So I'm going to give you a chance to prove me that I can rely on you too do something for me. Which I'll cut your outstanding debt in half.

At least I know you won't be misled about his whereabouts. If there's no women involved to send you off on a wild goose chase.

Seeing how we have cleared up several of are other matters successfully for the other girl here. Daryl I want you to fully understand that I'm not going to tolerate failure.

So I need you to listen to what I've to say. I need you to locate a person for me. His name is Mr. James Baron. The guy is into me for three, grand.

Now this is right up your alley. Money is the one thing I know will get and keep your attention when there aren't any women could except for me."

"Now you got my full attention. I'm listening and you can be assuring he's as good as found. Now can we get back to us, and are pressing business?"

"No, not yet. I serious about this. Finding his is very important to me. This Mr. Baron is a very important person. He's a scientist."

She took up a more serious position. Stepping back away from him to lean back against her desk. Putting more distance between Daryl and her as he stood before her.

"Daryl I don't what him only found. I don't want him to know he's been found. The other thing I want you to do for me is. I want you to steal something from him.

It's a book that's more like a ledger.

This book has nothing but, names and addresses in it. I need you to locate it, and steal it for me."

"Sounds important?"

"It is. Up until two, weeks ago. When he just upped, and disappeared, or just stopped coming here for some reason.

Daryl it's essential that I find him. I need to know that he is alright, and unharmed. Believe it, or not. I've more invested in him than I do in you that goes beyond just money.

He's been covering his gambling losses with formulas associated with the work he's been doing.

He's a worse gambler that you're, and he also loves the ladies. It appears that losers and women always go together.

Sweaty what I'm about to say most assuredly will astound you, and make you think that I went off the deep end but, believe me I'm serious. That's why I need your undivided attention on what I'm going to be telling you.

Daryl let me ask you. How would you like to live forever? I seriously mean forever...!?"

"You're kidding, right?! Seriously?!"

"No, I'm not. Believe it, or not. He's been working on perfecting the means to regenerate life by using genetics that virtually restores human tissue. The nearest I can figure it involves cloning and stem cell research.

He claims that he can make one come back to life young again. Whether it would be male, or female... and that he would soon be able too even alter one's appearance, even one's age. "

"Now that's extremely farfetched. I knew science has progressed a lot over the years but, not that far. If such a thing was possible, there would be no way it could have been kept secret."

"I'm serous... I've been dealing him for mouths. In fact, I have practically everything he's achieved thus far with the expectations of some key equations down on paper. That he hasn't divulged as of yet.

However, what I need to find out is who's footing the bill for him to be able to conduct his experiments.

I also need to be assured that someone hasn't put the snatch on him, and that I can find him when I need him.

I need to know that what he's been dumping on me is authentic, as well as conceivably possible, and I don't understand anything he's been giving me but. I am convincing by what he's been telling that it sounds believable.

I've tried everything to find out who his backers are, and where he is. As well as if what he has given me is actually believable.

I was under the impression that I knew practically every name in that book of his, along with their addresses also down on paper but, I don't.

Those I thought I did have. Until lately I came to discover that none of those other scientist he's claimed to have been working with ever existed. Including as well the secret institute he's been claiming to be conducting his experiments at...

I know because I had them all checked out, and if they did exist they don't any longer. Where I know for a fact. That the damn institute did at one time. Where it's now nothing but, an empty abandoned warehouse plot

As for those names and addresses. I myself even went to a couple of them myself. Too discover that no one by the name he had listed has ever lived there never lived there.

That's not all of it. It gets even far more complicated but, before I tell you anything I want you to know. That I don't even trust myself with what I've been finding out.

If you do this for me. I have to depend on you not to try to double cross me. That's why I'm trusting you to do this for me. There's no way in hell I could trust in anyone else not to double cross me.

I'll not have you, or anyone jeopardize my chances of living forever. Daryl honey, I wouldn't be saying this. If I wasn't certain it was possible...

Like I said, at least he has me convinced that it is, and even though I'm still young yet I'm still getting older every day. If I find out that he's be ling to me I promise you I' make him regret the day, he was born. Besides if it is true. I want to be the one who is possession of the formula.

Do you have any idea how rich I can become?! Hell I can't even imagine it, and I have one hell of a creative imagination where money is concern!"

She over zealously raveled on trying to express her excitement regarding what she was attempting to relate to me.

"I understand. You know there isn't anything I wouldn't do for you."

"No, don't patronize me! No, I don't understand, and neither do you! But, we're about to find out. Honey this could be the best thing that could happen to us...!

Think of it...! Me and you would never want for anything ever again! But, you better understand this.

What I'm asking isn't going to be easy. You're going to have to devote almost all your time, and energy on finding him!

What I haven't as yet told you is that this professor James Baron could be anyone. If in fact what he says is possible, and actually perfected the means to alter one's human biological structure. As well as rejuvenates their body chemistry to make one young again.

What I have come to discover is that even the governments been looking for him, and they haven't been able to find him. That has to mean that word has gotten out about what he's been doing.

Daryl if he has. That could mean that he's possibly altered himself. He might not even look like I last remembered he looked like but, I do remember that there still might be a descriptive way to identify him.

He had a birth mark on his buttock just above his tail bone. His other deceptive characteristics leastwise when I last saw him was.

That he was also capable of passing himself off as a woman but, there's no mistaking his features from that of a man. Even with all the cosmetic alternation that his body has been put through thus far.

The girls who have been with him tell me. He has more feminine characteristics than masculine.

That his sinuousness is that of a woman but, still has the hands of a man but, are unmistakably recognizable too be familiarized with a women body chemistry biologically.

By the way he's able to manipulate them into becoming aroused sexually. Mostly in patience and sinuousness. Describing the possibly of him being a transvestite.

I'm thinking that he was affected by the experimentations he's been preforming. He had to have been not only using himself but, human females as Ginny pigs to prefect the procedure to have gotten as far as he has. To where it's not effecting his manly feathers, and characteristics.

I've every reason to believe that he's actually altering himself without having to go through surgical operation into becoming a woman.

The problem is. I don't know if he actually seceded already. All I know for certain is that he was still physically a male two weeks ago.

Nancy one of the ladies who's been keeping me updated on a regular basis. Tells me that he hasn't been reacting like a moral male the last several time she's been with him.

She said when the average guy reaches a certain point. They forget about being affectionate but, where he's concern. When he reaches that point he doesn't.

He erotically accelerates his jubilation by concentrating on the erosions zones that only a woman would become hyper- sensitively effected by. While he withdraws himself from satisfying himself.

She said that when it happens the first time it was truly scary as hell. She said that she's been with a lot of men sexually, and what she was experiencing with him lately wasn't at all natural.

That she couldn't figure out why but, there was something very uncanny going on with him, and she's rarely if ever can remember.

Only a few men that would pay attention to intensifying the sensation for the women depriving himself of raveling in the acceleration of the moment of his own gratification.

When I first became involved with him it was strictly business, and it took a lot of convincing on his part to get me to go along with covering his losses. Even though while he was doing so he did a lot of technical talking that I didn't understand.

So I got him to start explaining what he was giving me for collateral, and wanted to document everything that he was telling. Where even them it didn't make all that much sense to me.

I admit that I'm not the brightest person on the block when it comes to all that scientific crap but, when I took what he was telling me, and read what he wrote on a sample page I took with me.

To someone who could understand, and relate to what I was reading off obviously did to the point where their ears perked up, and attempted to grab that paper out from my hand.

That's when I felt sure that I was onto something, and kept backing him but, only up to a point where I was certain that he wasn't ling to me.

So that I could obtain more information along with the formulas on what he was working on.

Where again just to make sure. I went to other scientists too ask stupid question, and they also all became extremely interested.

In finding out who I was getting my information from, and became very discreet about replying back on whether, or not what they were hearing was any good as they jotted down what I was saying taking notes for themselves.

Lucky for me I only took bits, and paces, and never everything that I had accumulated what he gave me. At least I was smart enough to lie to them about my name and where I lived. Otherwise they would more than likely be all over me like flies on shit.

Honey, I know that I'm on to something here. I just can't let it go, without finding out for sure if I'm right, or not. I'm depending on you to help me find out one way, or the other.

Love, you know me. I'm not going to bull-shit you. Yes, I hooked up with him. Even though I have only been with him but, once.

You know more so than anyone else that once I turn on the heat. That no man alive could just settle for just once, not to desire me again.

Believe it or not, that wasn't the case with him. Has hard as it is for me to believe where he was concern. He wouldn't let me near him afterwards.

I don't know if it was just me and I was harder to please but, I didn't feel anything to the likely my girls were telling me it was like having sex with him.

Then a few days afterwards he suddenly upped and stopped coming in, and never even bothered to phone me too try to hook up with me again.

Don't get me wrong I'm not saying that I'm more disable than any other women are but, I know damn well.

There are very few women who could compete with me when it

comes to keeping any man thinking of nothing else but, wanting to have just one more time with me.

Sometime back when I first meet him say about maybe seven months ago. I was told that he suffered a stroke. That he was paralyzed on his right side.

You're not going to believe this but, I saw him with my own eyes. He had no feeling in his right side and was restricted to a wheelchair, and had to be pushed around.

I wanted to take Nancy with me. Making a house call by appointment. Being informed that he was rather old I decided to one, of the oldest women I had working for me. Taking her to that damn warehouse. That is now a vacant lot.

Where when I first saw him he appeared to be a middle aged man in his middle 50's. He also looked withdrawn, even older than he was looking like an old man who had nothing to live for.

Daryl you're not going to believe this but, he virtually reconstructed himself within a matter of several mouths from when I first saw him.

During that time, I was even with him several time too his laboratory. That was located in that old warehouse building.

The two, of us sort of established a rapport between ourselves, and he was paying me for Nancy's time. Is where I became interest in him.

The closer I got to him the more he was opening himself up me. Telling me about what he was involved in. Actually convincing me to believe him.

Daryl that laboratory it doesn't exist anymore. Where I personally wheeled him inside and locked him inside an impenetrable transparent chamber.

I saw him myself lying in that transparent capsule. That he claimed was going to reestablish his bodily function back to moral again.

That's how I know that what he was working on did have some

altering side effects attached too what he was doing.

Where nothing much actually happened but, during that time which was only a matter of a few mouths he was actually being to walk again.

When Nancy started to bring him to the card room. Saying that he wanted to play some poker so she brought him.

At first he was doing alright for himself. However, when he started losing he lost big and just didn't recover, and came to me.

That's how I came to accumulate what I now got on paper by giving him a credit line and only extended it whenever I felt he was a sure winner but, to my own surprise someone else had the better hand.

However, that's when the two of us really started getting personal. Not physically Nancy was handling that aspect of things but, intellectually and he started explaining more of what he was writing down on paper.

Where I even went with him a couple more time back to that warehouse and overlooked him going through that bazaar process he was putting himself through.

I don't know all the particulars that was going on in that chamber but, I do know that it has something to do with some sort of chemical alterations to one's blood.

That it associated, or had something to do with omitting an extremely high pitch sound. That the dome covering the chamber that the cylinder was sealed within.

Absorbed most of but, not the vibrations that it generated. That literally shuck the cement foundations of the warehouse floor.

I'm so sure that this guy is the genuine article. That I'm will to stake everything I got on the fact that he is. That is, if in fact he's still a guy, and alive.

It was due to what Nancy was telling me. That was the reason I started to take notes on any changes he might have went through. Documenting when, and how he was making her feel when she was with him.

I talked with her. Asking her if she's heard anything from him during the two, weeks he's not been around. She claims that she hasn't heard anything from him.

I ask her just how close she got to me. She replied back saying. "We didn't talk much. Moistly I did what he asks, and he paid me. Then I left and that was it. "

"Come on Janet you can't seriously be expecting me to believe this?" I disbelievingly walked over to the wall bar behind her desk, pouring myself a scotch in a tall glass saying.

"You don't need me. You need another mad scientist." I sarcastically replied trying to talk my way out of wasting my time. When I was already working diligently on another case that I was finding more realistic to handle.

"Hell...! Janet with your resources you could find the devil himself."

"Daryl as far out as it sounds, it's real! As for bringing anyone else into this. If knowledge of what I know ever got out.

I wouldn't stand a chance in hell of keeping what I've for myself.

As it is those who were collaborating with him must know just as much, or more than I do. If they find out that I had what I have.

I know that they would stop at nothing to get at me, and those notes I've acquired. That's why I'm keeping them hidden where no one but, I myself will know where to find them."

"Janet just suppose I did believe you? Why would he up and disappear?"

"The last time I saw him. He said that it had enough of being dictated too. He was really

frightened about something but, he wouldn't tell me what.

The nearest I can figure is. Whoever was funding his experiments are starting to use what he's achieved for their own selfish means, and might feel they don't need his services, or his colleagues any longer.

I got the impression that everyone who was working with him were beginning to feel threatened as well.

It's also my guess he did something to ensure they couldn't get rid of him, or still weren't able to fully find out what it takes to work that thing he invented.

In order to keep them from discovering what it was capable of doing, and it's all in that book he has.

I don't need him as much as I need that book. I can always find a scientist related to the field he was working in.

Seeing how all those names I already have are fictitious to begin with. What I need is the hidden factors. That only he alone has written down in that damn personal book, or journal of his!

I regret now not connecting with all those he was working with when I had the chance too and concentrated my interest only on him.

I'm hoping that in his personal leger I'll get lucky and he wrote down who was collaborating with him.

However, I'm no fool either where they are concern not thinking that they're also running sacred. Who most likely won't help me, or acknowledge having any knowledge of what I'm talking about.

At this point I sort of feel certain that the only three, people who know that I've any notes at all on what Baron was working on.

His him and myself and now you. That if anyone did, someone would be breaking down my door to get at me, and those notes.

With him suddenly being gone under mysterious circumstances. It forces me to take precautions for my own safety.

I already have my personal bodyguards on alert not to allow anyone to get close to me. Without me personally okaying it first with the exception of you of course.

That's why I'm also going to need professor Baron. To get what worked on him too also work on me before something does happen to him.

Without not having ownership of that book I might not be able to get him to collaborate, and see thing my way, and it's the only means I'll have to use if he need to be persuaded.

I've already spent a hell of a lot of time, and money getting what I've, and I can't do a damn thing with it without either him, or that damn book. Daryl I need that damn book!

I honestly believe that he's already achieved the impossible. That he's been talking about too me.

That he's actually perfected the procedure to the point where he could place a person in a state of extended hibernation. Too when he could use him, or her to sustain life.

With the other person being him himself using the other body for a temporary periods of time, or even permanently for all I know.

My God, Daryl do you have any comprehension of the possibilities and how endless they would be?!

Even if he hasn't already gotten that far. Where I don't know if in fact he was using another life source but, according to those other scientists I went to.

The way they say it is. That it wouldn't be possible without using another living source to sustain the changes long enough for them to become permanently.

There's so much I've to find out, and I need your help to do it. I can't trust anyone else not to betray me."

"Surely Janet he has to know who they're if he is suing someone else, and there would be reporting them missing? As for those he's been working. Surely they must know what he looks like as well as himself knowing them as well."

"I'm sure that they do and he does. I even have been attempting to describe some of them as much as I could remember about them on tape including the way he last appeared to me but, what I could remember could describe hundreds of people.

Where I can't afford to have any attention brought onto anyone of them, or the fact that I'm out looking for him, or them.

Questions will be asked that I couldn't answer. For the very reason that I've no idea what happened to him, and anything I say could possibly get him killed. Where I stand to lose out on everything that I managed to obtain thus far. I need your help."

"You've it. As for anything else I don't want to believe a word of it but, I've to see this guy with my own eyes.

I can't believe he's some sort of a super human biological freak as you say. You mean he honestly refused to sleep with you?"

"You don't have to rub it in. It's embarrassing enough just to have to tell you. I still can't bring myself to believe that I was rejected by a man."

"Maybe your bitch man, is now a bitch with bobs, and is hiding right under your nose?"

"You know I never thought about that but, at least now I've someone I know who can find out for me, as well as trust.

Even if this does turn out to be some sort of hocks. At least I know I didn't miss out on the chance of my lifetime."

She walked over to the bar saying pouring herself a jigger half full of brandy." Tell me Daryl dearest how are you going to manage working on two, cases?"

"You let me worry about that. You just tell me everything I need to know about this Mr. Baron, and all those he could have been associating with. As for my fee take it off my bill.

Seeing how all are business is done, and we both got are personal frustrations behind us. What about picking up where I left off? My mind is beginning to have lapses of memory losses…"

"Well, I can't have that now can I?" She took my hand in hers. Leading me back over to her desk. Where she stopped pushing the red bottom.

Opening the wall behind her desk. To expose an elegantly decorated bedroom suite. Leading me inside as the wall slowly close behind us as she finished unzipping the side of her dress.

Chapter 6

"Well Mary I guess it worked I'm officially dead, and here we are alive and still kicking." Steven Morehouse stood before his wife in his wife maid room with her as she was believed to be over in London. Who became the temporary clone of her personal maid Ginger?

With him becoming the temporary clone of one of James Baron's colleagues Paul Murray. As they both still laid in a hypertonic state in a hidden location that Steven Morehouse previously set up for him and his wife to be cloned

Until such a time where Mr. Morehouse could from someone that Paul Murray could go through the transformation himself.

While not only maintaining his level of intelligence but total dominance over Paul Murray's memory level of intelligence.

Using their combine intelligence that allowed Steven More house too temporary take mental dominance over Paul Hurry after going through physical altering feathers where he could no longer be recognized as Steven More house.,

Where his wife Mary temporary took over her personal maids Gingers physical feathers using her own level of intelligence to remain in control of her own mental fatalities.

"Where soon we will once again regain our financial status that we once maintained. Thanks to my foresight some fifteen, years ago.

I told you investing in the future was going to pay off big, and I was a right. Look at us now, and tell me I wasn't right in investing in cloning research.

Now all that's left to do is to get rid of that Sandy Peterson, and that asshole husband of hers and we'll have everything we could ever want for as long as we want to keep it all for ourselves.

That is after we find a suitable duplicate to take that wife of his place. Along with putting suitable alterations in place that will be in are control to manipulate.

Until them of course Norman will be able to keep his millions while we regain control over his empire. Which rightfully belongs to me.

Dear, I'm going to be relying on you to keep Sandy interested in that Henderson character until his usefulness is no longer required. Where he's going to come in very handy to be used as the sap that he is.

Where I'm going to be relying on him to be taking full responsibility for all those, who are going to be eliminated but, for also attempting to extort millions from the mentally unstable Mr. Peterson. Which is also going to end in his death as well.

Honey it's all going to work out just the way I played it. It's just going to take a little more time, and patients on you that's all.

Now dare that idiot think that he could pull something over on me, and with Normans own wife. With her thinking that he wouldn't find out about her betraying him.

Especially with such a dumb imbecile as that Daryl character. You should have no problem what-so-ever keeping her under your control until we can duplicate her.

We got them right where we want the both of them. Neither one is going to know what's going to befall them until it's too late for them to stop it from happening.

As for are dear, Professor Baron. His usefulness is no longer required. Knowing him as well as you do. I feel certain that it's only a matter of time before we find him and his notes. He can't continue to keep on eluding me for too much longer and now that I'm considered dead. Along with having this new look about me he'll never recognize me.

I know he will pock his nose out where I can get at him where I can be rid of him once and for all. He's been a pain in my ass for far too long. Besides what he thinks is his, is mine. I bought and paid for all of it.

We got the jump on him. Even if he wanted to find us there's no way he could. Not knowing what we look like, or where our own lab is located. Where I took a special interest in making sure no one, will ever find it.

I hope that you are keeping up are location like I told you too? We are going to be needing it diligently maintained for when the time comes to make certain that all James secrets died with him.

Now that we've taken the initial step to go through with this. We can't let anything stand in are we to stop us from being successful. There's no going back for us now."

"Relax sweetheart I've everything under control." She consoling spoke out trying to place his concerns at ease, and that she wasn't harboring any regrets over taking the action they did.

"I must say Steven dear. I'm utterly amazed with the change in you. You're more than 20 years of your younger self. This rejuvenation of yours is nothing less than staggering to say the least.

So when is it going be my turn to make my miraculous transformation again? I don't trust my old self holding enduring long enough to see this scheme of yours through. Ginger wasn't much younger than I, and not as healthy I might add?"

"Soon my dear, very soon. You must be patient until our daughter inherits what is rightfully oar's first, before your alternate transformation well be able to take place.

We have covered all the unforeseen complications that might arise. We can't alter things now at this point.

Let's not rush things too fast. You still have to die mysteriously yourself. If things are going to work out the way, we played them too.

We must make certain to preserve your body so that it will last till your final hours. That duplicate clone we improvised has limited function. It was only intended to get you away and not that much longer. Maybe possibly another week at the most.

Don't forget that of what we mostly used was taken from Ginger who is steadily going to slowly pass. The rest of her is going to be surviving because of you sustaining her chemical composition to do so.

I'm still hoping that using Paul's body will eventually give me James location, and where he hid those damn notes.

Thus far I'm not getting anything on his whereabouts, and I can't trust jeopardizing using Paul's memory cells. When having to keep my senses about me to find that damn James.

I was lucky enough to get those two, who I've been training on the side to help me make the transition as it is.

Where the only thing keeping them loyal is the money I've been stealing from Normans' accounts.

Everything depends on finding that damn note book of James.

I'm not all that sure that things have turned out the way they should have just yet, and won't be until I can verify the procedure I used with those notes, and calculation of his. Seeing how Paul was that much help to me seeing how he was close to dying as it was from cancer. I was just fortunate enough to be able to use him in the condition that he was in.

Don't forget it took James closest ally Paul. The one I'm using to sustain myself to get everything set up as fast as I did.

I knew when he suffered that minor stroke that I had to get ahead of the game where James was concerned knowing that he was up to no damn good himself.

I had too much invested to let him turn on me knowing that once Norman discovered the millions I stole from him. That he wouldn't hesitate to get me arrested for embezzlement.

I had no choice but to us Paul knowing that it was my only hope to elude everyone, and still come out ahead of the game, by making sure of the outcome for the two of us.

I'm handling my end, but I wasn't the only one that caught on that

James was abandoning the project, and took most of what he invented along with him as well.

We needed time to protect ourselves. Where they also are doing likewise and also out trying to find him while having to struggle to survive with the limited assets that they were left with after Paul and I absconded with most of what James left behind.

Even them even with all the knowledge I obtained working with Paul it's still not going to be easy. That's why I desperately need those two, I latched onto until I can bring Paul back to correct all the mistakes I obviously have made.

Then there's still James himself to consider, and not knowing what he's up to attempting to protect himself, and everything he's achieved.

Where I just know, he was holding out on everyone with entirely new advanced that he achieved behind everyone backs.

It was Paul who perfected the means to automate the procedure to where it could be used on a timer.

That gave me the idea as to how to gain control, and overpower him long enough to use him to preserve myself.

So that I could be able to accomplish all that I have but, I'm no damn scientist! Otherwise, I wouldn't be here using one, of Paul's experimental chemical composition. Attempting to alter my own. Using those two, I'm having to depend up now.

I know it's only going to be a matter of time before they double-cross me that's why I'm not letting them learn too much too soon. Which isn't also not helping my position one bit.

That's why time is imperative from here on, and things have to work out just as we played them too.

Honey, I need you to stay close to Sally like the loyal maid you are. To make sure everything goes the ways we planned it where she's concerned.

It's going to take time where her, and the money are going to be concern. After Sally has everything.

Then all it's going to be, is a simple matter of gaining control of her mental capacity for us to secure are financial futures all over again.

Hopefully by then I'll have perfected the new procedure and gotten rid of the threat of those who would dare to take from us what is ours'.

I spent millions on making it ours' and no one is going to be taking advantage of what's ours' but, us.

Honey, she's our daughter. We are going to need her alive and healthy for all are benefits without her catching onto what's going on around her."

"Steven I don't like having to used Gingers body. She was a loyal servant to me as well. I really hated to do what we did to her. Are you sure there isn't any chance of returning her back to herself again after this is over?"

"I don't think so. These bodies are only temporary we ourselves are going to have to find new bodies. One's that won't be recognized by anyone. We can never go back to whom we were again.

As it is, I have no idea what James was up too. When last I saw him he had that body of this badly mutilated.

Then when he upped, and left he left behind the remains of several of the women he was actually attempting to change his appearance of himself into that of a woman. That netted him no obvious beneficial results, by what I could notice.

As fascinating as it is for us to be here. This truly isn't me as I want to be but, it's still go enough to move about without being recognized.

I'm far from being anything but, what I am as you see me. Let alone being capable of altering my gender.

I know how to make money to be able to afford to pay people to do for me. I need time dammit! Along with people I can trust not to double cross me.

Let's not forget that I'm not the only one out here trying to get ahead of the game here. I made it appear as if someone actually murdered me where I had to do it to myself.

I'm not out there actually murdering people like someone did to Miss Perking's. Luckily with you overseas you'll be safe. Where with myself already dead. I should be able to move around freely to do what I've to do.

Speaking of that. Honey I really can't stay too much longer. You know where I'll be, and only call me if it's an emergency.

I'll only call you when I want you to meet me. Now remember when you here the name Milton. That will tell you to come meet me down under the pool house.

As for me, with all our money, once again intact. Where I will know, we are safe from harm. I want to start all over again. Say from about ten, years old.

With my mind fully in tacked there's nothing I won't be able to accomplish, and I'm going to want you with me as always."

"Steven, what about those others who are involved in all this?"

"They won't be any concern. We'll simply handle them when the time comes. Just like we did to all those others prior to recruiting the two, we are using now.

Honey, I admit that in my hast to obtain what I have. I had to move recklessly but, we were able to recruit the loyalty of two.

Whereas the rest I'll have to devote more of my time into locating them. I hope you realize what I'm going to have to do to insure are security of us not being discovered."

"You just do what you've to do. Just don't let me know about it, and you damn well better always come back safe and unharmed to me."

"Never fear dearest I'll find them, and when I do I'll take care of them permanently. There were only nine, not counting James, and the two of us. Of which I have already taken care of two. That should only leave nine excluding us.

However, I can't be certain until I check out the other locations. If in fact that there are others, that is.

I sure wish that Paul's memory would start seeping into my brain more quickly that's confusing my train of thought just by lingering about mixing me up.

That's only one of the problems I'm having to deal with. I need to find a way where I can store his memory until I can use it to my benefit

I'm getting nothing but, only fragments that I can't associate with. Hopefully everything will come eventually I know it will because his mine is stronger willed than my own, and I have to prevent that from happening.

As difficult as it is to handle the inconvenience I'll just have to deal with it as best as I can for the time being.

Meanwhile we can't leave any witnesses behind to tell about any of this that's for sure. We also can't risk acting to hastily either, where we would endanger ourselves.

We have been covering are tracks up to know. There's no reason why we can't continue to keep on doing so.

I only know of one we have to be concerned about. That's James himself then that's only until we find his notes. Then I'll find someone else to take his place.

Where I think that he established a good cover for himself to keep everyone looking for him.

By creating himself as a loser in that front of a card room actually risking his own health sleeping with whore's.

Getting that stupid bitch of an owner to actually believe in his bull-shit. So that he could leave a lasting impression. Having everyone wondering about what in the hell, he was doing.

In order to keep everyone attention on worrying about who might be looking for him because of her running about asking a lot of stupid question amongst other scientists.

Attracting their interest just enough to keep all are eyes and ears concentrating on his, and their whereabouts. Leaving himself free to move around freely to elude anyone he wants to avoid, like me.

Was utterly genius of him. I have to give him credit for that, and for actually pulling it off right under everyone's noses.

With that being the only exception everything is working out perfectly. All we need to do is keep that idiot detective concentrating his efforts on Sandy for a little while longer until we can get things set up for that husband of hers' Norman.

To take his rightful place in the scheme of things I've planned for him. To which everything is happening just as I planned them to happen.

Damn Mary I'm feeling fantastic!" Steven zealously blurted out. Grabbing hold of her waist walking her backwards towards the bed. Until she plopped down backwards upon the mattress with him coming down on top of her.

"No, honey . . . Not again? Are you sure that you, and Ginger haven't been practicing already? Oh, my god, Steven . . .!"

* * * *

I laid with Janet hugging up against me. Under the cooling satin sheets of her bed, smoking a cigarette. Still not being able to shake Sandy from my mind. While there I was lying with the only woman, I ever truly felt anything for.

Arrogantly trying to tell myself that Janet wasn't good enough for me. Honestly believing that Sandy was, and I never been as close to Sandy has, I have with Janet physically, emotionally, or otherwise. Let alone have anything in common with her as I obviously did with Janet.

Denying that all it was. That it was I really comparing her to Janet, and that I became obsessively frustrated over my sexual attraction for.

What I was able to get close to, and became compulsive with wanting a lot more than what I got, and not wanting it to stop once I got what I wanted.

Putting plainly in terms that I could understand. I was just being my greedy myself never wanting to be satisfied with what I already had.

"Janet I've just been lying here thinking about all you have been telling me about this professor Baron of yours pondering over if such a thing was possible?

I realized in this now day generation anything is possible. I mean it's 1995 and science has made some miraculous discoveries.

However, even with all the new advances in science, and technology being developed. But? Someone being capable of being regenerated as someone else. Now that's too incredible to even comprehend. I'm not saying I'm doubting you?"

"Don't say it honey." Janet cut me short from finishing what I was about to say." Just have faith in me. I know what I'm talking about, and believe it is possible.

I seem the impossible happening with my own eyes. Like I said it was within a matter of several mouths like I said before he was actually up walking around.

Not looking like the same person I first saw. Believe me honey, even I was having trouble believing my own eyes.

He was actually changing his appearance putting himself through those bazaar treatments that he was subjecting himself too.

I'm telling you he wasn't the same person. I couldn't have been imagining what I was seeing him putting himself through. He was virtually taking years off his appearance and changing physically as well.

I was there and saw him being place inside a transparent cylinder next to someone else lying in another cylinder. That where placed inside an even larger transparent dome structure.

Where all sort of diabolical looking equipment was inside with him. Where a group of people where manning the controls, I guess to monitor what was going to happen.

Where suddenly from out of nowhere this extremely this high pitch frequency sound came ear piercing into my ears.

That became so loud I couldn't hear it anymore. Where I started to feel vibrations that were being omitted throughout my entire body becoming so intense that I thought I actually past out from the turbulence I feel myself shaking so profusely.

However, when I thought it was all over I found myself still standing bewilderingly disturbed by finding myself still on my feet and no longer dizzy, or feeling even faintly dizzy.

I admit that I didn't see what actually transpired with my own eyes. However, what I did see was one person appearing to walk out from that dome by itself afterwards.

What I found even more alarmingly shocking was when I looked at my watch. Shockingly discovering that several hours have passed. That I wasn't even aware of noticing went by.

Then the next think I saw was professor Baron emerging from another door greeting me saying.

"You see I told you that I would be all right."

"I was at a loss of word to say other than. You did?! But, you didn't look anything at all like him?" I stood there replying seeing him all pale, and withdrawn.

Looking lifeless, as if he had no color to him at all but, it was him no less, and he was standing up straight.

Even several hours afterwards. When his color started to return, and he began looking the same again. He still didn't but, then again it was him like I said, and he was walking. Not steadily but, walking none-the-less.

I don't know why he allowed me to see what he was allowing himself to put himself through. However, he convinced me just by him standing straight up, and actually walking gain that he had something incredible going for him, and I wanted to learn more about what it was.

Where I spent a couple days with him several days later just walking around with him. Listening to him talking about how great he was feeling, before I had to come back here.

Even though I wasn't allowed to meddle into what everyone else was going down below, or even speak to any one of the others doing whatever they were doing, and sort of restricted just to his living quarters above what was going on down below.

I did however manage to get him to feel comfortable around me. To where he would speak freely, and confided in me not to ever tell anyone that he was researching cloning.

I didn't have any idea what cloning was. Even when he was trying to educate me about it. All I cared about is what he was doing to himself was actually doing to him. Seeing a golden opportunity flashing before my eyes.

I was only intimate with him once but, that one time when I was he put on a hospital grown and wouldn't take it off but, I couldn't help to notice one particular change in his appearance.

When that gown tangled up, and he had to remove it in order for me to help him put it back on again.

I notice that he had a large dark birth in the small of his back that ran down to his tail bone.

The reason that it drew my attention was that Nancy described him has not even a single mold anywhere on him. Before he started subjecting himself to undergo those treatments.

Those treatments had to had done that to him. Thereby it's a way of being able to recognize him if he doesn't look the same anymore.

It's like a pitch black streak about an inch wide that must have effect the back of his spinal colon down to the crevice of his ass.

There's another thing you have to know. After those few days were over, Was the last time I saw him where he just upped and disappeared.

Where prior too then. He kept coming back losing, betting recklessly as if hoping to regain his losses. Continuously giving me more, and more pages from out of that book of his.

While telling me that what he was giving me was worth more than he was losing. That I was only holding onto them for him until he was able to pay me back.

I kept taking them because of what I saw with my own eyes. Eventually winding up with peoples, names, and even addresses of those, he was working with. Along with a lot of gibberish that I couldn't even begin to understand.

Where without his knowledge. I took it upon myself to find out just what it was he was dumping on me but, I already told you all of that.

Daryl I wouldn't be so dead set in getting you involved. If I wasn't certain that I'm onto something miraculously life changing here.

You know me, and that I'm not one to be easily screwed over by anyone but, you. Someone has to be damn good to pull a con over on me, and if he did. I want to make damn sure that he's not going to get away with it!"

"Janet a thought just occurred to me. About how many names were in that book?"

"I counted Twenty. Why do you ask?"

"Well if they're not the right names, and addresses of those who were other scientists, or collaborating with him. Maybe they were the names of the other people who were involved backers maybe. I would like to get a look at those names and maybe check a few of them out for myself.

Now mind you now the through just came into my head. I was just thinking that maybe that some of those name could be associated with someone that might have been used for the regeneration procedure itself, and who have already been reported missing, or never existed.

Say, being used for others who have already gone through the process, or scheduled to be going through the regenerating process. That he may be handed them to you. For whatever reason I have no idea as of yet.

Another dreadful thought also occurred to me. He also handed you the means of how what you saw could possibly work.

Which means that you could also know who's going to be popping up someplace else. Maybe starting new lives for themselves, or have been reported missing

Even though it's only conjecture on my part. I was just thinking that you having that list could be placing you in a very precarious position.

If it should become known that you're in possession of that sort of information. It could place you in a very hazardous position with other people who might have an interest in what he was into.

If in fact this is some top secret stuff that someone doesn't want to become known, and that someone will stop at nothing to keep it a secret."

"Jesus . . . you sure do get smart once you apply your mind's attention to other things besides sex. Not to mention frightening.

I never once given any thought to anything like that. You could be right. I even said it myself. That someone else might be out looking for him, now didn't I?"

"Janet, this book what does it look like?"

"It's a ledger. An account ledger. It says on the front." Past due accounts. The way I figure it, the values in it must be some sort of code. I sure as hell can't figure that part of it out.

Baron said that the names represent the values being their address, and the figures, and values underneath. Are in code that only he himself can decipher.

Maybe that's why I can't figure out who they are, or that they don't live at what I intrepid as their addresses.

Dammit! Daryl! That's why it's imperative that I locate him. Especially if you're right about there being others.

Each time I was with him. There was never more than maybe six, other people who always had their faces covered with masks. I figured that it was due to the condition inside that dome. So you could be right.

There were, or could be a lot more other besides myself who could have been working with him that might also be holding other sections, or pages of that damn book of his.

It might even be his way of protecting himself against any reprisals for him disappearing, preventing any harm from befalling him if he is discovered.

Knowing that not just one other person has possession of what's needed to make what he achieved work.

I can't believe that I was that naively gullible to think there weren't others who weren't being involved in what he was doing. I mean I just took it for granted that I was the only one, he was entrusting his findings too.

Excluding those who have already been there with him, and possibly others as well. By not paying them all that much attention. To even ask what functions they were taking on and what they were doing.

Hell I never even bothered to even ask any of their names. Even though I was restricted, I should have had the common sense to do it anyway.

Once again Daryl had no idea that Janet was using him to aid her find the others who could have also allured being discovered who had to be eliminated in order to prefect Baron's secret identity.

That she was colluding with him to locate all the others who worked with him to prefect his procedure that Baron already promised he would perform on her.

Dammit Daryl there's so many if's, there's no telling how involved, or complex the contents on those pages can be describing.

He told me a little bit about how he came about experimenting in the development of that contraption of his that I saw but, never went into detail as to how it really worked or derived at perfecting it.

He said that he was recruiting funding for his invention. That it was only in theory, hoping to get investors interested in funding it.

After which he even made some major breakthroughs. However, there were still numerous complications that had to be worked out in the process, that he felt sure where too dangerous for him to precede safely

He said that he went to his investors, and told them that he wanted to stop the experiments but, his investors thought otherwise, and threatened to take his invention away from him. Then have someone else pursue completing it but, instead of taking that route.

They took another one. That left him no choice but, to comply to their demands to finish it.

That's when he told me about him having a daughter. He said that they kidnaped her, and threatened to kill her if he didn't do what he was told.

He wouldn't go into detail, or say how long ago that was but, I got the impression that it was quite a few years ago.

Where during that time he diligently devoted his life to completing his invention, and to his knowledge they still had possession of her, and his invention was still far from being completed."

"How old is she?"

"I have no way of knowing for certain but, by the way he was talking. That a great many years have passed, and by the way he was always referring to her as being innocently young I would guess maybe around ten, or so.

I would guess say maybe in her twenties now.

Where the nearest I can figure he had to be working on achieving what, he started out to accomplish for about twenty, years, maybe.

Where he let it slip that he received his first investor some fifteen years ago. So basically I figured her to be at least in her twenties.

According to him they let her see him from time to time. To ensure him that they still had her, and that she was alive and well.

Honey, the way he talked. Those investors involved could take over Nations, that's how influential, and rich they're.

It had to have costed millions to set up that lavatory I saw, and he said that he had two, others just like it, and that they were only being operated just by him, and only a few of his colleagues. Leastwise the one I was in was.

When I went to find him. Not only was the warehouse he was conducting his experiments in gone but, so was the lavatory inside it. All that was left was a deep hole. The entire area was undergoing reconstruction.

I asked around to find out what was being built. It's going to become a plastic factory owned by Peterson enterprises.

Whoever dug up that warehouse had to know what was in it. That entire place came out of a science fiction novel. It just couldn't be picked up and moved overnight."

"What about the other two locations. Couldn't he be at one of them?"

"All I know is that another one is located somewhere near Las Vegas. I don't think that he went there. I think that he's still here trying to find his daughter.

I do know this much. That formulas that James used that could possibly create an alternate clone of himself, or other people can't be done alone.

I'm no scientist by any means but, I know what transfusions look like. The method he uses starts out with a clear tube.

That a cloudily liquid is being used to fill the entire contraption of glass tubing that he uses. To where no one has to monitor what in the hell is going on inside them. Where still another one was also monitoring what was going on inside those cylinders.

If what I saw is any judge of how many others were needed to successful conduct the procedure, I saw him go through. I would say at least six, possibly seven.

Then I saw it with my own eyes. Them using multiple other flexible clear tube of some kind. Leading form his brain I suppose into the others people's brain in the other cylinder but, don't quote me on that.

Even though I feel certain it had to be another person I have known a way of knowing for certain? I was standing on the upper level where everything was going on down below me.

As bazaar as it sounds and as grotesque as it looked the procedure apparently most have worked. I can say that because I saw it with my own eyes, and him standing tall and walking again with no signs of paralysis what so ever.

Where all it took was a matter of several hours to achieve the end results. Now that I can't swear to for certain. My watch could have been affected by what was going on during the procedure itself.

Like I said, the professor was paralyzed. From his right side shoulder down to his legs that was also affected by the stroke.

I saw him rise up then later on actually moving his arm about while lifting and wiggling his right leg, and walking firmly upon it.

Get me that book, and I'll get us both immortality. Think of it honey! Life for as long as we want to live. Being anyone, and any age, you want to be!

I honestly feel that I'm so damn close! But, I still can't figure out what happened to make him suddenly runoff.

With him knowing that they still had his daughter under their control but, something happened to cause him to do what he did.

Honey I might be way off base about this but, I honestly believe that it's his daughter who is the key to get him to reveal himself.

I honestly believe that one or all of those who were working with him were in on her being kidnaped. Where I also think that you are onto something with those names. Anyone could know where she's being kept.

If we were to find her, we could be the one, holding all the cards and him under our control. To where we could force him to divulge all his secrets. If we were to promise him that in return, we would tell him where to find his daughter.

I could care less about anyone else especially any of those traitorous colleagues of his. It's a sure thing that they would help us.

So if we have to I'll give t hose who might have also got away to him. To let him deal with them as he wants. All I'm carrying about are us."

"Janet maybe he didn't runoff? Maybe his usefulness just ran out, and they disposed of him?"

"No way! Without that formula they have nothing, and as far as I know I have the original pages that he ripped out of that damn ledger."

"What if he gave it to them in return for his daughter already, and doesn't want to be found?"

"Now that's a possibility. If he did, he would have to have something else to insure his wellbeing, as well as his daughters. Both of them know too much to be allowed to live."

"Well that shoots that idea. I'm getting tired of all this thinking. It's giving me a headache."

"Speaking of a headache. You're becoming a major one. With me having to foot the bill for you carousing with my employees.

I received a bill from Doris for an office call visit. Isn't it enough that I allow you to use my girls for nothing. Now you are wanting me to foot the bill for you on the job antics with them as well?"

"Would you rather I go elsewhere?"

"That's not funny! I can't see why you can't be satisfied with what you have with me. I'm more a woman for you than you can handle as it is. There's no need for you to go to any of my girls.

"But there is. They tell me what you don't. You tell me as it is, and the last time I got myself fucked up good was because I didn't listen.

Where because of it I'll never be the man I once was where you're concern. You make me face the fact of how it once was between us, and it could never be the same again.

With your girls they say the words that I need to hear. As for you footing the bill. That's of my doing. It's on me not you. I'll talk to her and make things good between us."

"Come on Daryl you're not doing so badly. You're still able to have sex, and you proved the doctors wrong."

"Yeah, I know . . . I guess I did show them, now didn't I? I guess that I have to give you credit for that."

"Honey, I didn't do anything but, give mature a little shove where it was needed. The rest came maturely. You only lost one testicle. The rest is functioning morally."

"You don't have to say that."

"I know I don't. I just feel that it's time you stop concerning yourself over nothing, and start looking on the bright side. "

Besides look at it this way. The sooner you find that book, or those who can get us to it. The sooner you can be twice the man you're now. Although your prefect the way you're now.

"If you want the truth, I like you better just the way you're now.

You're caring, compassionate, and sincere but, you're a man with a deeply seeded ego problem. Who thinks needs to prove to himself that he himself is the best even over himself. Who is also easily offended by the least bit of criticism."

I hate to say this but, at times you were really brutal with me. Women love being made love to. They don't like being pulverized by an insidious masochist."

"Was I that bad?"

"I'm still here so you couldn't have been too terrible but, there were times when I actually dreaded the thought of submitting to you desires but, I'll always still long for you to hold me in your arms.

You men can become so primitive at times. I guess I became too accustomed to the way you were. I mean we have been together since junior high school.

"Honey, I'm not like any one of my girls. Sure I had my flirtatious affairs but, it's been you all along. I did what I had to do to get where I am, and I'm not regretting any of it."

"Janet it's been you all along with me as well but, you need more than me. You had to get out and make your own mistakes.

God, knows that I made some real dozy. And there's always the chance that something could happen to me, and has as we both know. With the exception of getting myself killed.

You are young, and far from being naive, or in need from being neglected where admirers are concern.

Even though you made me the proudest, any guy could hope to be, you yourself have rose to levels I could only dream of achieving, regardless how you did it.

Who am I to judge you, or anyone else. Where if it wasn't for you. I wouldn't be where I am now. You make me feel majestic just lying here beside you.

Honey, look where you're now, and you are only 30, and you are still young, brilliant, gorgeous, as well as very successful.

Where I'm still struggling to make something out of myself, and all I've to show for my effort is getting myself busted up, and severally wounded several times. One of which has marred me for life.

Janet I admire you more than I do Randy. You are extremely important to me but, the way things are. There's not very much I can offer you that you haven't already exceeded in obtaining for yourself.

As much as I hate to say this but, I do love the way it makes me feel when I even think of it but, I do look up to you a great deal.

Not because I feel indebted, or obligated but, because you always have and will be the only women I'll ever want to be with."

"If you're attempting to flatter me. You best be careful. I'll hold you to everything you say. So why don't you shut up."

"I'm trying too but, when I look at you something in me wants me to relive every moment I ever spent with you.

Your beauty is bewitching. Your sinuousness inflames me with majesties of the devil himself you so inflame my wanting desire for you wanting to feel your loving warmth embellishes me beyond my wildest fantasy."

"What's wrong honey? Why can't you just come right out and tell me that you love me as much as I love you? Instead of using excuses to keep you from admitting the truth."

"I can't. Especially now I can't but, you've no idea just how much I do love you but, my love is only standing in your way from finding the love you so richly deserve."

I climbed out of bed saying not another word. Picking up my clothes, and leaving her laying covered up with her silk sheets.

Chapter 7

I left Janet's place around 2:00 A.M., and returned back to my office. I sat thinking over all Janet told me pondering whether or not to pursue the existing case with Sandy Peterson that I was on.

Along with what Janet told me. Both cases seemed to become tangled up together. As if they were making some sort of a connection in my mind's way of thinking.

To where I found myself thinking of them as one in the same case. Even though they weren't associated with each other.

I was finding it extremely hard to believe what Janet told me. Asking myself. 'Could in fact really happen?'

Rationally thinking warranted that the outlandish things she told me. Could only happen in some science fiction movies.

Where at the same time. The very thought of it really being possible terrified the hell out to me along with intriguingly fascinated even my wildest imagination.

Cloning people, while altering their appearance, and actually being able to retain their own memories, and intellectual fatalities. Whereas even giving a person the possible means to be able to live on forever.

Thinking how stupendous such a break through it would represent, and the miraculous possibilities, it would generate alone just by applying it to eradicating the disease factor alone Why the achievement alone would in itself become astronomical to say the least.

Where one, could actually achieve eternal life. How to me that was just too incredible to be realistic.

Where there again, if what Janet was telling me could be believed. It could obviously be happening.

Not being much of a science enthusiast myself I had to admit that science in general has overcame insurmountable obstacles in a great many areas?

Then there was Janet herself. Knowing her as well as I do. I felt certain that she wouldn't lie about what she saw.

No matter how I looked at it, I just couldn't seem to resolve myself to accepting all of what she said.

Sure some maybe but, I had to see it with my own eyes if I'm going to become convinced that she couldn't have been over exaggerating.

Janet was known to partake in tampering with an assortment of drugs. She was also in the business of distributing them as well from time to time.

Especially about one's body slowly being able to be transferred, or actually taking on the configuration, and appearance of another person body, and characteristics. While even being able to convert oneself from male to a female.

The question I had to answer right now was. Where to start looking for that professor Baron, and on how to keep an open mind, about who, he was, or who he could be now. If what Janet said is true, he could be anyone?

The fact of him being able to become another person, and actually being able to take on the appearance of that other person left a hell of a lot of doubt in my mind.

Where at the same time opened up an entirely whole new realm of inconceivable possibilities. That left me pandering the feasibility about it actually being possible.

If science did in fact become so advanced. That it was able to actually achieve to be able to duplicated another person?

Which startlingly brought up another alarming question. What would be happening to that other person while they were being used?

Multiple question kept popping into my mind like. 'What happened to the person the professor was, and where did the persons he may have become, come from . . .? Certainly they had to have existed, and established some sort of identifying history?'

Thinking right off. 'Find that person, and follow their history, and that would lead me straight to that Mr. Baron the one Janet wants me to find.'

I needed to go back, and have Janet describe as best as possible just who he was beginning to appear like, and go from there.

Thinking that it might even be someone that was named in that book of his, and with a possible description of him as to now he might look like.

I could cross reference his description along with the names in that book, and come up with a possible resemblance to where I would know who to look for.

Thinking also to search out the missing people's data base on the computer, and the police files of missing persons. Which was going to take up a lot of my time, not knowing from what state, or who they could be?

That's when my minds' thoughts came upon the present case I was involved with. Where two, people were already murdered, and that I was already in over my head in.

Realizing that I was already being held accountable to the police as being a person of interest in both cases.

That I had no choice but, to concentrate on getting those cases resolved before dealing with Janet's problem.

The question was how I was going to go about not obligating my promise to Janet? Knowing there was no way I could work on them both at the same time. Knowing that I was good but, not that good. Not to be able too without getting help.

Instinctively something drew my eyes' attention towards my open office door. To the bottom of the outer office door.

Where I saw a very distinctive shadow blocking out the light. Filtering in under the door from the outside hall light.

I reached into my center desk drawer, pulling out my revolver. Then slowly got up from my chair. Where I crept up to hide behind my open office door. As I could hear the main office door opening creepily slowly . . .

"Past, Past . . . Is anyone home . . .?" A woman's voice whispered out asking." It's I . . . Daryl are you here . . .?"

It didn't sound like Sandy's voice. My gut told me that if I answered I would regret it. I did the only thing I could do. I waited with my finger in the trigger.

"Damn it Joan! I told you this wouldn't work." A man's voice whispered out with an uncertainty nervous tone to it."

"I know he's in here I saw the light on in his window before coming up here."

"That might be but, you don't know that it was he, and not someone else. Now whoever it was knows that we're here as well. Shit . . .!" He nervously replied back.

"Relax Tom I've the situation under control. Mr. Henderson if you can hear me, you best come out where I can see you. All we want to do is talk to you.

We were very fond of Jenny Perking we know she's dead, and she went to talk to you. We're here to see Mr. Henderson.

If you're not him, we won't hesitate to shoot . . . You need our help Mr. Henderson, and we need yours.

Mr. Henderson we're walking in towards your open office door. We're armed Mr. Henderson . . . Here we come Mr. Henderson . . ." She skeptically stepped inside the outer office door.

Creeping slowly toward the open door of the inner office door as she continued to whisper out talking making her presence known.

The woman's voice came became louder as she entered the outer office, as she continued to keep on talking. While she entered inside my door. Being followed by some guy entering my inner office behind her.

"Stop where you're!" I yelled out moving to position myself standing behind them with my back against the open door hastily closing it behind me. Trapping all of us inside my office pointing my revolver at the back of the one, who entered first.

"That's far enough! Drop your guns on the floor, and step inside up to my desk. Then slowly turn around so I can see who came to visit me so early in the morning."

"Mr. Henderson . . ." The women slowly raised her hand holding the gun above her head. Calmly spoke out.

"We're the only. As well as the last people who can help you. We can't go to the police, and neither can you. "

She walked towards the desk. Leading the guy walking in behind her. "If you know anything about what's going on. You'll know why we're hear."

"Lady, if you knew that I was here. Why did you come creeping into my office with guns out?" I walked up behind them, then around beside them. Positioning myself beside my desk as they stood before my desk. "Now just put your guns down on the top of my desk, and step back."

"Mr. Henderson I was only sure that you were here. I didn't know who-else could be here with you. We didn't want to just come upon you if I was wrong. I might be holding a gun but, let me assure you I'm not very good at shooting it.

We value our lives too much for that. As well as you should yours. One of the reasons we came here is to warn you that your own life is in danger, just as Are's is.

People are being killed. If you were to be the next, we didn't want to get involved. We saw who killed Jenny Perking. We were supposed to be protecting her.

A needle projected from an air pistol killed Jenny by a man by the name of Robert Anderson he was the one who murdered her."

'Robert Anderson. Isn't that Mrs. Peterson chauffeur?' I startlingly said to myself recognizing his name immediately.

"Are we going to talk Mr. Henderson, or are we going to stand badgering each other back, and forth accomplishing nothing? Where it's getting too late for bickering where every second is becoming more crucial."

She places her gun down on top of the desk stepping back from it just barely out of reach from being able to grab hold of it if need be.

"All right let's talk." I stepped in front of them behind my desk. Still, pointing my 38 at them. Where we all then sat down about my desk.

I sat giving the woman a visual good going over. Not, for a second taking my eye off the guy sitting beside her.

Nervously watching his hands, while using my eyes to scan over the women face. Diligently taking special notice of her facial expressions and her body language.

She was a very attractive. Who appeared to be in her middle 20's. Her hassle colored eyes accentuated her brunette hair, that kept attacking my eyes' attention for some reason.

Mainly because they looked provocatively unstable, and were becoming nerve-racking to look into Through those wide rimmed glasses she was wearing.

From what I could see of her sitting before my desk. Her body structure conformed to her figure elegantly.

Emphasizing upon her finder qualities, and though her face was attractive to look upon. It reflected the look of high intelligence that projected an intimidating image superiority about her.

"Mr. Henderson my name is Joan Staples. You wouldn't believe it by looking at me but, I hold five, master degrees in science, and chemistry. I'm a scientist. My main field is biological chemistry I'm also a renewed genealogist.

For some years now I've been involved in experiments that up until two, years ago were only a dream. Evolving about Stem Cells research, and biological cloning.

That has become a dream come true for all who were participating along with colleague Tom here along myself. That has now turned out to become a disastrous biological nightmare.

If any of what we achieved ever became known that it became a reality. Life has you know it now.

Could, and possibly would become extinct with the exception of chosen select people establishing a new order in which those who did live would be made to live by.

If something isn't done to stop what has been discovered from becoming a reality before its time.

Along with seven, other scientists. We've discovered how to not only stop aging, but reserve it as well. However, there were some unforeseen developments in the process.

The human body wasn't able to tolerate the restructuring process. Therefore, another means had to be developed, and was.

We discovered that all aging occurred in a certain portion of the genetic structuring of one's DNA. That had a major effect on ones' mind comprehending processes that was associated with the minds retention process.

That evolved around the aging process, and aided the deterioration of genetic organisms that are critical to normal bodily functions.

That during further examinations. We also discovered that all that was needed. Was to reproduce those cryogenic cells. Was by reducing them into billions of molecules.

Breaking them down into a molecular composition by self-insemination. Categorizing their importance, and their relationships to other specific functions. Necessary to retain normal developing bodily balance.

While energizing one molecule, or a group of others to surpass another. Creating a rejuvenating process such as is used when creating a test tube baby.

A single cell when integrated with a certain additive, or depressant element. That could in fact become regenerated, or depleted.

When interacted with the composition break down, with alternate cell structures. Such as in the atomized cells associated with age, and when the chemical additive was applied.

We not only discovered the regenerations of human growth, and devolvement was able to be controlled.

During which we also came to discover that it would be possible to create another living being by duplicating the restructuring process.

We also were capable of determining the sex, and age of the alternate clone and actually modify it to our own specifications.

Such as using live human skin to generate more like it. That's been being used in skin graphing on burn victims for several years now. With there not being very much of a difference being added to the original procedure.

During which we have been able to also perfect the ability to be able to be capable of taking on the actual human genetic chemistry of the person it was being regenerated from.

Besides having also other biological altering capabilities that are too extensive to get into right now.

The altering procedure wasn't believed to be totally perfected as yet. To where the persons being cloned, along with the clone itself being able to take up the other's appearance.

TIME CHANNELING

Our both placed into suspended hibernation, and intravenously kept alive until the cloning process is completed. As projected this process entails two contributors to produce one clone

So that the procedure can be repeated until the new identity has been totally adsorbed from the others bodies energy, that will then eventually die over a period of time.

Where the same also goes for the alternate, or primary person the clone is to represent the one, using their body as well will also suffer the same fate.

However, it's only going to be a matter of time before the longevity might be possible to become permanent.

At present the transition as it is right now could last up to a year, or more. Before the other person's body can't be used anymore.

By being able to undergo several more transformation. The formula and the procedure are good but, it needs perfecting there still remains some risky flaws associated with the process.

The key is the brain stem, and the extraction of the bodies accentual DNA cell that keeps the original brain cells alive and which brain is going to be the prominent brain being used in the clone.

Over time the strengths of either, or both brains diminish, and start to break down, and the user has to go back to be regenerated.

Even to the two of us as well. It's the memories that must be maintained. It's accentual to keep the link between the two, brains connected.

We've been experimenting with long term memory cells to enhance the stronger of the two minds.

Where it took weeks maybe even mouths for it to take effect it takes a lot sooner. But it's still inefficient to replenish itself without having to go back to regenerate the duplicate cell.

Using ontogenetic in conjunction with lite responsive proteins are genetically inserted into the brain cells.

Then with the use of lasers to find out what they do. We have learned that by engineering the neurons, by inducing electrical current. Combined with the laser light to enhance the weak brain cells.

Reestablishing not only the long term memory but, also enlarging the neocortex. Which we're hoping that will increase the short term memory as well.

By scientifically converting the cells through light regenerating the short term memories as well that were already there.

Achieving hopefully long term success in the transplanting procedure from the drone being used, to the person actually extracting from the combine memories to keep the superior one stability dominant.

However unforeseen complication's development where I'm sure, you have been made aware of. Where all nine, of us including professor Baron had to have to reestablished special locations on our own where we can continue the process.

The way it was set up so that everyone would benefit from all the research was that we all apply our own special individual fields to achieve certain specific efforts.

To which we were to concentrated on until perfecting particular portions of the formulas and procedures needed to be combined together.

Where we would go back and reduce it all over again until each stage was perfected where it could be applied.

Where professor Baron and his primary colleague Paul Murray would compile the results and delegate how each of us should precede.

Professor Baron empathized on how essential it was that we all refrain from collaborating with each other. To avoid getting ourselves involved in the other's project that might influence our own.

It was working out great for all of us. Seeing how we were all benefitting by perfecting discovering that which was necessary to continue to the next level in oar's. Whereas it appeared that the more we contributed the further advanced we became.

It's for that very reason why I can't go into detail from this point on. Which bring me to the point we came seeking you out. Hoping that you will help us in locating professor James Baron.

We can't stress enough how it's imperative that we find professor Baron. Because without him and his notes, and the formula.

This could very well be the beginning of the end for all those dictated scientists that invested so many years of their lives in perfecting this breakthrough.

Without your help are life spans are going to be short lived. With any luck at all the most we might last is possibly two, years at best.

The preservation of are alternate life forms have to be extended. If not. Once the other body's dies it will only be a matter of months before we'll virtually dissolve from lack of bodily energy.

Where are existing body fluids will become dried up and these bodies you see before you right now will most likely decompose and literally turn to dust.

Only through stem cell research, along with more biological, and anatomy restructuring can we have any hopes of completing the necessary research needed to prefect what we have achieved.

Now that Jenny Perking's. Mr. Morehouse's secretary has been killed along with Mr. More house himself. One, of are primary founders.

Where now along with the professor himself, and his colleague Paul Murray now also missing. There's only seven, of us left. Where we too will eventually die along with are counterparts.

The more of us that do especially at this point. The more humanity is going to lose out on the most spectacular discovery of mankind.

Yes, your right. I know what you're thinking right now. At present it is costing human lives, and you have every right to think that way but, eventually once perfected that could be totally avoided.

The possibilities of this newly found discovery are limitless. As too how far are discovery could benefit the human race. Think space itself just for starters.

Whereas also think. We are not the only ones in danger here. Anyone that had any association with what's been taking place, or had knowledge of its existence. Is as well in danger of being killed in order to keep this a secret.

These experiments took years, and millions in perfecting, and I'm sure the ones who were funding us. Won't be spearing any expense on seeking all of us out.

Something prompted professor Baron, and his close colleague Paul Murray to disappear without telling any of us what it was, or why.

There by forcing the rest of us to also do likewise. Which isn't benefitting any of us, who have managed to survive being murdered. If we hadn't of acted in our behalf like we did.

However, as things stand right now. Eventually all parties involved will eventually die if something isn't done to preserve what we've already accomplished. So that it can be revealed at the proper time.

When science as well as the human race can accept it's potential, and use it for the proposes it was intended to be used. That of preserving all of mankind, and not just a special few for their own personal gains.

Where the ones such as ourselves. Who place themselves in the forefront of having to lead the way. By sacrificing ourselves, by putting ourselves through the transfers, and are forced to continuously go through others.

All over again so that the human race can benefit from the sacrifices that the few of us have dictated are lives to contributing to the human race.

This is a pure example where the few are truly sacrificed for the preservation of the many, and it can't be allowed to be used unjustly for personal gains.

Mr. Henderson you won't believe it by looking at me, but I was once

77, years old, and Tom, here was 65.

You don't look shocked Mr. Henderson. Why is that? Could it be that you already knew? You do know, don't you?"

"Let's put it this way. I was aware of the possibility but, I've never seen the living results. That's if you're the living results?"

"I assure you I am, and so is Tom along with others that I know of. That brings us to the other reason why we are here.

Along with professor James Baron. Some four months ago. All the data on are experiments disappeared along with professor Baron and just recently professor Murray. "

* * * *

"That's where what she was telling me didn't connect. Janet told me that this professor upped and disappeared some two, weeks ago.

Whereas she was now telling me, he's been gone for some four, mouths. Now I wasn't any mathematician but, there was no way that was going to add up.

Which makes me wonder. If what Janet was telling me was in fact true and she was visiting him at his lavatory at some warehouse.

It had to had been at an unknown location where those would be originally working with him wasn't able to find him for over three, and a half mouths.

During which his colleagues themselves had enough time to also relocate and set up a lab all of their own also in isolated inconspicuous locations.

* * * *

"To duplicate what we accomplished. Where without the data we accumulated will take us another lifetime. Someone is trying to stop us from going any further by taking away are means to complete our research.

That someone has already murdered a critical member of our group as well as Jenny Perking are only link to are primary founders by also killing him as well.

Without Miss. Perking's her vast knowledge of who was backing him we're virtually cut off without any funds as well as being informed on future projection regarding funding so that we might be able to order some new equipment.

If it wasn't for her informing us regarding professor Baron suddenly up and disappearing when she did.

We never would have possibly escaped what could have possibly already befallen either the professor or professor Murray, and without one, or the other.

Our situation will no longer appear to be hopeful. That's another reason why it's imperative that you find one, or the other, and quickly.

It came to our knowledge though Miss Perking that Baron has been handing a lot of the documentation of what we have been conducting over to Mr. Morehouse.

Where when I myself last spoke to her.

She told me that after speaking to his wife. That she wasn't aware of seeing anything looking like confidential documents.

She said that she checks his office safe and it was empty but, there was a note in it. Reflecting that some documents were missing. That means that Baron was obviously giving them to someone else.

If at all possible I need you to find that someone else. If in fact they do exist. We can't have anything out there that would remotely connect that research to what we were working on, was ever out there.

Or that he alone could have been hiding for himself, or withholding it from the rest of us that could be essential to our survival. Where now we discovered that by what Miss. Perking's told me before she was murdered.

That Mr. Morehouse was no long with the initial group who has been founding are experiments.

That someone else has bought out his interests, and has been founding us for quite some time now.

Mr. Henderson you've to find professor Baron, if in fact he is still alive. He's the only one who possesses the knowledge to duplicate the procedures that took so long to prefect.

I'm prepared to pay you $1,00,000, to find him.

Where judging from your response. You're obviously the only one beside those already involved who knows about the existence of what I told you.

Could it be that you've already been approached and given an offer that night be exceeding the one I'm offering you?

"I felt certain that I was right about you. When I learned that Jenny went to meet you. I know that she didn't live long enough to tell you too much so that can only mean that someone else is already involved.

"However, I also must inform you. That I do know that you became involved in this though your connection with one of the persons personally involved with professor Baron as well as also could be involved in what is going on.

A woman by the name of Janet who was closely associated with professor Baron along with one Mr. Steven Morehouse who was also just recently murdered.

Which also places you in as much danger as all the rest of us. How I came to find out isn't important.

What is, is the fact that whoever it was who told, or approached you has knowledge that you know about the experiments that have been going on.

I've no proof of this but, I'm sure that others beside Tom and myself could have also gone through the transfer process for their own protection.

As for the professor doing so himself. Beside here there's only two, other places that might have the capabilities of helping him to do so.

It takes special construction to be able to handle the capacity of the equipment. Plus, a lot of special electricity excess cables, but getting the power supply to handle the high current output.

It will take to conduct the transference has been reduced to unitizing multiple gas generators so that wouldn't be a hard obstacle to have to overcome.

It's mostly the space, and location that would be accentual because of the conditions that take place to complete the actual transfer.

The accentual components mostly consist of specialize equipment and monitoring stations to regulate the insemination process.

However, both of the other places have been shut down. One, was located near Las Vegas, and the other in Tennessee.

Where the one place here has already been demolished but, Professor Baron did however mention something back about another lavatory that was being discussed about being built. I think I know where it could be.

He's several times talked of this island he lived on when he was a child. It's my guess that he's gone there if he's gone anyplace that would make him feel secure.

Seeing how he's the only one, who could have the resources as well as the results of using all the updated experiment. Leaving behind only the antiquated equipment for the rest of us to improvise using.

The updated equipment was constantly being altered, or modified to make changes that were mainly improvised as attachments to the older chambers.

Then used to create the upgraded version once the attachment was proven adaptable worthy, that professor Baron was constructing.

It's those outdated versions that I'm sure the others also improvised to reconstruct the upgrade that were applied to the latest version as Tom and I have done.

It's my guess that either he was reconstructing the one he was copying at the lab with us, or had somehow managed to transport everything before anyone was able to catch onto by disassembling the equipment in a short period of time when everyone was gone.

Like on the weekend that he disappeared, and is most likely attempting to put it all together by himself.

As for professor Murray I can even assume what he might be up to. Everyone is taking up fending for themselves until they're certain no harm is going to befall them.

I don't know for sure but, I've every reason to believe that a Mr. Norman Peterson was one of the men funding the project.

I heard tell that he was Mr. Morehouse's senior partner then bought out his booker business about a year ago.

He owns Peterson's enterprises to which Steven Morehouse once owned outright along with his Broker Agency.

I'm not certain but, his name is the only name I can come up with that keeps popping into my mind for some reason.

Seeing how you already became involved when Jenny Perking's was murdered, and you are also associated with that friend of yours Janet.

Who owns that card room who has established a connection with Mr.? More house, and the Peterson family as well. Especially with Mrs. Sandy Peterson. Who has been seeing a lot of Mary, Mr. Morehouse's wife.

There might be a connection there between them as well. Miss Perking's surely thought there was when she was telling me about how the three, of them are getting really chummy together.

Where there is you. I don't know about you but, I do see a connection between all of you even if you don't.

The way I see it. If anyone can find out what's going on. It's going to you. See that you already have knowledge of what's been going on already. Will you accept my offer to help us?"

"I don't see how I can say no. Seeing how you know so much about me, and already know whom I've been having associations with.

If what you're telling me is true. Whether I like it, or not, it appears that I'm in no position to contradict the position you obviously place me in, or your offer. Seeing how I might be needing a good attorney before this is over.

I've to admit I can understand why it was you sought me out. You just made me aware of why I was thinking that there was a strong commonality of acquaintances that were puzzling me and why I felt uncomfortably close.

Where seeing how you came to me already assuming that I knew something about all this. I feel certain that my name has obviously came up amongst other whom I haven't become acquainted with as yet.

Where you're making it apparently obvious to me. That you're not the only one, who's thinking the same thing about me, and placed me in all this. Whether I want to be, or not but, I want to know everything.

I want to know just what it is I'm going to be expected to take on. So that I could be at least prepared for more visitors popping up, and hopefully a lot less people dying around me. Whereas you did mention money, and that always interests me.

Let's finish taking about my first condition first. Then you can tell me the rest. If I decide to accept the case.

The way I see it. All this is merely assumption on your part, and I'm still the one with his hand on the gun undecided whether, or not to trust anything you say.

"Yes, of course. Where do you want me to start?"

"Where you left off will be fine but, I need more convincing if you don't want the price to go up. Risk costs and I don't come cheap especially when there is murder involved."

****

"Damn but, your one gorgeous lady . . .!" Sandy stood before her full length mirror saying out loud admiring herself wearing her sexy negligee.

" I sure know how to pick them, and now that Mr. Steven More house is gone I've all the time needed to find my daughter.

No one is every going to suspect who I really am. Not while I am who I am, and I look like this.

I must admit that stooge detective did open me up too really getting to know my new me. I wasn't expecting him to enlighten me the way he did but, I'm sure glad that I let him bring out the new me.

Once Robert finds out where Steven's wife Mary really is at I'll finally rid myself of both of them. To think I did it all right under everyone noses. What fools they are . . .

Once Norman signs those separation papers I'll close up the house, and continue my experiments in privacy.

That fool Norman actually thinks that he has it all. That sap doesn't realize that he's the one going to take the rap for those who must die to insure my secret".

Sandy startlingly stopped talking out loud to herself. Hearing someone knocking on her closed bedroom door.

Collectively composing herself making sure she covered up all female parts that were visible to the mirror she was standing before speaking out.

"Yes, who is it? Yelling out answering the knock on her door.

"It's I Mrs. Peterson." Your chauffeur Robert may I come in?"

"Just a minute." She answered going to slip on a cotton bathrobe, before going to answer the door to let him in

"Yes come in Robert." She opened the door saying inviting him to enter. Closing it behind him as he entered, and stood facing her standing in the middle of the room.

" Yes, what is it Robert?"

"I just wanted to tell you that Miss. Perking Mr. Morehouse's secretary has been taken care of, and that the lavatory is set up in the cavern under the house here."

"That's terrific Robert. Now what about Mr. Peterson's secret monitoring room?"

"That's been taken care of as well. Damn! James' I can't get over how you look . . . I still can't bring myself to believe such a transformation was possible?!"

"Me neither, Mrs. Peterson is quite the woman. She took off 40 years of my life when she gave me all this."

She opened her bathrobe giving Robert an ogling view of her ravishing splendor clearly visible from under that scanty negligee.

"Damn Professor! You sure make it hard for me to be a woman hater. I'll be glad when this is all over so I can be my old self again."

Miss. Kate Olson now occupying Robert's body. Spoke up complimenting him on how ravishing he was.

"You never told me that your husband was a homosexual. Between your husband, and that cook Carl. I don't see how I can found the time to do half of what I'm being expected to do?"

"You needn't concern yourself about my husband. He'll be gone prominently by tomorrow morning. As for the cook, and the staff, maybe within a couple of weeks depending how things go.

Then we'll be rid of them as well but, you're still going to have to stay close to Norman. I want to know everything he's doing, and for him to be around. When it comes time to really get rid of the last of those Morehouse's once and for all.

That rotten contemptible Steven is going to pay for what he's been doing to me all these years. I know he's been the one behind me being forced to do his bidding!

I think that it's only deserving of their fate. That they all go together along with that daughter of theirs.

Seeing how they were the ones responsible for accomplishing this miraculous miracle of transformation. I most certainly do look gorgeous don't I?" James flattery twirled around slowly showing off her beautiful self before Robert.

"Clam down honey we'll get them when the time comes. How are things going with you, and that private dick Henderson? "

Robert walked up placing his hands on Sandy's youthful naked breasts asking. Commenting on how pleasurable they felt to his fondling touch. Smirking grinning saying.

" Nice . . . Really nice indeed professor." As he fondly squeezed the pungent firmness of her breasts while she just stood patronizing his curiosity enviously recalling her own femininity.

Knowing that she wasn't fraternizing the real Robert Anderson but Kate Olson one, of James key scientists who once was Paul Murray's lover who was now fully devoted to James.

"Just the way I wanted things to go. He's my connection to that close friend of his Janet. After I'm though with him he'll do anything I say without question.

You damn well better be gentle! I'm very fragile, and I went through a very excruciating ordeal once already."

"Sorry professor but, I just can't believe you're inside this gorgeous woman body. It's been so long since I felt womanly.

I don't mind telling you I didn't like in the least having to take on your chauffeur's role but, it sure helps me do what I have to do.

Beside it will teach you to appreciate me a lot more when we finally revert back to our own genders again. I certainly envy you. You're so extravagantly gorgeous . . .

You do so remind me of my youth. I can only hope that once this is all over. We'll find me a woman as stupendously radiant as the one you obtained."

"Kate You know I love you and always have. I promise you once this is all over you'll be twice as beautiful as I am.

I will make good to that promise. Have I ever let you down? Honey, if it wasn't for your effort we wouldn't be here now. I can't believe that Paul was just using you to benefit himself like he was planning on doing

I just couldn't allow him to do that to you I just had to tell you. It's always been us from the very beginning.

I admit I was extremely jealous of him and wanted to do anything I could to come between the two, of you but, you became smitten by him, and wouldn't have believed me unless I could prove it to you.

I hated myself over letting you make a fool out of yourself over a jerk like him but, you left me no choice if I was to convince you of my love for you.

You meant everything to me where he was just manipulating you to get at me and what we were creating together.

I had to get you away from him before you allowed him to use you for his own deceitful purposes and ruin everything we worked together for.

I know that contraption of his was never going to work yet you were going to let him experiment on you and most likely kill you.

Because you became infatuated with him because you were sexually frustrated and he was appeasing you where I wasn't.

I'm sorry that I wasn't the man you wanted me to be and let you down sexually but, I just couldn't let you destroy your life over the likes of him. Nor was I going to allow you to ruin all are plans so I did what I had to do to insure you wouldn't.

Lucky for you that I did. Otherwise you would be dead right now just like those two, other women he attempted to get that contraption to work and failed on.

I promise you I would do right by you and I will by finding you even a better body than this one to replace the one, you once had with even a lot fewer years of less wear on it."

"Let's not get into that right now dear. Right now all that's important is for us to get the upper hand over your husbands vast holding. So that we can maintain control of the company in order to have it pay for clearing up all the loss ending Steven has dumped on us.

"I know. We both have lost out on so much. The years just past by for both of us but, now we can relive all those years a hundred times over again without having to struggle just to survive from day to day."

"Kate I promise you that it's going to be just the two, of us for now on. If it wasn't for you I wouldn't be standing here now but, there still is the problem of relying on those others.

I'm hoping that all we have on them will keep them loyal until we won't need them anymore. I don't trust any one of them.

Somehow we've to prefect are methods of preforming the transformations without the aid of the others. Just in case something should happen to one of us.

We're risking everything by endangering are welfare. By being forced too continuously being separated. Having to handle the things that need to be done by ourselves.

Between having to deal with my husband, and now that detective, and you having to do everything having to move everything around, and doing all the dirty work. It's just not fair to you.

Then having you being responsible for eliminating everyone one, by one. It is really making us very venerable to detection if the slightest mistake is made.

Honey, we only began to start making the selections to replace those who can expose everything we are trying to achieve for ourselves.

Don't forget that I personally don't like any of those Morehouse's still being around. They are not to be trusted.

At the first chance that wife of his gets she's going to turn on us. You know as well as I do they're only for themselves and now she's split for London where we can't get at her, and them theirs that daughter of theirs."

"Yes, I know, and that's where I come in. So relax I know them for what they're. There not going to get over on me."

He amorously ogled her now exposed breasts while opening the entire robe to reveal her bodies' exquisiteness. Becoming increasingly impetuous to become more aggressive to familiarized himself with Sandy's femininity.

"Now Robert let's not get to inquisitive . . . I'm not quite use to myself as it is yet. Being a woman is nothing less than mind boggling . . . They're so emotionally unstable, as well as vivaciously impressionable. So I've been finding out.

Oh, yes . . . That really does feel so good. You do have the magic touch I must say." James slumberous sighed out as Robert's hands flirtatiously stimulated all the right spots.

"No, Katy. We mustn't do this! We can't trust that man in you not to ruin everything. If you know what I mean?

"Well Mr. Henderson you now have it all."

"I sure do, and what makes it worse. Is knowing that I can't do a damn thing with any of it. If word of what you just told me ever got out. None of us would be safe from political tyranny. The only thing open for you is to disappear but, you can't do that. Knowing that someone else is looking for you, and not knowing who they would be.

The only other way is for you to keep going through the changes yourselves, and there again I have no idea just how many times you can do so.

Before it becomes too dangerous to do so safely where that's not going to benefit anyone. With me only being the one, everyone will be able to recognize.

I don't mind telling you that I don't like in the least being drawn into to this, and having the knowledge that I do know about all this.

It's obvious that I can't find people who don't want to be found. Having to seek them out under such adverse conditions as I'm being expected to operate under.

I have my way of finding out about the whereabouts of people but, only if I've something to go on, and neither of you has given me anything to even be able to find out.

If you are who you're saying you are. Legally I can't take you on as a client. Without you proving that you are whom you say you are.

Officially I can't even be held accountable for not repeating every word that was said here. Which if I was in my right frame of mind. I should to protect myself if nothing else.

You do realize that I could end up going to prison if I'm not careful, and I can't see how I can be. Not knowing who the hell too look for, or where to start looking for them?"

"I hate to repeat myself Mr. Henderson but, you are in no position to decline to collaborate with us. However even if you did reveal what I told you. No one would ever believe you.

Where for another if you did. You would be exposing yourself to those who aren't aware that you know about any of this.

Doing so will must assuredly be placing yourself in a very adverse situation. Making yourself out even a bigger risk of being approached, or worse.

Maybe even kidnaped, or even tortured until you reveal all that you do know, possibly even killed afterwards, or maybe even used to replace someone else.

It's going to be for your benefit to work with us, instead of against us. Like I said. We aren't the only two, who has taken precautions to protect ourselves, and if they are as frighten as we are.

There might be no telling what they might do to keep their identity unknown. You do see my point as far as your position in all this is concerned?"

"I have one, question. Where are you keeping those that are being used for these transformations, and are they still alive?"

"At the present. That information has to remain unknown. As for those that are being used at present. They're in hibernation, and yes, some are still alive with the exception of those who were used first.

Too where I can't say anything about their present condition. Seeing how when we went to the laboratory everything was gone even those that we had.

However, none of the scientists that we worked with have dared to make contact with Tom, or myself but, them again I can understand why they might be reluctant to attempt to do so.

You see the first experiments were done on persons already dead. It worked but, the transformation didn't last long.

That's when we started to used air, being injected into the temples on mice. When we discovered that it put them in a hydroponic state of unconsciousness. That give the impression they were dead but they were induced into a comatose state of mind.

Where we also discover that doing so coagulates the main arteries, so when they embalmed them.

Their biological system would become clogged, and them easily extracted for us to implement using certain drugs to preserve them until we could run experiments on them.

Which made it easier to examine and even prepare them to go through different stages of the chemical restructuring to prepare them to go through the transition and to be examined afterwards

I realize that it sounds gross, and inhumane but, it had to be done. Where we did so as humanely as possible.

You must also consider where we have to perform the initial induction process. It had to be done right there at the funeral parlor where we would exchange them with the others that were already used, who were actually dead.

All the ones we selected were taken to one particular funeral parlor under are control. Where the dead were buried, and the ones being transferred were taken to the lavatory.

Then placed in hibernation to preserver for future use. If it becomes necessary to have to do the process over again.

We have advanced extensively since them. I can't tell you the methods that are presently being used but, I can assure you. The method is painless to those chosen.

However, without the formula, and the updated equipment we're severely handicapped. The people behind this also know all the scientists who were working on the project.

Where neither they, nor we know who they're now. Whereas if the location where we're keeping those we're using for ourselves personally were ever located.

We would be sitting ducks. Just waiting to be picked off by those who might be seeking us out, and that even includes you now.

This is so futuristic no one would ever believe us without proof, and we aren't about to expose ourselves to anyone but, you that is but, then again it's only Tom and myself.

Even if we did up and tell anyone about this. There would be no hope for us being able to obtain new lives for ourselves. Where we would most likely become experimented on ourselves.

Whereas even if we were able to.

There would be no guarantee that the procedure would be effective. Each time we have to preform it using the antiquated methods that we are using at present we run the risk of something breaking down while having to unitize such outdated equipment.

There's a ledger that contains all the names of those involved. None of those have died thus far, or have been delivered to the funeral parlor. Where we can only assume that they could have already been eliminated, and we're the only two, left.

If anyone is unable to go through the transfer again within 24 hours upon their actual death. Death will be the ultimate end result.

It takes only two, to perform the transformation, and knowing professor Baron like I do. It's only a matter of time before he prefects a method of doing it by himself.

We've to find professor Baron, and somehow force him into going through another transformation. So that we can duplicate the exact procedure. Then preform it on ourselves so that at least the three, of us will know who we're.

Yes, we're going to be including you. Seeing now you're all we have to intervene for us and if anything should befall you. Hopefully we might be able to preserve you as well.

If something happened to one of us. The others would know who did it, and what to do to restore the other if possible to do so.

Mr. Henderson I can't stress how important it is for us to find a solution. Our time is running out every second we are being held hopeless, and unable to complete are experiment. The risk of it falling into the wrong hands multiples.

I say concentrate your efforts on Mr. Peterson chauffeur. He's the one who killed Jenny Perking. He has to be working with professor Baron, or has to know where he is."

"What about Steven Morehouse is he, or isn't he also dead. Can I discount him? He's was the one who hired me to watch Sandy Peterson who at present I'm now working for."

"Yes, we know, and you do bring up a good point. Until we find out for certain, I wouldn't eliminate him. That also goes for your close friend Janet.

If you want my opinion, it's her that you should concentrate most of your attention on seeing how she's the only one who has been known to have associated with everyone involved. She could be the connecting link that will able you to locate professor Baron.

What amazes us is. With everyone watching everyone else. How it was possible that professor Baron could have been able to do all this. While still being able to elude everyone without finding out about what he was up too?"

"Easy." I interrupted her saying." No one was watching him that's why."

"Someone had to be. He's not wondering around as himself, and that someone could only be that professor Paul Murray who was his closet colleague.

It's my guess that both of them were colluding with each other right under your very noses, and are still together somewhere."

Mr. Henderson do you see this pendant I'm wearing? It's a radio activity detector. If I get close enough to either of them, or any of my colleagues. I'll know them by this.

A portion of the formula requires using radiation. That is concentrated through sonic vibrations at high pitch levels. To create a molecular balance to keep the heart beating during the transformations.

Without it the regeneration of the skin texture wouldn't be possible. It would lose its density, and become dried out, and crusty.

Which has to maintain a certain moistness form the inside out. Of course special lotions will have to be used to keep its texture looking natural as well.

Without that radiation continuously regenerating from the inside. It would age the body rapidly, and eventually will cause it to dehydrate and possibly disintegrate into a pile of dust.

However, it leaves what appears to be a birth mark on the buttock. It's cause by a chip that's implanted before the exchange.

It's only purpose is for us to detect who's supposed to be who. This detector will light up when it detects that chip.

That ledger holds the real name of those attached to that chip, and it can't be removed. Doing so will set off a flashing alarm on are monitors if it is shutoff, or removed and removing it from the spinal colon would not be an easy taste.

It has growing properties that attaches itself directly to one's spinal colon that over time would make it impossible to be removed without a major operation.

We all know that we know how to detect each other, and that it can't be removed without serious complication developing that might be irreversible.

What no oneself but one of us will know. Is that now you will know who's one of us when you come upon one of us." She handed me a watch.

"Take this. If you happen to get close enough to either of us. The crystal will illuminate but, whatever you do. Don't let on that you discovered them.

They'll kill you for sure! Don't forget they can change, you can't, and you'll be dead. The best you could do is follow them, and get their descriptions. All you've to be is within 15 feet of them."

I took the watch, and put it on my wrist after removing my own. Sure enough it glowed.

"Why doesn't your pendant glow?"

"We've Are's treated with a special coating. The stone in are pendants will turn black. As you can see. So you will still be able to know if you come upon any of our colleagues.

Where your watch will also be able to detect sonic levels as well. If by chance you happen to be in range of an actual transfer taking place.

Which in that case the minute hand will start to vibrate to where you will feel it against your skin. Where oar's will react differently where yours don't need to be the same as ours.

Another way to detect one of us. We can't eat meat. It will cause a violent reaction. There are still minor setbacks to the process that would be noticeable if one knows what to look for.

Although they're minor, they could produce severe reaction that will take at least 24 hours to recover form. That would mostly appear as allergic reactions of some sort like hives.

We were working on them when all this started. I still have my notes along with Tom's here. We also know where some of Baron's notes are but, they're incomplete, and worthless without the rest."

"Just suppose we should pull this off. Just what do you intend to do with the formula?"

"I know you're not going to believe this but, I've dedicated my life to science. The world isn't ready for what we've discovered right now, and it's obvious that it's being exploited already.

Science today is experimenting with cryogenics, and stem cells. With are discovery there would be no limit to how I could help those who can't afford the outrageous fees to get the help they so desperately need.

I'm not going to lie to you. I'm also in it for the money, and recognition. I'm not a crusader. I realize the unlimited potential in what we've discovered but, it's not going to do me any good if I'm dead. We were all supposed to be sharing in equal shares as well as the recognition.

I've a second chance at life. I want more chances. No one wants to die but, with the right people controlling the amount of information being divulged.

Hopefully humanity could benefit from the innovations that could be developed. As it thrives to benefit the development of the human race.

Meanwhile people like Tom here along with others like him, as well as myself could use the money to continue evolving the human race. Instead of destroying it for personal gain.

We need time not only to break it down. We also need to all get together so this discovery can be used to preserve the human race.

Think of it, cancer could be a thing of the past. Along with deformities, mental retardation, even Alzheimer's could also be abolished.

The preservation of the world genius will be maintained they will not have to die taking their knowledge with them but, continue to aid in the advancement of the human race.

The opportunities are limitless . . . Where we could explore space itself without the fear of dying exploring the universe."

"Sounds fantastic. But, I'm a realist. Though it's a noble gesture, you haven't convinced me that you haven't been dedicating so much of your time, and energies to unselfishly just give it all away."

"Your right I'm not. I worked hard, and long. Sure we all did, we're all entitled to reap the rewards for are labors.

It belongs to me as much as it belongs to the rest. No one should have it all. Being young and beautiful isn't enough. I want all I'm entitled to, and I plan to get it but, the work is still far from being over.

I didn't apply myself to wind up dead, poor, and destitute so one could have it all. You don't feel the same way as I do now but, once you experience it.

You'll never stop from wanting to experience it again, and the beautiful thing about all this. Is that no one needs to die.

Those who're already hopefully can be saved over time. Like I said. There still remains a lot to be perfected before it should become known.

The processes are far from being perfected as yet. The eternal organs between men and women. Although similar, except for the reproductive organs, could be severely damage or even mutilate if the proper procedure isn't used

Men might become a woman in appearance but, internally he'll still be a man, and vasa-versa. The damage could be irreversible physical as well. Such as mental disorders, and even have severe internal complications.

Thus far no list has been composed of those who might be compatible for the transformation that I've been aware of.

Its possibilities are very limited now. Where DNA plays an extremely important part in the availability of suitable substitutes.

Professor Baron has perfected a formula that would establish a common bond suitable for the transformation but, it wasn't suitable to both male and females that I was aware of.

To do it randomly could be disastrous. That data, along with his formula is what is crucial to a successful transformation, and even them are still in the experimental stage."

"Meaning what?"

"Meaning the genitals. The woman's virginal in fact could be deformed. As well as the male's penis, and their prostrate. There's no knowing what forms of deformities could develop if one isn't extremely careful and even then there's no assurance. Even if it's preformed within the same gender line.

The fact that some are coming through it all right doesn't guarantee that we haven't endangered ourselves eternally somewhat or seriously.

A great many previous attempts all met with failure. Unless certain conditions were, or are present.

Even though it might appear that everything turned out right. Internally they could be messed up, and there's no reversing the mutating effects.

Altering genders should be avoided. It's far too dangerous at this time. To my knowledge it was never done successfully but, that was before professor Baron perfected his new formula. That he must have done outside the group."

"Do I dare ask how many suffered from failures, and whatever became of them?"

"Let's put it this way. Two, minds joined together. Where one, has to be controlled by his, or her brain?

The most superior mind must prevail. Therefore, a small sonic transmitter is implanted with the frequency set to the one taking possession of the others brain cells.

As for the failures. They're beyond your concern now. They're much better off dead I'm sorry to say."

"They might not be worth concerning about but, what about their relatives, and families?! Just how long have these experiments been going on anyway?"

"Some 20 years for me and about 10 for Tom. Others' as well have dedicated practically their entire lives to the research, and we're still years away. We've only touched the threshold of are discoveries.

Up until 15 years ago professor Baron never had enough money for what was needed. Then suddenly from out of nowhere. We had money coming in on a regular basis.

Where were able to devote all are time to are research instead of just some of it. Maybe in the future it might be possible to computerize the procedure but, computer technology is still in its infancy stage. For anything that we've achieved to be trusted in other people's hands.

What I can't figure out is how you got involved in all this? There has to be some reason why Mr. Morehouse came to you. I hate to say this but, you don't impress me as being all that successful in what you do."

"That's a matter of opinion. If you evaluate success by appearances I guess I'm not but, my rates are affordable to anyone.

TIME CHANNELING

I measure success by proficiency in what I do. Time is money, and I don't like sitting around paying someone else to do my job for me. And I'll have you know I do have a rather high successful rate."

"I'm not referring to your investigative abilities. Your abilities for deductive reasoning are commendable.

If you want my opinion Mr. Morehouse under estimated, you. You don't impress me as being the half-witted no account you are trying to make yourself out to be.

You remind me of a sleeping giant. Who's trying to hide his enormous size. When you get yourself wound up. I'm sure all hell breaks loose. Which we can't afford to let happen right now."

"Let's hope I can continue to keep on sleeping. I'm too big of a target as it is, but I must tell you I work alone, nor do I like anyone following me.

The two, of you are going to have to holdup someplace until I settle this matter." I reached into my pocket pulling out my key ring. Removing my front door key. Then wrote down my address and handed them to her.

"Go hold up at my place. It's not fancy but, it's clean and safe. I want the two, of you where I can find you.

No one would bother to look for you there. It's somewhat secluded. Just stay in the house, and keep the nose down, and the shades drawn, and you will be all right.

You best walk up to it, and leave your car a good distance away from it, and don't go directly to it from here.

You might be being followed. Stay here for an hour, or so after I leave." I rose from my desk saying.

"Where are you going?" she asked

"Just to snoop around."

"It's 4:00 A.M. in the morning . . .?"

"That's the best time, now just do what I told you. I'll get a hold of you when I find out anything."

Chapter 8

I left my office and, drove to Sandy's house certain facts that Joan Staples brought me attention to rang bells in my head. That related directly to Sandy.

Those pictures I took of her kept bugging me. There was something on them, or about them that I was ignorant about that was bugging the hell out of me. I knew there was something but, I just couldn't see it.

Then there was that no sex agreement. Something about her just wasn't adding up, and I didn't know why.

Even after the last time I was with her, where I confined that she was all female. I felt sure there wasn't anything else I could have possibly overlooked. If there was some weird about here. I had no idea what it could have been.

I parked my car where I usually park it across the lake downstream from the lake that ran past her property.

Where I took my roll boat up to the dock of her boat house, and entered feeling confident, I was unnoticed.

Immediately checking my equipment. Discovering that it was still the way I left it. Where I then turned on the recorder to check out what, I might have picked up on tape. Where it appeared to be usually blank which I thought to be weird before it occurred to me.

That she said that she removed my bugs. Where I then annoyingly too check out my telescope, and check out that it was still focused in the way I set it.

Noticing that her bedroom drapes were drawn but, her balcony double doors were open. When a thought hit me to go listen. Thinking that I might catch something being said that would benefit me.

I went from the boathouse, and crept up to the house. Her bedroom was on the second floor where it had an extended balcony. That she would constantly walk out on to show herself off in the moonlight.

I was in the house several time, I knew the layout pretty good. The servants lived at the back of the house behind the kitchen at the other side of the house. So I was sure that I wouldn't be spotted by any of the staff. Positioning myself directly under it.

I instinctively looked at my watch. To make sure that it wasn't glowing realizing what Joan told me. That I had to get within 15 feet, so that told me why is wasn't glowing.

I heard Sandy's voice speaking out as she came out from her bedroom out on the balcony. Where I once again instinctively ducked into the clump of bushes underneath the balcony.

"My, but isn't it beautiful at this time in the morning . . ." Sandy stood at the railing letting the breeze hit her face saying to Robert.

As he came out to join her wearing only his shorts standing behind her, while she stood facing the iron railing in her negligee.

"It sure is Sandy." Robert replied, wrapping his arms around her waist. Hugging her back up against him." You make it even more beautiful. Now are you feeling?"

"Fine, my only regret is that I'm not perfect."

"You will be. It's going to take time that's all. You are used to being the one being romantically aggressive.

Where your new heighten passions Our still new to you, and we are both having to suppress are true

selves. Emotionally being apprehensive over not knowing how it was going to feel being the recipient. Just as I was having to be. Having to be expected to perform as the male.

I wouldn't concern yourself too much. We'll have plenty of time to work on are insecurities. You mustn't let it up set you."

"But, can we Robert?! I don't know if it's possible? I'm all mixed up inside. I might never be able to undo what I did?

Maybe I acted too hastily but, things were moving so fast due to that damn asshole Paul and that double-crossing Steven Morehouse."

"Relax we will undo it. We did it once we will do it again now that we've everything working for us."

"That's easy for you to say. You're not in my predicament. Being a woman isn't what I consider pleasurable. I don't know if I can deal with all these mind-boggling emotions . . . We've to start immediately!"

"We can't, and you know that. There's still so much that has to be done. We can't start changing things now, and disrupt all we've worked for."

"Robert, you've no idea just how nerve-racking it is! Where could we have gone wrong?"

"Stop! Just stop it! Don't go getting yourself all wrapped up in regrets. Not now, we can't afford it! We could be loss everything. Hell! It's not that big a deal. It still worked out, now didn't it?"

"Yes, I guess you're right. I've to concern myself with my priorities but, I never expected it to be anything like it was. Everything was there! But, I just can't get close enough.... It was madding I'm telling you! Why are you women so damn complicate anyway?!

Even now, I feel like I'm being torn apart inside. I feel so off balance, as well as unstable, and most of all confused! I can't go through life like this!

I need to be able to keep my head about me. I've come so far. I can't let what's happening to me dominate my every thought."

"It's all my fault James."

"No, it isn't. You just acted normally. I'm the one who's at fault. I should have never of let it start to begin with. It didn't seem to bother me before."

"Before? You mean you let someone get to you?! Who?! When dammit? When?!" Robert despondently yelled out. Spinning Sandy around to face him.

"That detective Daryl Henderson, the other day. Because I had too, that's why! It was the only way I could eliminate any doubt he might have about me.

He as much as insinuated that I wasn't a woman. I couldn't let him continue to harbor those suspicions. So I let him find out that I was all woman.

I didn't let it go any further than petting but, I guess he had more of an effect on me than I thought.

I never felt the actual sensation of being a woman becoming sexually aroused and it's been haunting me ever since.

When you came in, I was admiring myself attempting to recreate what he was inducing inside me. All the emotions of an aroused woman were there. Then when I let you fondle me. I just lost control.

Things started to happen to me. I lost all conception of who I was, and got wrapped up in what I was experiencing trying to analyze the sensations that were besieging every nerve and muscle in my entire body . . . I kept jumping back and forth fighting a power struggle with myself.

"Robert, it wasn't I...! She wouldn't let me maintain control I just know there has to be a flaw? The chemistry is all there but, it's not mine!"

"All right James now just calm down. You're going to be all right . . . It's just sex. It's all in the mind . . .

I was supposed to be in control, and was until those blasted male hormones started to take over. It's just something we are going to have to tolerate for the time being.

I'm not going to let you ruin things. You didn't let it get in the way when it was the other way around and you're not going to make a big deal out of it now.

By tomorrow not even Norman will be able to find anything transpired between us, and whatever what you are going through will be gone as if it never happened.

Believe whatever the frustration is you are having to deal with won't last. You forget that I was once going through the same things you are experiencing right now.

Believe me your body, as well as your physical emotions will adjust. You just can't keep on placing so much importance on the act itself. It's all in the mind.

All that you feel is your body chemistry responding to that which you're concentrating on thinking about what happened to you, and not mentally comprehending the after effects.

You are a scientist treat it as research and derive all you can from the experience and denounce that which makes you feel uncomfortable.

Honey, things are going to start happening really fast now. I need you with your wits about you.

Now go take yourself a cold shower. That should pull you back together. I've to get some sleep, it's going on almost 6:00 A.M. in the morning. I'll see you later."

He leads Sandy off the balcony back inside the bedroom. Shoving her off towards the bathroom as he got dressed and left.

I ran back down to the boat house. Focused in my telescope, and waited for her to come out while loading the camera, and mounted the telephoto lens.

Wanting to see ever luscious inch of her up close, knowing that lens would see everything better than I could.

Even though I saw, and felt it all before. I had to make sure that she wasn't hiding something I didn't recognize, or overlooked before. Hoping that the lens was bond to see the same things all over again.

'If only I wouldn't have given her those negatives, and all my duplicate copies.' I said to myself. Impatiently waiting for her to come out of the bathroom.

As I impatiently waited, something both Janet and Joan said suddenly rang alarms in my brain.

'The birth mark!

If Joan never seem her undressed. How could she know if she would have a birth mark? Or, am I just assuming that she's actually involved in all that going on?

Just because Joan wind up with one doesn't mean Sandy could have. I have to find out for sure. At least it would prove just how wrong I am about her, and her not being who she said she is.

For the life of me I'll never understand how I got the idea that Sandy wasn't who she said she was. The damn thought just popped into my head and it just won't get the hell out.

Then again the one thing I never did take special notice of was. If she did in fact have a birth mark on her buttocks?

All I know for certain was that my eyes were never drawn to the fact that she did even when I had her practically naked on film, and was looking right at her through the lens of the camera.

As for Janet she did say that she was with him when he went through some sort of a transformation...

She told me she saw it. But it was on that professor not Sandy there's no possibly way that it could been him. Could it...?

What if my suspicions are right and she's not who she's claiming herself to be? Who the hell could she be if it's not him?

I know what a woman feels like and she was all women there was no mistaking that. There's no way she could be leading me on, and even if she could pull it off. Why... dammit?! Why...?'

Sandy came out drying herself off with a large towel. Standing before a full length mirror totally naked examining herself. First her breasts then her pelvic region.

Seeing her totally naked for the first time focusing in on her frontal view. There was no doubt about it. She was all women alright.

The telescopic lens made a believer out of me... That how close I focused in on her facing towards the lens.

That's when I notice something very peculiar. That I didn't pay any attention before. The light over the full length mirror was casting a reflection that actually blurred my vision by making a glare on the lens.

Reflecting what I imagined she appeared like naked, and I was obviously carrying that same image when I developed the negatives. Forcing me to ask myself. 'What did I actually see...?'

* * * *

The lights went out... As I felt a crushing blow crashing against the back of my skull by someone hitting me with a sludge hammer.

When I opened my eyes I found myself strapped to a slab made out of wood with my wrists, and ankles strapped to it.

To see that chauffeur Robert standing beside me. Looking down at me smirking, grinning from ear to ear. As I scanned my eyes to focus in to see where I was. Discovering that I was in some sort of a lavatory...!

"Well, hello Mr. Henderson I'm glad to see you came back to the living. I thought that I might have hit you too hard. You really shouldn't go around snooping into people's windows."

"Yeah, sure you made you point. Now let me loose." I struggled to attempt to break myself free, argumentatively being defiant. Not wanting to just lie there strapped to that wooden plank I was on.

"I don't know if I can do that right at the moment but, if I were you I would think about the reason you are lying before me.

Where you might not be if it wasn't for you stopping by at the most inopportune moment. It was just simply bad luck on your part that I'm unable to decide at the moment.

Now I honestly don't know what to do with you...? Your doing so disrupted all my plans, and I do hate using alternatives."

"Plans for what?"

"You mustn't concern yourself with my problems, when you've problems of your own that are obviously more pressing."

"Why did you bring me here? Surely it wasn't to get your kicks...?"

"There again I'm afraid that I can't tell you that at the moment. I admit Mrs. Peterson is very beautiful, and even more alluring in the nude but, to come all this way just to ogle her.

When I hear you have obviously done more, doesn't make any sense. Especially this early in the morning."

"I came to get my equipment. Beside I'm an early riser, Maybe I just decided to stop by to say good morning, and a cup of coffee."

"No good Mr. Henderson. That's not going to hack it. You're going to have to come up with something better than that.

I couldn't help but, to notice that expensive watch you were wearing. Where did you get it, or should I ask? From who did you get it?"

"I bought it!"

"Try again. You couldn't afford a watch like that. Even if you could. You wouldn't be wearing it. A man in your profession would only break it.

Beside the technology that it took to make and design it. Is to far advanced for you to understand how to even wind it.

Now I'm trying to be nice about all this but, if you leave me no choice I can make you tell me all I want to know. I do have the means to do so."

He raised his hand showing me a hypodermic syringe." Sodium

Pentothal I do believe it's called.

Mr. Henderson your usefulness is about at an end... I'm afraid that your time has just about ran out. If you don't start telling me what I want to know...

You are going to force me to do what I do so much enjoy. To those who think that they're able to outsmart me, and you are so damn pathetically bad at it.

Yes, that's it. Struggle to break yourself free. Like you I had many on this table. They too struggled but, it did them no any good either. I'm a patient person but, only to a point."

"Fuck you! Asshole...!" I yelled at him struggling in break loose from the leather straps holding me at bay. It was hopeless he had me strapped down good.

"All right Asshole! What where those questions again..." I spoke out asking using my last resort. My procrastination delay tactic. In hopes to keep him from sticking me with that damn needle.

"Now, that's much better. Now tell me, why have you really came here?"

"Have you forgotten Mrs. Peterson happens to be my client. I only came to check up on her.

People are being killed. I've an obligation to look out for her wellbeing. Besides I never go anywhere without leaving a message on my recorder telling where I'm going.

If I don't show up at my office someone is going to know where I went. You don't want any more than you already have snooping around sticking their noses in your business, now do you?"

"Good answer but, not good enough..." He stuck the needle into my arm saying. Was the last thing I remember him saying?

The next thing I remember, was opening my eyes being blinded by the sun's rays. Finding myself sitting behind the steering wheel of my car.

Parked in front of my home holding my 38 in my hand.

It didn't take a genius to know what happened. I checked the cylinders. All six, bullets were fired.

I got out of the car, and skeptically approached the house. Stepping up the steps of the front porch. Knowing who I sent to hide there. Finding the front door was as I figured it would be. Unlocked, and partly opened.

Cautiously I entered, nervously looking around. Anticipating coming upon the worst. Spotting blood splattered all about the walls as I entered the living room but, finding no bodies lying around.

I went to check out the kitchen. Finding more blood spatters but, no bodies but, noticing that some sort of a struggle did take place in both rooms, and the two, I sent weren't to be found.

I stood looking down at the gun I was holding in my hand. Then at the back door leading out of the house from the kitchen.

Then down at the floor following blood spots out to the back door leading down onto the driveway.

Pretty much analyzing what took place. Fingering that I was just set up to being the fall guy for what took place, and the less I know about how I did kill them. The guiltier I would make myself look. If in fact they were already dead.

I walked back out into the house and back into the living room attempting to compose my thoughts. When the phone rang. As if knowing who was calling me. I went to answer it.

Pretty much fingering out who it was going to be on the other end, and what was going to be said as I picked up the receiver, slowly raising it to my ear.

When I startlingly thought that I heard Sandy's voice coming though the receiver. Skeptically speaking out saying.

"Who is it?"

"It's me Sandy, Daryl I just thought I would call, and see if you were alright. I heard that you might be in deposed.

"Yeah, sure you did...! Now did you get this number. I never gave it to you?!"

"No, you didn't. I call your office, and there was no answer. So by chance I ask

Robert my chauffeur if he knows of a number where you could be reached.

Luckily he said yes, and give me this one. I must say that was nice of you to tell him where you would be."

"Cut the crap! Just what in the hell do you want?! "

"My but, you're cranky in the morning. What's the matter didn't you get enough last night?

I just called to tell you that I'm a free as a bird now. Norman and I just settled, and I won't be needing your services any longer. So I'm officially discharging you.

I also took the liberty to deposit the agreed amount in your checking account. Plus, giving you an added bonus for the great job you did.

As for those other matters I'll have my attorney deal with them. It's been nice doing business with you. We must do it again sometime. You will remember me now, won't you?"

"Lady, forgetting you is the last thing I'm going to do! Where are they...?! What did you do to them...?! It's been you all along...Hasn't it!" I rebelliously yelled into the receiver.

"Now Daryl dear heart, you mustn't get so upset" She smugly replied... "You should consider yourself very fortunate that I allowed you to get as far as you did.

However, there comes a time when all good things must come to an end. You mustn't get discouraged. I'm sure if you let it end right here. You'll find more important things than me to keep your mind occupied.

I have to admit. You do have a way of getting yourself into predicaments. You do have this propensity for literally jumping in, and not even be able accomplished your purpose behind your objective. Which only substantiated the loser I figured you for all along.

Hopefully this might teach you to stay out of things that your level of intelligence isn't able to comprehend. I would hate for your ignorance to come back, and make even a bigger idiot out of you.

You can thank me for taking the initiative to look out for your welfare but, if you persist I'll not be able to control, or protect you any longer. Seeing how I hear it. That you are the one holding an empty gun in your hand at the moment.

If I were you I wouldn't want any of those bullets that were once loaded in it. Turning up in some unidentified bodies, now would you, and you not being able to present that very gun that I do believe is yours knowing what you used it for, now would you?

Be content of your good standing with me, and go back to taking on clients that are dumber than you are.

If that's at all possible, and you just might live a long prosperous life as the want-to-be that you are.

By the way I've also taken the liberty of sending back all your equipment. I'm wondering however whatever is on this film that I found in one of your cameras.

That I have thanks to you. However, I can see why you would want me to have it. When they are all about you holding that smoking gun standing over two, dead bodies lying about your house.

Thanks for thinking of me.

Why I don't know seeing how I'm not really into that sort of hostility that you obviously must be. I'm sorry but, you are just too volatile of a person for me.

Something are very risky to have possession of but, I'll do my best to hold onto them for safe keeping for you.

However please due refrain from sending me anymore. I don't want to get any more involved with you than I already have.

I know that they a say. That pictures speak for those who can't speak for themselves... I mean both of them, and in cold blood the way you did... Really...?"

"You really think you are so damn smart don't you?! Well let me tell you lady...! You just out smarted yourself...!"

"Really Daryl...? I don't have the vaguest idea what you're talking about but, just to clarify my position. I'm not responsible for your actions.

All matters pertaining to my case were closed when I dropped myself from being your client and according to my attorney that was more than two days ago. If you don't believe me buy a newspaper and check the date.

That's why I fired you. Because you've been gone off doing something for some two days without notifying me where you were at or what you were doing either.

To also assure you of what I have said. I will be forwarding you a legal document to that fact through my attorneys

Involved me in anything relating to you personally, or what has transpired between us up too two, days ago. And my attorney will sue you for everything you've.

Where in doing so they have informed me that I could even turn states evidence against you if it becomes necessary for me to become exonerated for anything illegal since I had the misfortune of meeting you.

For I know you could have even been responsible for poor Mr. Morehouse's death as well. You really should get that hostel disposition of yours checked out. You are a very dangerous person if you ask me.

You are on you own Mr. Henderson! You can't connect me with anything but, need I remind you. It isn't the same with me. Don't force me to divulge what I know about you...? Especially not after you supplying me with such incriminating evidence against you. I hope for your sake I'm not forced to get involved."

"Maybe not you but, I sure as hell can. Your chauffeur Robert I know who he is, or should I say she, and that she killed Mr. Morehouse's secretary Miss Perking's

You might think that you have the upper hand but, I wouldn't be too sure of that if I were. I also take it that you are very familiar with an Mr. Paul Murray? Now do I have to elaborate on just how well?"

"I have no idea of whom you're referring to. I don't know any Paul Murray.

What could you possibly know about him having to do anything with me? There's no way a person that I don't even know could know anything that transpired between us. It's pointless to even bring him into anything you can't prove.

Especially where you would go so far as accusing my own chauffeur Robert of murdering someone.

I honestly think that you are becoming mentally disoriented You should really go get yourself checked out. I think you are getting things all mixed up with some other client you had dealing with.

The way I see it, It's you who's getting yourself involved in your own uncontrollable actions that you created for yourself that you are now finding no way to get out of.

As for my association with Mr. Morehouse. The last time I heard anything about him, or even seen him. Was sometime ago when my husband bought him out of the business they shared.

Before coming upon him finding him dead, and your favorite police detective already cleared me of any wrong doing in his death. Which I might add doesn't exclude you by the way.

Do I need to remind you of your situation, and who has the evidence that could convict you for two, murders that I have pictures of you holding the gun in your hand over their bodies lying on the floor?"

"Lady I admit that you and that chauffeur of yours set me up good but, I still have an ace up me shelve...

You should have killed me when you'd the chance! Now I'm coming after you...! You forget I'm no longer obligated to you, and what I don't know I can sure as hell make up.

Making you answerable to whatever I say. I don't think you want that sort of exposure with all that you have going on.

However, I do know that I will be leaving a lot of unanswered questions that's going to be drawing a lot of attention to you.

Where I've answers to questions the cops don't even have to ask that will cause them to want answers too. So, sue me lady! But you damn well better prepared to do some explaining. I'm not going down alone...!

Lady you don't know the first thing about making a set-up stick. I'll see you in hell lady...! "I slammed the receiver down shouting into it.

Picking up the receive again calling Randy immediately asking him to come to my place saying that I was desperately in need of his help.

I waited impatiently for him to arrive. Knowing that whatever Sandy and that chauffeur of hers were up too that they had me cold.

Where I still didn't know why they were doing what they were doing or their reason for setting me up the way they were doing.

Only assuming that the chauffeur Robert could be involved in what I got myself involved in and only assuming from what I heard them talking about that Sandy herself was not who she was claiming herself to be.

Knowing that I might be able to walk away but never knowing if I could rely on either of them not turning those pictures over to the cops. Having to constantly live under the fear of either one of them dropping the hammer on me.

I wasn't trying to play ignorant, but there was no way I could prove anything against anyone. When all I had was a lot of talk and nothing to substantiate any of it where four people are already dead two, of which I wasn't sure that they were.

However, if I couldn't figure out a way out of the predicament I got myself in. The only certain thing I'm going to wind up in is the electric chair or spending the rest of my life in prison.

I didn't hesitate. Upon Randy's arrival I immediately showing him the place, and my gun. While I preceded to tell him the whole outrageous story.

What amazed me, was that he didn't disbelieved me, and accepted everything I told him at face value. Not asking me to repeat myself or cross questioning me.

"Alright Daryl you told me your story. As incredible as it is to believe I honestly do believe you.

No one, not even you can concoct a story like that. Besides it's the first time I heard your version officially.

Beside after going over your documentation I smell that something was stinking where that Mrs. Peterson was concern but, didn't know what. To tell you the truth I still don't know what their motive is behind setting you up the way they are.

With them never knowing of you, or not harboring any resentment towards you, or having a personal vendetta to settle. None of this makes any sense.

Especially considering the elements this is all associated with, there being scientists involved. I mean scientists researching cloning people. How I the hell could you have gotten ensnared with something like that?

However, I have to admit that it's not the first time I've heard something similar to what you are telling me happening elsewhere but, only about the cloning research nothing else.

The fact that you've just been keeping me up to data, and thus far you've been checking out clean.

All I have to go on is an empty gun, some blood that could belong to a rabbit maybe, and some unsubstantiated allegation, that you have been set up.

All of which I have to check out to determine if in fact a crime has been committed. Which still doesn't give me enough to conduct an official investigation to even question Mrs. Peterson, or that chauffeur of hers on anything. With the exception of the death of Mr. Morehouse.

Legally I don't even have probable cause. Let alone act on you suspicions that she's not who she said she is.

Which no one would believe me if I can't come up with something to get a warrant to have her examined.

Which I would really like to just to find out for myself even if there's a remote possibility of what you are saying could in fact be true but, like I said the topic as come up very recently in fact.

Two, FBI agents contacted me shortly after I returned to the station. After the killing at the restaurant. It's too damn bad you lost that watch. I could have surely used that to convince my captain."

"FBI?!"

"Yes, and do they ever want to speak to you. If the two, you told me about are dead. That will make four known killed, and if what you are telling me about Mrs. Peterson now being someone else Which you are assuming could be one of two persons.

That professor James Baron, or someone else by the name of Paul Murray another scientist. The best I can do from this point is have those names checked out and go from there.

The question remains. Could she be alive and if your suspicious about the chauffeur might be correct six, total Thus far.

So where are they hiding the bodies of all these people. There appears to be at least four unaccounted for, where there again how in the hell are we going to prove that those two, aren't who they say they are.

Listen Daryl if it looks like a duck and it quacks like one. It's a damn duck. I can't even finger print either of them to find out, and if I did and they came back that they are who they say they are. What them?

Daryl there's no doubt in my mind that you've been set-up but, if one of those two, show up dead. You're as good as in the hot seat.

You can't prove your innocence if you weren't aware of where you were, or what sexually transpired for the past two, days.

Then there's your own gun that has been fired that you know for sure six, times. That you're aware of. Of course I'll have the place checked out by forensics before I leave.

If they have you as good as she claims they have I'm sorry but, not even Janet, will be able to get you out of this one.

The main question is why you, when it was Mr. Morehouse who hired you and no one else knew about you =even being involved with the Peterson's.

"Randy, my office! I taped everything that goes on in it."

"Good but, not good enough. They're not admissible in court. I couldn't even act on anything that was said.

It's protection by client confidentiality, and there's no way you could prove that it wasn't obtained was under dress, or under the influence of being drugged, or without being coerced under stress, or that could be misleading.

Tapes are good for remembering information, but not very much more. Without court orders which would entitle probable cause.

Which you didn't have to begin with. The law of confidentiality makes them useless, and you know it.

Technically you were still representing your client when the conversation was going on. If you hadn't of told me that she discharged, you when she talked to you over the phone.

Then maybe...?

The money, your gun, and your connection to the people being killed or missing. As for where the law is concerned.

Someone is going to be held accountable, and that someone is going to be you. If you can't figure a way out of this.

What gets me is why they moved the bodies. They had you cold... Unless that is they're waiting to use you as the scape goat again, or they could possibly still be alive and being held somewhere.

They could also be hoping that you'll do something they can't do like lead then to others.

The only thing you can do is bade for time until they pull the plug, or you find some way to clear yourself."

"It sure sounds like they are up to something that's for sure. They've me locked up good and tight. It doesn't figure that they are going to sit on top of what they have doing nothing knowing what they know that's for sure.

Randy I'm positive it was the chauffeur who's doing all the killing. I know for sure that he was the one who killed Miss Perking's.

The phone call from Sandy leads me to believe that she's going along with everything. I overheard them talking together. There's no doubt in my mind that she is in fact involved in everything.

The more I think of what I overheard the other morning the more I think that she's in the position of overseeing everything as well. There's no way someone might have something on her, or she's doing all this against her will.

It's my guess that the case they're using to establish my connection with what's been going on. Is the case that initially connected me with Mrs. Peterson to begin with.

That, that Mr. Morehouse hired me for. It's his dead that has to be the missing link that is what's linking everything else together.

You can't expect me to just sit around doing nothing just waiting for them to do something that's going to build a harder case against me for me to have to get out of.

What about the FBI? You said they're involved in what's going on?"

"You could go to them, but I don't see how they can help you and possibly make your situation even worse than it is right now. At least your still free to help yourself out, for all the good that might do you.

Even if we did catch the one's responsible. Without a confession they still got you for at least two, murders if not three, or more.

Let's not forget Steven Morehouse who you are linked to and still a suspect in his murder. He too was also one of your clients. As for motive. Any rooky DA could come up with one, and make it stick.

Even though you even might not have committed the murder yourself you can't prove not being an accomplice to it.

The burden of proof will be on you, not anyone else. He'll just present the evidence, and believe me there's a lot of it.

Like the statement that I took from Mrs. Morehouse over the phone pertaining to you ungentlemanly conduct towards her."

"What...?!"

"That's right. She alleged that her husband caught you trying to make advances towards her. That the two, of you argued, and he was forced to dismiss himself from being your client and for his wife safely sent her away to ensure her will being."

"That's a lie...!"

"Sure, it might be, but it's her word against yours, and it does give you a motive for killing her husband. I wouldn't fall for it, but a jury might.

The second she leaned of her husband death so immediately contacted the police in London. Saying that she was in fear of her own life, and is afraid to return back home. Until she can be assured that no harm will befall her.

I had the police there repeat her statement to a stenographer here so it has to be entered into evidence against you.

If I can prove that you were involved in her husband's death in any way I'm going to personally have to arrest you.

Whereas Miss. Perking's is concern. Even though as you claimed she agreed to meet you at that restaurant.

You can't even disprove complicity that you couldn't have conspired between an accomplice to silence her. From divulging that Mr. Morehouse hired you on his behalf to spy on Mrs. Peterson.

She did however state that her husband did hire someone to obtain some evidence on her husband. Pending on a lawsuit against him, challenging the legalities that forced him into selling his shares in the business he shared a partnership in.

Going by what you have been telling me and what's being related to me. I have known doubt that you are being targeted to take the fall for whatever is coming down, and if you want my opinion it's not yet over. There's most likely more going to happen that you are going to be held accountable for.

I have been a cop for a long time, and this is by far the best frame job I have ever come across. Whoever is behind this has got you sitting in the chair now just waiting for the right time to pull the lever.

You've to find that something that links you with everything you just told me, and even them. Just maybe you'll be able to pull yourself out of this. If you can prove any of this outrageous fabrication about people being cloned."

"Hell Randy who do I know who could even be remotely connected to any of this, or would even believe me?!"

That's when my mind snapped saying.' Yelling out. Janet...! Janet that's who...! It has to be her. She's the only one not exposing herself alienating herself of not even being connected to any of this...?!'

"What are you thinking about?"

"Nothing...! That's the trouble... I can't think... Randy whoever it behind this had to know a hell of a lot about me. If what you're saying has any validity to it.

There's only two, people that knows me to know anything about me that well to be able to trap me like this. You and Janet."

"Hold it right there! Don't start bringing Janet, and me into this. Just because you're pinned against the wall!"

"I'm not. I'm only saying that I might not be the primary target. It could be either of us... Both of you are a lot more connected to than I am to anyone remotely connected to shit like this.

Whoever is behind this must also know that it could be either you or Janet that I would go too. Hoping that you would help me.

Just suppose it's not really me they're after but, one of you, and they could be using me to draw one or the other out too lead them too who they are looking for. Knowing that if I was placed in a no win situation that you would go to any extreme to help me.

Janet was involved with that professor James Baron who seem to be the primary person behind all this. Where you're closely linked to both Janet, and I. The only one who doesn't connect is Mrs. Peterson.

She could be nothing more than a ploy to divert everyone attention onto her away from the someone, or something else they are hoping that either of you might lead them too.

Where I'm linked to both of you. You know the sort of people Janet deals with, and you're a direct link to what's going on in this city.

I'm only looking at this objectively. You, or I telling Janet about what's going on concerning certain people she might be concerned about by simply manipulating us into discussing them or what it is.

Where upon then Janet goes telling who knows who, about what we say. While not even knowing she's divulging anything..."

Playing all of us as stooges with me taking the fall for everything such as murdering those they're looking to get at before someone else does.

It has to be about this cloning crap. It's the only thing that makes any damn sense. Someone is attempting to quite anyone who's been involved or even knows about the break though that professor Baron as made.

Where I'm the one that everyone has out looking for me to capture what they have dictated their entire life for that he has in a damn leger or journal."

"That does make sense, but sitting you up to take the rap. Why, and why you. What's so special that they selected you?

I can relate to the Peterson's, and the Morehouse's over business affairs but, where do you fit into all the rest of this bull-shit? You just don't fit in.?"

"I sure as hell do! I'm the one who's connected to everyone involved in what's going on because of Janet no less.

From Mr. Morehouse to his secretary, even Mrs. Peterson, and straight to you and even the FBI. Who are all going to be out searching for me wanting to arrest me for murdering the two, scientists who came to see me. Which I sent here to hide, while I went to investigate what they told me.

I'm being used as a human decoy to help those wanting to rid themselves of all those who were accomplices in all those experiments that were taking place.

Where they need a patsy knowing that the government it's was going to become involved who have been onto them all along.

Just say that Mr. Morehouse was the original founder of the research, and Mr. Peterson discovered what Mr. Morehouse, and professor Baron were making great strides in.

Now say that Mr., Peterson planned to take over everything that was achieved so far for himself to benefits by, and found a way to stall it out from under Mr. Morehouse.

Now let's say that this professor Baron found out what Mr. Peterson was up to and got scared and had to do something drastic.

Which I would have no idea what that would be but, in any case. Ran scared thinking only of himself leaving all his colleagues behind with nothing to where they would become exposed to the FBI, and possibly end up in prison for what they were doing. Maybe even murdering innocent people.

So they too ran scare when now that professor found out and felt threaten by what they knew and had to figure out some way of shutting them up, and that's where I come in.

From there I don't have any damn idea what my part in all of it was going to be other than one or the other is hoping to use me to seek the others out.

Too use me too dump the blame on leaving me taking the rap for all those who were, or are going to have to be killed.

With everyone knowing who I am and me knowing nothing about any of them making me out the prefect pasty by not being able to explain my whereabouts, or how it was possible that I was always the one being involved in what was going on.

Where they have nothing to loss. Where I've everything to lose by not being able to prove my innocence.

The extenuating circumstance involved that I'm going to be the one to have to explain where there's no way I can, because no one is going to believe a word I might say.

As farfetched as it sounds it makes sense dammit! Maybe not all of it but it does fit it all together.

From Mr. Morehouse too Mrs. Peterson, then to Janet as well as you, and the FBI, and me and the situation I'm not in.

Now the question is how do I get out of it, and where does it take me from here? That chauffeur made it a point to place in here for some reason.

Then there's the fact, now in the hell did they know that I sent someone here, and who those someone's were?"

"You know that makes a hell of a lot of sense… Everyone's attention will be on you. That could only mean that more are yet to be killed."

"Yes, more but, the question is who and how many. The only thing that tell me is that nothing is going to happen until the last person standing only remains. Randy that book Janet wants me to get my hands on."

"Book…? Yes, that damn book that I might add you waiting until know to mention it. Where now you feel that it's relevant to what's going on.

A book I might add implicates all those who could be involved who now become extremely critical.

Yes, I agree it would be but, it would have made a hell of a lot more sense if you mentioned it long before now.

Which raises still more questions such as. What does Janet have to do with this book, and if it is the primary key to link everyone why is it so important for her to get her hands on it?

Now you brought it up attacking her name to the damn thing and arouse my curiosity about just how deeply involved in this whole thing.

I was curious why it was that you kept on mention Janet's being involved and now you attack her to what could be the primary key evidence associated or behind what's been going on.

Where yes, it could be essential to why you were the one chosen to be the fall guy. Where you obviously have special interests in why to avoided to mention it.

You do realize that her being involved in all this does place her in risk of becoming a victim of this as well, and you ignoring her importance could have increased placing her in even more extreme danger.

Where once again it would mostly likely place you as the perpetrator of the one who most likely be the one who murdered her adding still another victim to your list of deaths.

Where who but you could get close enough to kill her. With the exception of me. We both know that she's made a lot of enemies that's why she keeps herself constantly guarded with the exception of the two, of us.

Just to place my mind at ease I want to hear everything about what's been going on between you and Janet, and I mean everything.

I opened up and told him everything Janet and I talked about along with that I agreed to seek out that professor Baron where I would not only locate him and that book but steal it from him for her.

When all of a sudden it all came together why I was visited by those two scientists who I was being set up for killing.

Startlingly theorizing why that damn Robert didn't kill me when he had the chance. That it all evolved about Janet and that damn chauffeur Robert. Thinking of him as another male not giving any consideration that he wasn't.

Mentally placing the two, main figure heads who was behind everything happening to me to produce a condensed version what the actual motive was behind having me become involved. Constructing a simple scenario as to how it was to go down in terms that I could relate to.

'I find this professor for Janet. Janet gets the book. Where the other wind up all dead including Janet. With me taking the rap with Randy, and the FBI chasing after me for all the killing going on.'

✶ ✶ ✶ ✶

inadvertently speaking out without stopping to think before blurting it out. "Dammit Randy that means that my office has to be bugged." As if having myself a shocking revelation.

"No one but, I knew where I sent those two, too. I even gave them the damn key.

That's how they could have been ahead of me all the time. Someone bugged my office... Randy it had to be one of Janet's girls or Janet herself who was having them bug my office. There the only ones who could have the time, and the opportunity to bug my office.

Randy a horrible thought just occurred to me. Do you remember when Janet took that unexpected trip Europe for a few weeks on personal business.

Don't quote me on this but, just suppose she's not no longer the Janet we both know but, one of those clones where she's been transformed? I'm serious. Don't you think we should at least attempt to find out?"

"Forget it. No one could get that close to her. Besides if she was why would they be using her? Janet's looking out for her own interests.

Besides if anyone would know if she was herself, or not it would be you. You know things about her that only she would know.

If she is colluding with anyone they're using her without her knowing about it but, the question is. Is she also using them? She can't be oblivious of the fact that she's being used to link us to her. Don't ever underestimated that woman she's too damn smart to let anyone put anything over on her. Unless that is you could answer me, why, and she would knowingly let them think they are...?"

"I think I can answer that. That professors Baron's daughter. That's why. Someone is using her to force him to preform those experiments for over 15 years now.

Where she has to be in her middle twenties by now, and he doesn't even know what she looks like because whoever has her has been keeping her restricted from him for the past 5 years.

Where he just upped, and disappeared some two, weeks ago, or so I'm told by Janet. Where I'm also toll that he never would up and disappear. Not without knowing where she was.

Just suppose those who already died. Were the ones who abducted his daughter, and he found out who all of them were, or maybe she might have already escaped, and went into hiding out of fear of not knowing who killed the only family she's ever had.

Randy the reason I could have become involved is though being involved with Janet because she was contemplating on using me to protect her not letting me know who she was, or that I was wanting to draw attention to who she was. If I'm right Janet must know who, and where she is

As to why? Because of someone found out about that the professor and her became close to one another. Where the one who is doing the killing is trying to find the professor where the two, who were caring for her were now dead. His daughter has no one else she can trust but, Janet to keep her identity a secret, and in hiding"

"Now you're reaching for straws..." You really are complicating things way out of proportion. You have to stick to the facts and stop jumping around confusing everything."

"I'm not. It would explain why I'm not already in jail, and my connection with all this. It's my guess I'm being used to bring the professors and his daughter back together as well as the one who aided her to escape.

I honestly feel that he's not going to stop looking for her until her finds her, and what's preventing that from happening is. That neither one knowing what the other looks like.

"If you want my opinion I think you're complicating things worse that they're already."

"What's going on with you?! Why are you being so damn difficult about this...?! Alright listen to this.

That scientist Joan Staples. She said that there were others that she knew about. At least five, others that she knew about for sure.

If Janet isn't the main one orchestrating everything. It also stands to reason that what might fit everything together is the Peterson's seeing how Mr. Peterson took over control of the research long before Mr. Morehouse was killed.

If in fact either one or the other is in fact the original master mind behind bring all this to light. Which I doubt because no attempt has been made on them of their lives, not was either of them killed.

Where the primary person of interest that originally brought all this about is he one Mr. Morehouse hired me to investigate Mrs. Peterson.

If one thinks of this in any other way than I already have it then starts to become disoriented. Placing her in the position of master minding what's going on.

Who would have to mean that he suspected, or knew that Mrs. Peterson was going to be in control of her husband's assets long before he was killed. Where when last I inquired about his health status he was still alive and kicking.

Whereas where Mr. Peterson is concern. According to his wife he is a full-fledged homosexual.

It also could stand to reason that just suppose he was Mr. Morehouse's' lover and the two of them had a major falling out?

Mrs. Peterson stated to me that her husband had someone special, and they were both partners for years. Where their original partnership was dissolved under duress.

Where Mr. Peterson ended up with the bulk of Mr. Morehouse's' money leaving him nearly penniless and himself loaded.

I sense a strong motive for resentment on Mr. Morehouse's' part, and a lot of concern on Mr. Peterson's part. Which establishes a motive for murder?

Once again don' quote me on this. But, just suppose that the Peterson's are harboring that professor Baron.

Which could mean the reason why he's still alive because he's now the major investor footing the bill for that professors Baron's experiments.

Someone has to be footing the bills for all the moving around that's been going on.

Thus far all those who have died were Mr. Morehouse, his secretary, and two scientists who thought him to be the primary investor in the experiments that were taking place. Meaning that everything that's happening is for the benefit of Mr. Peterson.

I just can't eliminate Mr. Peterson as not being deeply involved in all this. Where I'm sure that he discovered that he just struck it richer than he already was from Baron achieving a breakthrough on the experiments he was preforming but, unable to benefit from it

Where I was just told by Mrs. Peterson over the phone. That they are separating, and that they made a settlement.

Placing their living environment in a turmoil that from the tone of her voice leads me to believe isn't effecting her.

Where her husband's financial situation must assuredly be stressing him out seeing how he is the primary investor and it must be costing a hell of a lot having the experiment being shut down and having things being moved from place to place.

The point I'm getting at. Is I being always lead to believe that by following the money always lead one to find out a lot of unanswered questions.

So I have been thinking to concentrate my sights on him just to see if I can find out why it is he spending time dealing with a separation and not what has to be costing him some heavy bucks.

I'm thinking that he might be harboring this professor Baron, or he's already got everything that he achieved.

If not the professor has to be close to the money and that could only leave one person, he could be held accountable too. Mrs. Peterson herself. Where if she that could only mean that she's been lying though her teeth up to now.

Unless it's been herself who's been colluding with that professor

James Baron himself. Where I'm being used to draw everyone attention on. Meaning that it's been her all along.

"She has an alibi." Randy answered him. You gave it to her and it's on record. You can't change yours statement now not without incriminating yourself as being the prime suspect. So you best forget that idea.

"Not so. That could only mean that someone has to be close enough to her to keep her informed and ling, or she was promised something...? If that's the case, I have a good idea who and what could have been promised to her.

Eternal youth...! They had to have promised her youth... She's settled with her husband.... If they aren't forcing her to comply.

There could only be one more explanation. That devious bitch is up to something rotten, and she's not alone.

Randy, Janet's been ling all along. She has to be the one who knows who, and where he is, and if she's involved with his daughter escaping. She could be attempting to play both ends against the middle, to get at that book.

Randy I have an insane idea. You're going to have to arrest me. I want you to book, and place me in a top security cell in jail.

If I'm right everything will have to come to a stop. It's my guess that someone will attempt to bail me out. I want to know who that someone is.

You're going to book me for the murders of Joan Staples, and Tom Randal. While I'm believed to be in jail. I won't be.

I'll be out following the chauffeur. While you will be following the one who came to bail me out. I'm willing to bet you your years' salary they're going to lead us straight to Mr. Peterson's house.

As well as us straight to where their bodies are, as well as those they already got to that we don't know about.

Once we find out where they're put those already murdered will have the evidence I need to clear myself

It will be enough to get me out of being anyone murderer. We might not catch the one's behind all this but, one things for sure. That whoever they are will have no choice but to have to get me out of the picture.

Because I'll be able to prove my innocence as well expose what's been going on. I'll finally be able to tell my part of this whole thing. Weather anyone believes it or not. It's all going to be out in the open.

It's my guess it's going to be that chauffeur, who's going to come bail me out. That someone who sent him has to be rich enough to put up that kind of money.

While that's happening I'll move the bodies. Once they figure out that they have been tricked, and now the police have become involved.

They'll have to move fast, so fast that they are bond to leave something behind to incriminate all those involved, and you will nail them.

All you need is just one for the rest to expose themselves. Either to shut the one you have up, or run straight to the one orchestrate the whole thing.

They will also have to go for Janet most likely too her to silence her from telling what she knows in order to cover their own ass's.

As much as I hate to even think that Janet is in this for herself. We both know that she's as sly as a fox and will stop at nothing even go as far as rebelling against either of us too get what she wants.

Whereas if she isn't already being cloned she'll do anything to stay young, and as beautiful as she already is, and having an eternity at just being herself."

"I don't know Daryl...? You're asking an awful lot...? I could lose my badge, and I'm up for promotion. If this plan of your backfires I could be charged with being an accessory to murder. I would be implicating myself as your accomplice?"

"Randy if it goes like I plan it will. You'll be police chief in a week, and I'll be free. I want tests made to prove that I didn't fire any gun."

"What makes you think you didn't?"

"There's no way could he be lugging me around standing while shooting up the place. Not with both of them being armed themselves, with them knowing that someone was out to kill them. That means they let someone they thought they could trust in.

It's my guess that two, guns were involved. My gun is a 38 that only carries six bullets, and that's all I had. Look around this place.

There's no way that anyone could have stopped to reload even if they had extra bullets without getting themselves shot.

Then the fact that there were two, of them and the blood spatter about this place. Where there's no concentration of blood piling up where they had to have fallen. That alone should tell you that there was more than one person shooting my gun.

Bullets are obviously lodged all about this place where to me it looked like they were all trying to dodge the bullets.

I checked the walls. there were a total of twelve, bullet holes. That means someone else had to be aiming another gun at them and firing at them as well while at least one of the was obviously returning fire dodging being shot at before he, or she was shot down.

Where they were standing with their backs against the wall beside the kitchen door." I pointed directing his attention to the blood spatters dispersed about the wall.

"I'm convinced that the blood spatters and ballistics will prove the bullets that killed them most likely came from my gun as it was intended however.

If I'm right their bodies will show that they were most likely shot several more times and that's why they didn't leave the bodies lying around to be found.

The paraffin test should prove that I didn't fire my gun, and that it was planted on me. I load my own shells I put a small amount of magnesium to protect myself against being charged with firing it without justification. You taught me that

All the bullets have to be in the wall. Even if they did have me fire it. They couldn't pin those murders on me.

Seeing how they had to save the bullets to make the kill shots. Meaning that only one of my bullets would have executed the fatal shot."

"Don't be so sure. They could have saved one, and fired it out the car window with you holding the gun.

True it might not be enough to convict you for murder but, that still places you at the scene of it with your bullets in their bodies?"

"The windows were up and the gun was in my left hand. I'm right handed. The asshole, just placed it in my left hand. The prints you will find on it will be from my left hand. They outsmarted themselves.

They should have killed me when they had the chance now I got them right where I want them. They got clumsy, and now it's going to bite them in the ass.

This couldn't have worked out any better if I didn't plan it myself. Sometime it pays to be a dumb want-to-be-detective."

"Alright I'll go along with you but, how are you planning on getting out of jail?"

"Simple. After I'm booked you'll walk me out the back door but, give me at least three, or four hours before you say anything to the press. I want my arrest published."

"I hope you realize the position this is going to place you in? If your plan doesn't work I'm going to have to cover my ass."

"Randy I rather have it brought out in the open now. They have me anyway. I've nothing to lose but, it might save someone's life besides my own.

This is a no win situation for me and if I'm going to go down I want to at least take a few who are plotting against me along with me."

"Aren't you forgetting about the FBI?"

"No, I'll leave that up to you. They can't get close to me without your permission for at least 24 hours, and once they know I'm in jail. They will have to follow protocol before they can get to me, or go over your head to your captain.

You just have to try your level best to keep him unaware of what's going on so that he would have to come to you to find out. Where you could hopefully stall things.

Once it starts I don't think that it's going to take long before the one's we will be waiting for to figure out. That they know that they lost their hold over me.

With me knowing too much for them to let me be running around free where the threat of me being out from under their control.

I have no doubt that there be scurrying about trying to cover their asses. Which will draw attention to what they are trying to keep secret.

Money talks, so let's see who speak the loudest too shut me up. Either way I'm a dead man as things stand right now.

I'll be depending on you too get to them before they get to me. Concentrate on Janet but, I don't want anything to happen to her.

I'll take that chauffeur. I want to thank him personally for all he's done for me by letting me live to face him once again."

"What about Mrs. Peterson?"

"She's too far gone for us to help. Besides I don't want her knowing what's coming down. Once she hears. It's my guess she'll start running to the one who can help her, and I'll bet she'll run straight to are Mr. Baron.

If I'm right he's more alive than dead and be skeptical of everyone including even Mrs. Peterson

Even though she might look like her don't let yourself be fooled.

Make damn sure that she is her you're talking to. There's no telling who's who at this point. "

"Who's the cop here…? I know how to do my job. One more question. Just so we're together on this. What about this professor James Baron and all the others ones involved?"

"Once the door is open. If I'm right about Janet that damn chauffeur will come after her. That will bring him straight towards the Peterson's.

Mostly likely Mrs. Peterson where the two of us should come together. If I'm still around to greet you.

Randy I don't want anything to happen to Janet legal or otherwise. I don't know how she became involved in all this but, she's not involved in any killings. I know that much, and so do you.

She's done a lot of lowdown contemptible things just as we have but killing anyone isn't one of them.

Regardless what might happen to me I'll still always love her. Just don't tell her that I told you that. I'm going to be depending on you not to let me down where she is concern."

"I've to hand it to you Daryl you never cease to amaze me. I never could have thought up a plan like you just did.

They had you cold, now it's you who has them… I'll try my damnedest to keep her out of this but, she's going to have to cooperate to the fullest."

"Randy sometimes in order to find out what's going on. One has to put themselves into the frying pan and seeing that's it I they are trying to fry and all the heat is going to be on me. It might as well be me

I just got lucky and jumped out before I was cooked. You being a cop limits you to work within the law. I'm not restricted and all this crap is really burning my ass!

You have taught me to think on my feet, and do what's best for best for me seeing how I'm going to be the who's going to have to live with myself over it.

Where survival has always been the means that I should always live by. Where up to now that philosophy as so far managed me to do just that. Thanks to you and all you taught me.

Where I couldn't, having to be looking out for anyone else but, myself when I was on the force."

I rose up out of the chair I was sitting in to stand before Randy before heading to what was left of the wet bar asking.

"Want a drink before we get started?"

Chapter 9

As planned I was arrested, and booked, and as requested tested. Then was out the back door 6 P.M.

I headed straight back home, and changed my clothes. Then hopped onto my motor cycle, and headed for Sandy's place.

Then hid in a cul-de-sac just so I could see the driveway leading in, and out from the main house.

I switched on my radio, and listened for the news.

It was 8 P.M. Sure enough there I was coming over the radio. With the commentator interpreting the events that led up to my arrest

"A murderer caught now in custody." The media announcer announced over the radio attracting anyone attention listening to the radio station.

A private detective by the name of Daryl Henderson otherwise known as Dice was arrested earlier today, for allegedly murdering one Mr. Steven Morehouse a stock broker, and was possibly involved in the murders of two, others scientists, and possibly others who appear to be missing.

The arresting detective Randy Collins says he'll have a signed confession from Mr. Henderson of his guilt by tomorrow morning. Now onto the sports.

"Hey, come on. Don't I deserve more notoriety like that?" I sat speaking out loud to the radio. Waiting for something to happen.

Having to wait until a good thirty, minutes later when Sandy's Rose came pulling out of the driveway onto the street.

Following far enough behind not to be noticed. The car leads me straight to a construction site, where her chauffeur Robert got out. Carrying a shovel, and went directly down into the constructed foundation yet to be poured with cement.

With me following him, and watched him digging for about ten, minutes down into the footing prepared to be poured.

Then went back to the car and dragged two, large sacks down where he dug and shoved the sacks down into the hole and refilled it. Then went back to the car and drove away.

Not heading back in the direction of the Peterson house but, in the opposite direction to which I thought was strange. Wanting to find out where he had me strapped down. When he first caught me unexpectedly.

Again following him as far back out of his sight not to spot me, as he headed towards the coastal region. Where he drove past a security gate shack as if he lived there in the community established behind it.

Where I couldn't just be able to ride pass the guards inside like he did. Not stopping at the security shack to ask if I could enter the area, I just sped passed it without stopping.

Then pulled off the road to hide, just in case if I was being chased by one or both of guards that were inside the shack.

Parking in front of two, parked cars in someone driveway, having to wait to make sure I wasn't being chased before pulling out again to go looking for the Rose.

Having no idea where the Rose, was heading, and having to wait for a good twenty minutes before I felt sure it was safe to attempt to go out in search of the Rose.

Where I had no choice but, to seek out the Rose by following the direction it was heading in. When it drove past the guard shack.

Taking a good twenty, minutes more before spotting the Rose, parked in someone driveway out front of one of the coastal cottages.

Where I then continued to pass until I was out of sight of the cottage. Where I stopped, and got off my bike grabbing my binoculars.

Where I then went to climb a tree to conceal myself while being able to get a good look at the cottage the Rose was parked in front of.

When I spotted a blue MG, pulling in parking in the same driveway. Where I saw another person climbing out of it.

Wearing very conspicuous clothes that looked out of place for the weather as if trying to conceal their appearance having their head covered with a hood.

Walking up to the front door of the cottage, knocking on it and stood acting impatiently waiting for in to open.

The door opened, and who should appear to be standing before him but, Alice my recently vacationing secretary. Greeting whoever it was warmly wearing a two, peace bikini as the mysterious person entered.

Seeing Alice really through me for a loop. Baffling the hell out of me. Prompting me to ask myself. 'What part does she have in all this?'

I couldn't hang around to find out. Knowing what that chauffeur Robert just deposited in that not yet poured foundation.

Knowing now imperative it was for me to get back to the construction site to remove those bodies so that I could place them elsewhere. Where I could tell Randy where they were.

Again I speed passed the guard shack check point. Heading back home to get my car to drove back to the construction site.

I dug up the two, bodies, and drove back to the house where I called Randy. Where I came to discover that sure enough Mrs. Peterson attorney was sitting before Randy's desk not taking note of the time that lapsed.

"Well I must say, you do have prefect timing." Randy annoyingly spoke into the phone saying to me.

"Randy listen up. I was right I found them. I've them in the trunk of my car. I need to get them put on ice, they're stinking bad.

That chauffeur Robert's buried them at a construction site at a warehouse distract on Maple drive. Then head to some coastal front cottage.

Something Palisades located on Sunset drive

It also appears that we have other players. I don't know who the other one I spotted is but, I sure recognize the another one. It's Alice my long trusted secretary who also works for Janet.

If I didn't know better, I would think that someone is attempting to venture off on their own. Using that chauffeur, Robert too put one over on Janet.

It sounds logical seeing how she works for Janet as well as I. Who better than she could anyone get to keep them informed.

There's a lot more involved than I figured and the number appears to be growing above my ability to handle. You better stick damn close to me on this one.

I think that I was right, and that I lite a fire under the pot I was in. Sure enough it was those two, I was supposed to have killed.

Randy I think I know where to find that professor, or maybe even his daughter. It's only a guess but, it could be that his daughter isn't missing anymore.

I can't prove it just yet but maybe she could have been hiding right under everyone noses all along. I saw someone also going into the same cottage the chauffeur previously entered.

Randy I'm sort of mixed up right now, as to who's who. I'll have to get back with you I'm not all that sure as yet about anything else.

I could be chasing my own tail for all I know. Just stick close to me I can't afford to be getting in any more trouble that I can't seem to get out of."

"Well you were right about help arriving you can't be too far off. "Randy spoke back," Not wanting to alert the attorney sitting before him. That he was talking to Daryl.

"I can't talk now. I've an attorney asking to see that creep I just arrested. I'll have to get back with you later.

As for your personal problems. Might I suggest you resolve them very fast. I'm a police officer not your house keeper. You clean up your own messes."

"Thanks a lot. I'm on my way to the Peterson house to see who else pops up unexpectedly. Keep a close eye on Mrs. Peterson's chauffeur I want to know his every move."

I hung up and left the house. Leaving my car again taking the motor cycle.

Heading back to the Peterson house. Thinking as far ahead as I could that Mrs. Peterson was the only one not being watched.

Going with my plan thinking to myself. 'Now all I have to do is make them think that I'm talking my head off. Hoping to put them on the defensive. Using what they felt they had over me would be out in the open.

Hoping to make everyone believe that once I did start talking I would make it sound believable hopefully get them to think. What reason would I've for fabricating such a bazaar story?

My luck was holding out but, it was going on 10:00 P.M. and things could become extremely more complicate where I'm discovered missing from my jail cell.

After parking the cycle across the lake I proceeded to head to the boathouse again to check out the place. Hoping that my equipment was still where I left it.

Thinking that Robert couldn't have carried me, and everything else that I had there at the same time.

Sure enough it was all still the same way I last saw it. Instinctively turning on the recorder, and checking out the camera's that were focused in on the same rooms hoping to spot Sandy. Only to find the entire place pitch dark, and not even a cockroach at home moving about.

Instantly the cottage came back into mind, and that other person I saw getting out of the MG, might have been Sandy herself, and not either that professors, or his daughter like I thought.

Again I went on the move heading back to the cottage. Where luck was with me as I made another speeding dash passed the guard shack. Spotting no one inside it as I streaked by it.

Not knowing where they could be. I diligently kept my eyes open hoping that I might continue to keep on eluding them. Slowing down to pass the cottage.

Spotting that both cars were still there but, something didn't seem right. As I parked the cycle in the same spot and, climbed my favorite tree again.

Noticing that all the lights were on but, I couldn't see any signs of life going on inside the cottage from the tree I was up in.

About an hour and 45 minutes elapsed since I left, and returned. The chauffeur Robert didn't come there to settle in for the night but, Why?

I felt certain that he was going to go back, and check on the bodies to make sure that they were still where he put them before they poured the cement.

That's when this startling thought came over me. 'Those security guards! They weren't there when I came back. I just rode right passed the guard shack!?'

Alarmingly I jumped down from the tree, jumping onto my bike. Again I sped back to the construction site hopping not to caught that chauffeur, or those two security guards.

Discovering that I already moved them but, no such luck! I saw three, men carrying shovels returning back to a park jeep and pulling away.

I panicky assumed that those two security guards were in collusion with that damn chauffeur. I jumped back on my bike and once again sped back to the cottage. Once again passing it noticing that no one was inside it.

Parking my bike by my tree again. I made it towards the cottage on foot using the beach. Knowing what was already out front, and if I had any hopes of getting to the cottage it would be using the beach.

Only to spot video cameras monitoring it, and that I was fully exposing myself to them. Kicking myself in my ass for not even considering that it would be monitored.

Realizing that I was already on film, and that I was already seen by the video cameras mounted on top of telephone poles. That were placed above the beach below, as well as on roofs tops of some of the cottages.

I made a fast retreat back up the slop I took down to the beach. To get back up to the street, and back to my bike. Thinking that if the worse was going to happen I would have something to get away on.

Still, spotting all the same cars still parked out front of the place. Really pissed off over how things were going, and that I was obviously seen heading towards the cottage using the beach. Blowing my own plan to hell.

I decided to do something drastic. To go busting in. Hoping to catch them all together thinking of going for broke. Accusing them all of colluding to frame me.

Hoping for at least one of them to attempt to do something to try to convince me that I was wrong and accidentally spilled something that I could use against them.

Thinking that it would be Robert if anyone who might get aggressive where I didn't have anything to defend myself with.

Thinking that Robert would be the only one I would have to overpower even though I was sure he was carrying a gun.

Thinking I would be able to get it away from him before he had a chance to use it. Hoping that I was right, and the other two were going to be women.

Where I took it upon myself to go barging me way through the front door. Knowingly setting off the alarm in the guard shack.

Half hazardously charging through the cottage. Not having the vaguest idea where I was heading hoping to catch one, or all of them together.

Startling discovering that no one was in the place, and that I just entrapped myself again and really blowing my entire plan to hell.

Panicky hearing sirens approaching in the direction of the cottage. Where I panicky half hazardous took a dare deviling leap through the bedroom window.

Coming crashing down upon the sand below drudgingly dragging myself down the beach. Hugging the sand slops, and bushy weeds to cover my escape as much as I could.

Panicky attempting to make my way towards the next closest cottage. Hoping to make my way back up toward my bike to hopefully get away.

Where two, people were standing on their back patio deck looking directly at me, and one of them panicky fired a shot at me. Forcing me to duck for cover, and virtually crawl on my hands and keens up the slop of the hill.

When two security guards suddenly showed up hot and heavy on my heels shouting out at me to stop.

With me only seconds ahead of them making it to the street above making it to my bike and just barely speeding off getting away. Before one, or both of them they took aim, and started firing at me as well.

I not only lost that chauffeur Robert. Someone also had to have spotted me spying, or heading to the cottage, and called me in.

Realizing once I stopped to catch my breath and check myself out for any bullet holes, that it suddenly dawned on me.

That even though I set the alarm off in the house. It still only took a matter of a few short minutes before those security guards were already almost on top of me.

When I only got a few feet from the cottage. When neither one was there when I rode passed it.

To me that meant that they came from out of nowhere within a matter of minutes.

Where it took me, a good five minutes after I passed the guard shack to get to the tree that I parked my bike in front of.

The only thing it could have been was another set up. To have caused them to be already on their way coming from wherever they were at. Which should have been a good five, minute distance away.

Where I couldn't have been in that cottage for more than two, minutes tops, and that's not counting response time for them to get to their jeep.

The only other explanation I could come up with as to why the place was empty. Was that someone had to have spotted me climbing that damn tree, and warned them, and they abandoned that cottage before I decided to go busting into it but how could anyone have known that I was going to go busting into the damn place?

Meaning that if I would have continued to use that beach I would have most likely run into all of those who were inside that cottage.

Hoping to make their way to someplace else using the beach to another location no knowing, who it was that was spying on them.

So who called security beforehand? There was something that I was missing again that's being used to track me.

Why that's it?! Dammit! I'm being tracked! And I had to be wearing it, and I couldn't strip naked I would be nailed for sure.

That's why that chauffeur went back. He knew I was there, and sitting outside the cottage all the damn time.

They had all the time in the world to set things up the way they wanted things to happen because they knew that I wasn't in jail all the damn time.

My plan was beginning to backfire on me all because of my own stupidity. I was acting irrationally and impulsively.

Without stopping to think doing more harm than good trying to think ahead of them trying to prove my innocence. Making it much more difficult for me to do so playing right into their hands.

By jeopardizing myself, and Randy helping me making things worse for both of us by not giving any thought that they could be tracking me.

Dammit to hell! Now that makes thing every more difficult than they were before as to whom could be the one, tracking me?

I looked at my clothes feeling about taking everything off checking every inch of the clothes that I was wearing.

Which I haven't changed for the last three, days, which meant that anyone I was close to could have planted a bug on me.

What also added Doris to the list of suspects of who could have gotten that close to me that I wouldn't have noticed it.

Which it also eliminates Alice because she was on her vacation for almost a week now so it could had been she.

Dammit! I had them on the run! Thinking to use my arrest to my advantage by placing himself out in the open, and I blow it royally."

Startlingly finding a tiny pin lodged into the back of my belt that I would have never noticed unless I searched for it. Pulling it out but, not knowing what to do with it, but wanting to smash the damn thing!

Figuring that I had nothing to lose now that my plan was shot to hell, and the only hope I had was the fact that none of those who were in that cottage could be sure that it was I.

Seeing how I wasn't reported missing as yet, and it was dark, and I was moving fast. Hopefully fast enough not to get a good likeness of me to be identified as me.

I was going to have to rely on a lot of if's but, that was all I had until word of my escape became public.

The other advantage I had was those bodies, and Robert not knowing where to find them in order to get rid of them. Where now that Randy had my gun on one could use it against me anymore.

Then there's still the evidence we gathered at my place. The way I figured it, was that I still had myself a good case to defend myself with.

That there was still hope I might make it out of this a free man. Even though I was hoping for miracles which would be one, if that ever happened.

Where now that I have their tracker I might be able to use it to my advantage. If there was only a way that I could track it to whoever is tracking me but, that's not going to do me any good right now. Where I need to get one, up on those framing me."

My first step was to find a place where I could stick that damn bug on where I could retrieve it when I wanted to get at it. The best place I could figure to place it was inside a cab. So that it would send them using it to follow me chasing my ass all about the city.

I rode looking for an empty cab where the driver was on a coffee break. Where I then noted down the number of the cab and stuck the pin in under the back of the front seat where the driver sat. While noting down the driver's name.

My second stop was stopping to call Mrs. Peterson's house. Going to saying I was the police, and wanted to ask her a few questions. Concerning her association with Robert Anderson her chauffeur.

Instead of her answering I got the butler saying that she wasn't home but, he'll give her the message that I called. Where I knew better. That he was just screening all the caller calling in to speak to her.

My plan was falling apart. I had to get things back to where I could control the outcome. In order to do that. I had to find Robert. He along with those other two women and maybe even those security guards went someplace.

It had to had been those security guards who told him that cause him to go back himself to make sure they were moved.

That only clarified that I was being tracked but, he still didn't know for sure who he was dealing with. Not being made aware that I broke out of jail.

There was no way anyone could have known that I moved those bodies. Where it was only Randy, and I, who knew what was coming down.

I randomly drove by all the places Robert might possibly go to. Hoping to spot him at one of them. One of them being my office.

Seeing how he could have Alice with him, and that there was no way he could make contact with anyone about my whereabouts without stopping to call the one who was tracking me.

That's where Alice would obviously go to check on the bugs she planted. Hoping to find out more about anything else that went on in my office. Since she's been gone vacationing on the beach.

Excluding the thought that she might have headed for Janet's because she was most likely with Robert and had no intentions of letting the two, or them come together. Unless that was, if Alice was collaborating with Janet already.

Listening to an alert news report coming over the radio as I passed my office building. Spotting no light on in my office window, or any cars parked anywhere around staking out the building.

"A major upset in the recent murder case involving a private detective by the name of Daryl Henderson." The narrator spoke up saying.

"It's just been discovered that Mr. Henderson a primary suspect in the murders of two, people. Has made a daring escape from the city jail not less than 30 minutes ago.

Although the facts as to how he managed to escape haven't been divulged as yet. What is to be considered is that he's armed, and considered extremely dangerous.

If anyone should see him. Do not attempt to apprehend him. Call the police immediately! His description is as follows."

I pulled over into an alley, and went to the nearest phone booth to call Randy. Being extremely careful not to draw any attention to myself.

" Yes detective Collins speaking." Randy answered the phone saying.

"Randy it's I Daryl. What in the hell is going on I was counting on more time?"

"I had to cover my ass dammit! And it's been already going on almost five, hours. I did the best I could before that damn FBI, went over my head. They are the ones who sounded the damn alarm."

"Shit! What else can happen?!"

"You're on your own. It's out of my hands now. I shouldn't even be talking to you right now!

They found those two, bodies in the trunk of your car at your place. After I told you to clean up your own mess! Now stupid is that?!

If that isn't bad enough. Someone tried to kill Mrs. Peterson not more than 30 minutes ago by taking a shot at her.

A man answering your description was seem running from her costal cottage. After several shots were fired. You didn't tell me that you were going to be armed dammit!"

My chief is questioning me about your gun, and how it disappeared when you did. I should have known not to listen to you!

You damn well better get me out of this mess! You gotten me into, and fast! I don't have a leg to stand on dammit! They are bond to find out that I was the one who let you out!"

"All right Randy just hold on. If you don't hear from me in six, hours tell your chief everything. You need to protect yourself.

Just to let you know. I don't have a gun, and yes there was a shot fired but, it was fired from someone standing outside on a patio deck. Randy it was as if he was expecting me to show up.

There were these two, security guards that got to the scene within minutes. Where they weren't anywhere around. Where it took me a, go five minutes after passing their shack to get to that damn cottage.

Can't you see it? I walked straight into another trap again. As if I was being expected to show up. When it was already over the radio that I was arrested. Something stinks!

There's no way I'm ever going to believe it's you. You have been like a father to me. Say what you what you have to protect yourself.

Say that I managed to get your gun using my own gun, and forced you to let me out, and then dropped yours keeping mine as I ran away. That you have no idea how I got hold of my own gun. That for all you know I could have snatched it from the forensic team without anyone noticing. That they were the ones in charge of it. Stick to that story, and they won't be able to blame you for anything."

"Too late. I already did that. Not only to my chief but, as well to the FBI. They don't believe a word of it! I'm going to be place on suspension if you don't pull my ass out of this!"

"Just hold tight Randy. You need to hang in there. Now that it's known that I've escaped everything might turn in my favor. Where's Mrs. Peterson now?"

"At County General under protective custody being cared for."

"Randy there's no way I could have taken a shot at her. She wasn't anywhere around when I was at the cottage.

The only three, I know for certain that were inside were that chauffeur, Alice and I thought the professor's daughter, or the professor himself.

Then when I busted in there was no one inside, and their cars were still parked out front of the place.

That could only mean that they had to have known I was going to come busting in before I got there, and did. How the hell could anyone have known what I was going to do before I even knew?

The shooting didn't really start until those damn security guards started shooting at me getting away.

"I don't care who wasn't there! You just made me an accessory. If they can prove, I conspired along with you.

To which it appears I'm going to have to do by confessing what I know but, can't prove. Incriminating myself of having the knowledge of you murdering two, people!"

"I understand Randy and I promise you that I'm working on it. Just hang in there with me. You can't let me down now." I hung up saying still having the uneasy gut feeling about Randy. Thinking to myself.

'The plan was too good to go so wrong so fast. Somehow someone knew what was going to happen, and they used it to make it appear that I attempted to get at Mrs. Peterson. Making it appear that it was I who made the attempt on her life. Hopping to absolve themselves, or herself of having any involvement in what was going on.

By using that damn chauffeur to lead me straight into a sure fired trap to take me out of the picture permanently.

In either case either Randy had to have something to do with it, or my place also had to be bugged along with myself. I never once checked it out.

I could have been bugged while I was out in my car unconscious, or long before they placed me out front in my car.? I had to make some drastic changes, and fast

. The killing isn't going to stop, and the more killed the more I'll be blamed for their deaths now that I escaped their attempt on my life. I have no choice but to call Janet.

I called Janet. We agreed to meet at our old high school stadium. She said not to worry that she could slip away for her bodyguards.

The meeting was set for midnight. It was now Quarter past eleven, and I still had no idea who was who, or where to start to regain some form of control.

Now that all my aces were played. Where I was now only going to be hunted, not only by the police but, the FBI as well.

I thinking to take a shot at locating Robert I headed back towards the coastal cottage. Again finding the guard shack empty along with both cars gone. Where the was an ambulance parked out in front, in the driveway.

Along with three, squad's cars, as I passed by heading back for my favorite tree. Questioning seeing what I was seeing.

Feeling certain that no one would be there. Seeing how so much time as lapped since I escaped.

Noticing that they were wheeling someone out on a stretcher. That I could barely make out who it was, only that it was a woman.

From my point of view up in the tree. Where whoever she was, she wasn't dead because they were giving her oxygen.

'Who in the hell was she?' I asked myself climbing down from the tree to climb back on my bike, wanting to follow the ambulance.

Once again saying to myself.' No one was inside the cottage when I went in?' I didn't know for sure that it was Alice until after I realized what hospital the ambulance was heading to, and got the jump on it.

To be there when it arrived when they wheeled her out of the ambulance, and I saw who she was. Noticing that it was Alice for sure. Instantly erupting another question in my mind.

'I thought Randy said that it was Mrs. Peterson that was being taken to the hospital?

If it wasn't she, where in the hell is she?

If in fact she was inside the cottage, was that the only place shots were fired? What about those fired at me?'

I looked to see if I could spot that damn chauffeur Robert but, there was no sign of him. So where in the hell was he? '

I ask myself again, again annoyingly not getting any answers for anything I was talking to myself about.

I walked in after them just to make sure it was whom I thought it was. It was Alice all right.

I Even attempted to try to get close enough to ask her about what actually happened to her. When I spotted three, men wearing suits approaching the gurney she was lying on.

The helmet I was wearing was covering my face. As I nudged my way up closer to Alice as one of the men approached the doctor standing beside her saying. "FBI" Showing his badge. "How is she?"

"I don't know yet. She's doped up pretty heavily. She nearly ODD."

"Doctor you've to bring her around. She's one of us. She has information vital to a case we're working on.

Someone did this to her, and shoved her into a closet. We've to find out if it was a man called Daryl Henderson. Now long before we can talk to her?"

"At least six, hours. If she pulls through."

"Say Matt." Another agent approached the two, men standing with the doctor. Calling out the name of the one talking to the doctor.

" Security says a man by the name of Robert Anderson, was passed through the main gate. They said that a Mrs. Peterson, called and gave her permission.

There's no record of any women by the name of Alice supposed to be there, or has she ever been allowed to pass through the main security gate. The security guards were under the impression that the cottage was empty.

That could only mean she was brought in by someone earlier who passed her through personally.

The guards also claim that while they were on duty. That they only left their post to pursue someone on a motor cycled who eluded them.

That they couldn't have been gone for more than twenty minutes' tops looking for whoever it was before returning.

Until they were called to the Peterson cottage by a neighbor, who saw someone breaking through the front door into the Peterson cottage.

Whom they then gave chase too but, whoever it was escaped because they didn't have any authority off the property to pursue whoever it was riding on a motorcycle.

The way I saw it. It was lucky for Alice here that someone broke in when they did, or she would most likely be dead right now.

If security wouldn't have decided to go back and recheck the place for damage and found her lying in that closet.

As for Mrs. Peterson who was brought in earlier from a gunshot wound. All we know for right now was that she was apparently shot by the person who broke in.

All we know right now. Is that she was discovered lying under the deck by security in a state of shock.

Who claims were chasing the guy who broke into the cottage so apparently the town was there when the break in incident took place.

That's when two, neighbors who lived in the cottage next store came forward to informed us that they spotted some man who matches that Daryl Henderson's description running away from the cottage.

After hearing a loud crashing sound of glass breaking, where her husband fired a shot at him but, missed.

Matt by question is. If that Daryl guy was supposed to have been in jail. How in the hell did he get way up here?

Even if he did manage to break out of jail without an all point bulletin being sent out on him? There's something very peculiar about all this if you ask me."

"Who's asking? What about the cars that were parked out front of this place?" Matt asked.

"Nothing much yet. The limousine belonged to that chauffeur a Robert Anderson who worked for Mrs. Peterson whom the car belonged too. That's about all we can substantiate right now. That could have been parked in front of the place.

If there were any other cars. They still have to be in the area they didn't pass through security at the main gate.

Security logs all vehicles coming in, and outgoing cars that come in, or out of this place, that's how exclusive it is.

Now as for this other case involving Alice here. The only two, other people who have been here is Mrs. Peterson's chauffeur, and herself within the past couple of days.

"Excuse me." The doctor interrupted saying. Pushing Alice passed them down the hall into the examining room.

I left the hospital feeling certain why Robert when to the cottage was because he knew that Alice was already there. Most likely already under the influence of being drugged.

Probably being watched by someone watching over her, and the reason he went there, was to bring a resupply of drugs to keep her sedated. When Sandy showed up.

Then before I left to check out the construction site Robert already left. Using the beach to meet up with those two security guards.

Where upon on my return Sandy was also going to leave. Using the beach for some reason.

Where the neighbors noticing all the activity going on at her cottage and heard the breakage of the window, saw someone running from the cottage and got frighten.

When just as Sandy was leaving. I came busting in. Storming through the place panicking the two, left inside. Where the one left to guard Alice panicky shoved Alice and herself into a closet.

Where when I heard the sirens. I panicked, and dove head first through the window making my escape. Not noticing Sandy hiding under the foundation of the cottage as I made my attempt to escape, and the neighbor took shot at me.

Where the bullet missed me and hit her. Just when those security guards got back and came to answer the emergency call, and attempted to catch me making my get away.

Where all it was, was just a major cluster fuck up on my part once again jumping in without stopping to think about what I might be getting myself into.

Because I was pressuring myself because of the time element I was thinking I could use to prove my innocence.

Leaving myself even more confused than I was originally. Not knowing who that other person was who was driving that MG.

What I also didn't know was why Alice was involved until I heard those FBI agents talking where I was once again assuming.

The reason for her going to her cottage was to hold up, because she was fearful of me escaping, and felt I couldn't get to her there.

Where I was also assuming when I saw her was that she was being held there by Sandy, and that Robert creep and those security guards were collaborating with them.

Which would have made her one, of them. Where all the time she was working for the damn FBI. Mainly because I never was made aware that Sandy had herself a costal cottage.

"Damn!" I blurted out criticizing myself for thinking how stupid I was. For actually convincing myself that Alice was in fact the professor's daughter.

That they were holding over her in order to force the professor to complete the experiments that he was working on.

Hoping to prevent him from finding her but, thought better of moving her, before I was going to get out of jail.

What I wasn't wrong about was Alice already being under some sort of drug like the one that Robert injected in me, and that someone not accounted for hid her in the closet, so that they could come back to collect her.

But, then again it was those security guards who discovered her and no one else when they went back searching the place to for the amount of damage was done when I broke in.

Where the cops were already there who obviously, have also searched out the place themselves?

Something wasn't making and damn sense again. That's when I recalled the announcement made over the radio about Mrs. Peterson being shot.

Where she claimed to have already been their checking out the damage that was caused by the break in when she was shot. Yet she was found by whom? Under the frame of the deck of the porch?

Then where in the hell was that Robert, when those two, securities got back and were chasing me. I saw three, guys climbing back into that jeep?

Why were they using my breaking in, to their advantage in hopes to exonerate themselves from having any involvement with me in what took place.

They were on the move. Hoping to make themselves inconspicuous using my own plan wanting to keep everyone attention on me instead of their own movements.

Sharping Alice by just keeping, her drugged up. For what? I need help desperately and there was only one place left to find it, and I was running late.

Where again Mr. Peterson suddenly popped into my mind standing out amongst all the other suspects, and players already involved.

Thinking that he alone would be the last person ever to be suspected as being involved in what was going on.

Him only being connected as the primary investor along with other investors. Who stood to lose a vast fortune by what was going on.

Having him, and all those other investors being totally obliviously unaware about what was going on without their knowledge. Right under their very noses.

As erratic as it sounded, he was the only one being exempt from even being involved in anything that was going on around him.

I personally I did even consider him as being a suspect at one time but, have been too involved in myself to ever stop to think about him. Until just now that is when his name popped into my head.

Suddenly realizing that he could be sitting back watching everyone chasing, and killing each other off. Just waiting to move in on who was left to take over everything accomplished thus far. As farfetched as it was, I couldn't ignore it.

Once it's in my mind I've no choice but to pursue it. Even realizing that bringing him into the picture now at this stage of things would be totally pointless unless that was he was the means to get me the hell out of the mess I've gotten myself into.

Chapter 10

I headed for the stadium to meet up with Janet. All the while not being able to shake him out of my head.

I sat in hiding in the dugout impatiently waiting for Janet to show up, looking at my watch reading 11:45, realizing how late I was but, also knowing Janet. That when she says she's going to be there she'll be there, even if I'm not.

As usual she finally showed up late as usual as I spotted her strutting across the open football field angrily has hell at me as I stepped out waving to her showing her where I was at.

Waiting to greet her anxiously grabbing her hand dragging her back into the dugout. Nervously looking around making sure that she wasn't followed by anyone.

"Jesus Daryl! You really got yourself in a hell of a mess this time. Not only are the police looking for you, but the FBI, as well. Just what in the hell have you been up to dammit?!"

"I know!" I unerringly answered her back." Janet you have to believe me. I've been set up really good this time."

"Come on. This is Janet you're talking too. No one-else could have killed all those people but, you. I personally spoke to Randy. Did you ever get him into a pile of your shit good this time!

Now could you do such an outrageously disgusting thing to him. When he's been nothing but, a father to both of us?

I'm not only appalled but, disgusted by what you did, and have been doing. When I ask you to get involved I never expected for you to royally screw things up this fucking bad. Where I can't even believe that you're innocent.

As much as I want to, I can't but, that doesn't matter now. What does, is how can I to get you away with everyone out looking for you."

"I know! I know it's hard for you to believe I didn't but, I didn't. Janet I don't know how they're doing it but, they seem to always be one, step ahead of me, and what make matters worse. Is the fact I can't figure out who's who, or what their next move is going to be, from one, move to the next.

They really got me good this time and I keep sinking in deeper and deeper playing right into their hands. It's like they're leading me by my nose right where they want me to be. So that I'm right there to take the rap for everything they're doing.

I'm serous dammit! Everyone seems to be connected to each other but, no one appears to be who they're supposed to be, and they're all dragging me along with them. To where I don't have the vaguest idea where too!

That even includes Randy himself. I don't know whom I can believe, or trust many more.

Janet I found a tracking device pinned to the back of my belt.

Someone been tracking my every move until I stuck it in the cushion of a cab. You are the only one who knows where I am at this movement so you don't need to concern yourself about being caught with me.

"Daryl, Randy, told me all about it. You got him to believe you, and look where it got him?

He could lose everything he's worked for all his life no thanks to you. I told you a hundred times to get out of this detective crap. That you were no damn good at it.

What's this bull-shit about you even suspecting me of betraying you? Now that was really low of you.

For the life of me I don't know why I even agreed to come meet you! By all rights I should have sent the cops to do it!"

The second she said that I knew she was lying. No matter how badly I would ever fuck Randy over he would never tell her what I suspected about her.

If he did, she wouldn't be alone. Which instantly lead me to believe that she wasn't alone, and I've been right about her all along. That even she's been involved in everything that's been happening to me.

"Janet I've this plan but, I'm going to need your help. I need you to get to Mr. Peterson, and talk to him. I don't know why but, I feel certain that he knows who been doing all the killing. I thought it was their chauffeur Robert Anderson but, he's only been cleaning up after the one who's been doing all the killing."

"Mr. Peterson?! What could he possibly know about any of this? Daryl you're losing it. You're suspecting everyone.

You are out of control. Frantically grasping for straws. Not having the vaguest idea who's doing what, or did what. Dragging all, those close to you down with you.

Forget it Daryl. It's over. From here on out I'll handle things. Once I find the professor. It will only be a matter of time before you are made into a new person.

That's the only way I can see you getting out of this without having to spend the rest of your life locked up in prison at best.

I want you to go to my place and stay there until I straighten this mess out. I need you to promise me that you will stay there until I come get you."

That wasn't at all like Janet. She avoids trouble like the plague. If there's any chance that she could get caught up in it with, no way to get herself out.

Harboring me would risk her losing everything she's worked for. This wasn't the Janet I knew and grew up with. Protecting, and supportive maybe but, nothing like the way she is now. Where with her she always came first, and foremost.

"All right anything you say." I slouched back against the wall gasping out saying." I'm glad it's all over. Tell me Janet why is it that you always come to my rescue?"

"I love you, you big dope, that's why."

"You must, to put up with all I've put you through. I don't deserve you."

"You can say that again."

"Janet I'm willing to settle down now. That's if you'll still want me?"

"Of course I want you. I've enough money now for us to live comfortably. I want to get out of this racket anyway."

"Me too." I placed my hand on her knee saying. "You know its times like this that brings back the memories of the time we spent in this dugout. I'll never forget that night."

I slide my hand up under her skirt onto her inner thigh. Fondly rubbing my fingers around nudging them upwards as she just stood smiling at me.

Janet's upper inner thighs were her most sensitive spots. Doing what I was doing would drive her up a wall but, yet she just stood there.

Letting me grope her not so much as being affected by it in the slightest. Even when I venture to fraternize her femininity. She didn't even attempt to snap her thighs shut to capture my hand in between them like she always did in the past.

"Now Daryl honey, this isn't the time to relive old memories." She placed her hand upon mine stopping if form pursuing its pursuits from going any further." I must get you to a safe place where we can be alone."

"What's the rush? I'm as safe as a baby in his mother's womb right here with you at my side. You know the best day I ever had in my entire life was that evening we shared together here.

You were so young and beautiful, yet you tried so hard to be so mature. I knew that night that I could never love anyone but you. You never cease to amaze me. You're even more incredible now than you were then.

I'll never forget how you responded to my touch. Now I would make your inner thighs literally ripple against my fingertips."

"Yes, darling that's when we were young and impressionable. Neither one, of us are anything like we use to be any more. "

She impatiently replied back still holding my hand at bay with my fingers not feeling so much as a twitch, or a quivering ripple.

"Yes dear as I recall you did have quite an effect on me, and you still do but, I'm under a lot of pressure worrying about you right now.

Where you are obviously distraught by all that's been happening to you, and are looking to me to make it all goes away, by allowing myself to patronize your frustrations. Where now isn't the time to let you do so at my expense.

I'm not going to allow you to use me like just some common tramp I'm going to be the women you are going to be spending the rest of your life with don't forget that.

Surely it can wait until we get to my place? I really don't feel comfortable here under the circumstances.

We can't chance getting caught out in the open like this and if I let you continue. I just know you won't want to stop with just caressing me."

"Janet if you did believe in me like you just said. Why is it that you don't think it when I say? That it's I who they are attempting set up?

When you know me better than anyone else. Do you honestly think me capable of doing what I'm being accused of?"

"As hard as it for me to say this. That's an easy question to answer. You're an unknown who is only really known by those who know you.

However, you do have a lot of connections where you do have the in's too, and the means that few other people have. Why do you think I hired you?

Where you know me when it comes to business. I want the best results, and you're always claiming that you're. Where even I knew better, I wanted to find out once and for all.

If you want my honest opinion. I think you did in fact kill all those people. Only the best would have the brains to use the system to prove his innocence and yes, I do know you.

I also know you're capable of killing without hesitation if it becomes necessary to do so. Like I said before. You're losing it.

This case is just getting too much on you. You need to stop before it kills you. The stress of having to deal with the fear, apprehension, and constant threats not only to you but to others as well was bound to get to you because you made it that way. When I ask you not to get yourself involved but, just to locate and steal something simple like a damn book.

I don't want to know why; all I care about is getting you back to yourself again where right now that's all that's important to me"

"What do you mean by that?"

"Come on honey you've to be guilty. Not even a lam brain idiot could compile so much evidence against themselves.

With the record you are creating for yourself no one would believe that you aren't the one, doing all the killing.

I myself never through you would go to such an extreme to find that book. What you're attempting to do is to insight them to start running.

So that you can get them out in the open where you can get at the one whose is holding on to that book, right?

Thinking that with that book you can change the turn of events that you yourself created for yourself believing what I told you about getting a new chance at a new life for yourself

Whereas in your way of thinking. It doesn't matter how many you might have to kill because you believe everything I told you, and that it's all going to work out in the end with us being together.

A bit childish but, effective none the less I must say. Especially where there be no one around to be able to point you out, or to incriminate you. Like I said before I know you,

Whereas if I didn't know any better, I would swear that this is your way of having yourself your last sensational fling by going out with a big bang so that no one would ever forget who you once were.

Honey I know how hard you tried to be someone. That's why you lived so recklessly all your life. All you wanted to do was to make a make for yourself where someone would remember you. Where now you have the golden opportunity to do so.

This is your opportunity of your life time to do what you want and get away with it but, you are going about it all wrong by attempting to expose the best thing that was ever achieved.

Doing so have already ruined Randy's, and cost several others because of your antics, and impulsive irrational thinking.

It's best that you let me take over from here before you do manage to get yourself killed and I won't be able to help you if that happens.

You're not going to be able to prove your innocence going about it the way you are. It's too late for that now. You need to start doing what I tell you and stop all this once and for all.

This crime spree you're on or endeavor is endangering everything and everyone who's also looking for new lives for themselves.

You forget they to have a lot to be held accountable for whom I might add are making it possible for me and you as well.

Listen to me honey, I want this as badly as you do. Why do you think I'm here risking getting involved with you in all this?

This goes far beyond just us where we are the ones who are going to be depending on them for are survival.

To be openly honest with you I like the way things are between us but, not the ways you're thinking when it's endangering is future together and it's going to have to stop for us to keep going on.

Taking you to my place isn't going to stop you but, it will give you a place to slow down and figure out what to do next, as well as to rest.

Right now all this has become mentally stressful on you. You need my support and I don't want anything to happen to you."

She stepped back releasing her hold on his hand stepping out of his reach. Making sure he was listening to her wanting his full attention.

"Daryl honey, I can't stop you from doing what you want, or doing what you feel you have to. I just don't want to know about it.

Just don't be around my place if you decide to leave it when I come back looking for you. Just encase I get a surprise visit from the cops, or even Randy.

I can't allow myself to get caught with you. Where you just might destroy my chances at getting what you are so willingly going too though away.

Once you leave there's going to be no coming back, and if you dare to involved one when you get caught and you will get caught. I'll see to it that you don't live long enough to be able to prove a word of what you say against me.

I want you to understand that I love you but, if you don't love me, or you enough to end getting involved any further I'll stop at nothing to kill you myself.

I'm serous I'll do it, or have it done before I'll let you ruin my chances at living forever. I just want to make that clear right here and now.

I'll call before I come to make sure you're there. I don't think that I'm asking too much of you to honor my wishes, and for Christ sakes, don't get yourself caught, or kill.

I can't afford to be getting involved with a known fugitive who obviously broke into me place. I have an outstanding reputation to maintain don't forget that, now shall we be going?"

"Before we due tell me. Just how did you manage to get away from your personal guards?"

"Why honey, you know that I sleep alone. I'm taking a nap my being here is just a dream I hope. Now we best be going."

" Hon, you best leave alone. I'll meet up with you at your place. Just encase something should happen.

I'm certain that the cops aren't the only one searching for me, and I don't want to get myself caught up in anyone coming upon you accidentally.

Knowing myself now, and the way, you describe me to be. Someone is liable to get themselves killed, and I don't want it to be I, so I best meet you at your place.

Beside as much as I love you if it happens to be I who gets himself kill. I can learn to live with myself where I'll never forgive myself if it would wind up being you who gets herself killed while I'm trying to keep myself alive. Besides you're the only one on my side."

"You just be there when I get there. I'm not going to come looking for you if you're not.

She walked away not waiting for an answer. Hastily creating as much distance from me as she could.

Avoiding going through the open baseball field using the nearest exit door leading out of the stadium that the players use.

After waiting for several minutes before leaving myself. I left the same way Janet did. Stopping to make a quick call to Doris. Saying that it was Dice who was calling. When she answered the phone.

"Doris it's I dice. Now I want you not to say a word but, only listen to me. I haven't a lot of time to talk. I'm sure you're aware of the trouble I'm in.

I'm calling you to tell you that I don't want you to return back to the office but, wait until I call you at home, and tell you where to meet me.

However, I'm going to need you to go to County General too check up on Alice.

I also need you to stick as close to her as you can get. I need to know what's been going on with her, and who comes to see her.

She's involved in the case I'm working on somehow, and I need to know to what extent, or if she attempts to leave.

Where I want you to follow her but, not too closely. I don't want anything happening to you so don't let anyone spot you. I think that it would be best if you ware men's clothing.

Now listen closely. If something should happen to me. I just want you to know that I think you're a wonderful person. I mean it Doris. If it wasn't for Janet being in the picture."

I abruptly stopped before saying something that I might regret later. Stopping to think before continuing. "Well anyway you take care of yourself now." Where I hung up without finishing what, I wanted to say.

Then I hopped onto my motorcycle, and headed for Janet's place that was another house just behind to card room where she lived most of the time when she wasn't managing the cardroom.

Thinking just to be on the safe side I should park the motorcycle some distance away, and hop a bus to ride that up to get close to her place.

Where I would walk the rest of the way making use I wasn't going to walk straight into someone waiting for me.

Getting off about a block away so that I could approach the card room from across the street where I could see the entire place before heading for the house behind the place.

Sure enough there was Sandy's car, but without the chauffeur Robert in it. Sitting parked around the corner about a half a block away.

Feeling that I had no choice but, to walk into what was waiting for me. Knowing that I was expected and if I didn't show up it would be telling them that I knew Janet was a fake, and she was sending me straight to them, and me without a damn gun to protect myself with.

Not knowing how many could be waiting for me just waiting to end all the bull-shit I stirred up by dumping me at that construction sight.

I walked to where the chauffeur's car was parked. I snuck up behind it skeptically peering into the windows and checking the doors to see if they were locked, or not.

The car was abandoned, and unlocked and I couldn't help but to notice that a gun was left behind between the driver's seat, and the center colon for the gearshift.

Anxiously I yanked the front door open, and snatched up the 9mm. Then silently closed the door swatting down beside the car to check out the gun to see if it was loaded.

Again I was in luck, it had a full clip. Thinking twice about taking it with me, knowing if I was wrong about Janet being one, of them, and something did happen, me having a gun could jeopardize Janet's welfare if everyone started to start shooting.

Thinking that they would most likely capture me and hail me off before killing me. I shoved it up between the gas tank, and the frame of the car. Anticipating on going for a little ride in the trunk. Figuring that they weren't about to take the chance of me sitting in the car with them where I could be hazardous to his health.

Figuring that if anything, it was probably going to be my last chance to find out just who's who, and knowing that this time they were going to be playing by my rules.

Telling myself that I was the one now in control with them thinking that they had me where they wanted me.

I crept. Backing away from the car far enough so that I could approach Janet's place using the driveway beside the lite up card room.

Making sure that I could be seen approaching the rear house behind the card room. As I walked up to the front door nervously looking around for any suspicious movement going on.

Boastfully ranging the doorbell trying not to look suspicious for anyone to take notice of my presence.

Now getting extremely nervous by not being able to take notice of anyone lurking about ready to pounce on me. Knowing that I wasn't alone by any means.

Startlingly hearing a women voice speaking out saying. "Yes, who is it? "Coming through the speaker next to the doorbell asking. That wasn't Janet's voice.

Where I skeptically replied back into the speaker. "It's I your long lost lover who just stopped by to play house, so come on let me in before I change my mind."

An electric buzzer sounded unlocking the security door. Where I anxiously entered suspiciously apprehensive over what, I was walking into.

Scanning about the dimly lit entry way while peering ahead anticipating that someone was going to come jumping out attacking me.

Where to my unsettling surprise all I saw was Janet standing in the middle of the living room, waiting to greet me. Waving at me with her hand to hurry it up, and get inside the house.

I hastily walked into the living room, and up to her as she stood impatiently with that annoyed expression upon her face wanting me to hurry up.

Then abruptly forced me to come to a stop by placing her hand against my chest to hold me at bay arm length away. Where she unnervingly asked.

"What in the hell took you so damn long to get here?!"

I bewilderingly answered her back saying "I took the bus." As I forcefully forced my way past her.

Walking through the living room up to the bar, pouring myself a water glass full of scotch, as she came walking up to me.

"Damn you Daryl! I was beginning to really worry about you!"

"Relax hon. I'm here now." I Walked from the bar to look out from behind the edge of the curtain covering the picture window.

Down the street in the direction of where I knew Sandy's Rosa was sitting parked while taking a large gulp from my drink.

Knowing in the back of my mind that she was up to something and I had to be out of my mind to have placed myself in this nerve-racking position that wasn't going to benefit me one damn bit.

Suddenly wanting to change my mind and get the hell out of there as fast as I could before what I was anticipating was most assuredly going to happen.

Where I was at the point of wanting to shove my fist down her throat, and find out just whom the hell was down inside her.

It never once dawned on me that she would spike the damn liquor. Where like the fool I was I just gulped it down looking out the window. Anticipating seeing that chauffeur Robert heading straight for the house.

"Take it easy with that stuff. Are you trying to get yourself drunk?"

"That's right!" I annoyingly snapped back.

"We'll all right, don't let me stop you. I've to be getting back to the card room before I'm missed."

"Yeah, sure you do that."

"Just what is this attitude of yours supposed to mean?"

"Nothing, you best be going. You don't want to be missed now due you?" I obnoxiously snapped back saying. "I'll be all right here. All I need is some sleep and about four, more refills of this scotch, and I'll be as fit as a fiddle."

"Daryl honey, I'll be spending the night at the card room. Don't try to contact me. I'll call. Let the phone ring six, times that will give you a good twenty, minutes get out. I don't want you here when I get home.

There's an extra key on the coffee table. Remember to only use it after I leave, or you know for sure that I'm not here. Otherwise you'll set off the alarm, and take a shower for Christ sakes. You stink!"

"Just get going I've some thinking to do."

"Honey." She walked up hugging herself up against me." You know I wouldn't leave you if I didn't have to. It's dangerous for me to be without my bodyguards and this is the only place that I can be alone.

Don't fool yourself they know that I'm going to be leaving you alone in here. You might see them but, you can have bit they're close by."

"You don't need to remind me. What gets me is how you could so easily fool them, when you can't me. Let's cut he crap!"

I shoved her away saying." Your no more Janet that I'm the man in the moon! The game is over Miss. Whoever you are! It's just you and I here now, or is it?"

"Lucky guess Mr. Henderson." Robert came walking out from the kitchen door pointing a 45 at Daryl saying." It's the three, of us now. Now go sit down and don't make any sudden moves, or I'll get a metal for shooting you."

I walked towards the bar pulling Janet along with me, and sat facing him with Janet standing beside me.

"So we meet again do we? And as usual it appears that you are holding the upper hand. Why don't you just shoot me and have done with it?"

"I would like nothing more, and most assuredly will oblige you but, not here. We're going to take a little ride out of the city into the county. Then I'll be more than happy to oblige you."

"Oh, well I never expected to live forever." I spoke up saying leaping up off the stool. Grabbing Janet around her waist, pulling her towards me.

Smashing the glass, I was holding against the bar. To hold the serrated edge against Janet's temple. Before he had time to surmise the situation.

Knowing that he was in Janet's house. With her doing nothing to intervene, or even attempt to say a damn thing.

That the two, of them had to be in on what he was trying to pull together. With Janet's bodyguards close enough to hear if he dared to fire that damn gun.

Using the only ace in the hole that I was sure I could depend on, was Janet's bodyguards not letting him in unless she allowed him in but, there was no way he would ever make it out alive if anything happened to Janet.

"Go ahead Asshole! Shoot! And she dies with me!" I threatened to kill Janet yelling defiantly at him. Using her body to protect mine as much as I could.

"No, no! Don't hurt her!" He panicky yelled back, lowering his gun.

"Drop the gun Asshole, and kick it over to me. Now!"

He dropped the gun on the floor, kicking it across the floor over to me. Where I shoved Janet away from me towards him picking up the gun.

"Now Ass-hole I've the gun. Now I want some answers, or the two of you are never going to leave here alive.

I'm as good as died anyway so don't fuck with me! I don't have anything to lose, don't forget that!

First question. Who the hell are you?!" I directed my question at Janet.

"I'm Janet you Ass-hole!" She snapped back yelling at me. Defying me to prove she wasn't.

"Like hell you are! If you harmed her in any way, I'll skin you both alive! As for you Mr. Robert's. Let me guess who you are.

That you're not whom you are claiming yourselves to be but, in fact you are one of those scientists who was involved in those creepy experiments, and you're some sort of clone or something like that?"

"What makes you say that?" Robert argumentatively snapped back. When you yourself can't prove anything, other than you're out of your mind. I don't know anything about what you are saying."

"We'll see about that. Both of you sit down. Neither of you are going to be going anywhere until you tell me everything I don't already know!"

"You're a fool Daryl!" Janet belligerently shouted out at me. "You could have had it all, right along with the rest of us. If only you would have left things alone.

If we wanted too, we could have killed your dozens of times. The only reason you're alive now is because a certain friend of yours insists that nothing happens to you.

Do you think that this all came about over night? It's taken years of hard work and dedication, and sacrifices by a great many. You're only one person. Kill us, and there only be more to take our place.

Whereby collaborating with us so we can do what has to be done and you can join us. Those who died, or who're going too, are for the sole purpose of protecting one, person.

Your becoming involved was strictly because you became involved before we gained knowledge of your precious Janet getting greedy, and nothing more.

You've no idea the inconceivable accomplishments that have been achieved here by using one, persons' genius. You are nothing more than an inconvenience that we had to tolerate because your only use is what you are doing right now which made you essential where you aren't any longer which make you expendable.

If it wasn't for you having the knowledge of the whereabouts of a certain vital person, we are searching for. "

"Let me guess. It can be no other than that professor Barons daughter, right?"

"Not exactly. True he is extremely essential that's why we have no choice but to hide him in order to protect the person that retains the knowledge of what he has in his head.

Professor Baron whom you are obviously referring to is a Johnny come lately but, he is the only link we have to the one, who's retaining the real knowledge. That was derived from all those who were involved in achieving the impossible.

Professor Baron was only touching on the threshold that's been achieve during the past five, years. His goal is to gain control over the only one who possesses the total knowledge. Which is the daughter of the original person who was behind what made this all possible.

Your right I'm not Janet, but no matter what you do you'll never find out who I am, or who it is I'm protecting.

My being here became a necessity because of your precious Janet getting you involved. As for any of those you are under the misconception I might be working for.

I can assure you that they are nothing more than rogues. That are behind us having to protect professor Baron.

We are the ones responsible for everyone seeking out his daughter where she never existed to begin with. We needed her like we needed you to divert everyone attention away from the real person we are seeking out.

Where you are never going to know of who, we are speaking of but, we know she is close by because someone is moving some extremely essential equipment around where it can't be located.

Equipment that only highly specialized scientists only know how to assemble and operate that are unable to do so without the detailed directions that only one person possesses.

You chasing us around were disrupting our plans of having you locate her for us. That's the only reason why you're still alive, and can continue to remain.

If you would only stop disrupting everything by drawing attention to us and just do what expected of you to do and let her come to you where we can get to her.

Doing so in return. We will grant you all of what your Janet promised you where you can become one of us.

Where the truth of the matter where you are concern is. If you dare to harm either of us. Will only warrant off any chance that you might get to come out of this alive.

That my being here is in fact because of you, and we didn't learn about you until a short time ago.

Yes, we have your Janet, and it was all her fault, because she became involved by sticking her nose where it didn't belong while she was over in Europe.

Where she became a victim of circumstances where she was nearly killed. It was all her doing that we were left with only one, way to go.

I shouldn't be telling you this but, it doesn't much matter now anyway that professor James Baron whom you have been seeking. Is none other than Sandy Peterson now.

He was, and still is the genius that must be protected at all cost but, he's using his importance to maintain his power of superiority.

He's in possession of the only ledger in existence that was used to transpose those very formulae's.

That was extracted from those geniuses who helped formulate the procedures that their minds possessed to create those formulas that were derived from.

It's those formulas that hold the key to the regeneration possess. It also contains the names of all those who took part in the experiments over the years. Along with those who successfully complete the transfers.

I don't know if it's just I, or if something is going on with you but, you're not looking to well. Are you getting sick? Well no matter. It's only a matter of time now. Please allow me to continue before time runs out.

To give you a further understand in the way professor thinks. Let me give you some insight to what he is looking forwards to.

For years now certain people have died without the recognition they deserve, or preserving the secrets they possessed.

Those are the people who held the secrets of nations. If that genius that was lost but, could be retained one, could gain world dominance.

By him eliminating those, who represent a deterrent from achieving his goal who he is in the process of doing.

Where regretfully he hasn't discovered whom they might be, or managed to locate all of them as yet. While having to resort to using others that he's already taken controls over to do his bidding for me.

As for Robert here. He's not all he appears to be but, underneath he's a she. Who was, and still is Baron's main collaborator. She is his most dependable as well as reliable person, that he's been able to become dependent on. He came along with the rest of us to ensure his ambitions come true.

As you are becoming aware of. There's far more too this than you can even begin to imagine. And yes, you have no idea who you can trust but, you know far too much to be allowed to roam around jeopardizing the welfare of others, and the reason being is.

That unknown to you. You've to have somehow managed to have gotten too close to discovering where the person is that came add to that ledger is hiding.

We need that ledger to preserve, and protect those still alive, and the one whose names are hidden that started all this from the very beginning.

We were lead to believe that the one who needed to be sought out has to be James Baron's daughter but, that still isn't all that certain. That's why we have been counting on you to expose her for us.

We are still harboring a great many doubts about Sandy's husband

Norman who now retains full control over the research that at present has come to a halt and she's attempting to gain full control of herself for herself.

Where most of the scientists involved are now having to use antiquated equipment that has previously been implemented.

You see we could be concentrating all are efforts on the wrong person. The one we are seeking out was blessed with a photographic memory. Her intelligence doubles maybe even triples that of professor Baron's.

Whereas those who are seeking her out for themselves are getting fewer, we are growing and we can't have a power struggle going on to prevent us from continuing the critical research that still has to be done to preserve are longevity.

When she was ten, years old she was kidnaped by the Morehouse's. It's due to her efforts that Professors scientists team advance over fifty, years ahead of its time.

Where the error where she is concern is when they allowed her to escape and disappear several years ago and when last seen by anyone she bared a very close resemblance to the Morehouse's' daughter Sally since then her appearance has become unknown.

Mr. Morehouse was professors' Baron primary founder until Mr. Peterson took possession over professor Baron's research.

Meanwhile during all that time over fifteen, years' worth the girl Mr. Morehouse was holding was memorizing everything that was taking place including the actual ledgers that professor Baron created.

Janet knew Mr. Morehouse long before she went to Europe. It was due to her relationship with him that she met professor Baron. Where Mr. Morehouse was determined to regain control over Baron's research again.

Meaning taking it back from Mr. Peterson where he was never going to allow that to happen.

That's where you came in. Mr. Morehouse got with Janet she was the one who recommended you to him to get you to get something on his wife.

I have no idea what actually happened but something happened between professor Baron and his most trusted colleague a Mr. Paul Murray. That set off a revolt within Baron's team.

Mr. Peterson tried to resolve the dispute between the team members but, wasn't having success when he discovered that Mr. Morehouse embezzled millions from him.

Where you weren't doing him any good where his wife was concern and Mr. Morehouse was on the verge of going to prison.

Where he took advantage of professor Baron and the dispute going on between his close colleague and had him put him through an experimental transfer. That Mr. Morehouse used his contact to put his wife through.

Which set off a chain reaction that force professor Baron to jump the gun himself, so that he could seek out his daughter.

Who was no longer under the Morehouse's' control, because far too many people were beginning to learn to much about how close the professor was coming to prefect the formula.

As well as the actual process to make actual transfers. Where he wanted the ultimate control over his achievement.

The sad fact about what all this interaction cause was. Even if professor Baron did find his daughter. He was going to suck her brain dry, then kill her assuring that no one else will have anything, and he'll have it all.

Where when Janet went to you to intervene in her behalf. Your constant intervention was hindering the rest of us from finding her before he does.

As much as he loved her. Her possessing the knowledge she did left him having no choice but to aliment her.

That watch you were wearing was given to you not only to locate the others but Baron's daughter mostly, nor could we allow you to get too close to Sandy wearing that damn watch. That's why Robert here had to take it away from you.

You were getting to close to the wrong person who we had to protect above ourselves. Where we know that she most of have been in close contact with Janet herself.

That's where I come in. If that was the case and she knows sooner or later, I'll know but it's taking too long. That's why you are still alive.

What Baron did was to achieve the impossible. He made a connection that can be undone baling him to transfer himself from one, body into another.

Even through Robert here has been with him Baron he has never been entrusted with his secret. However, what we do know about what happened still doesn't make sense. It appears that he took Robert's dying body then his life, and then connected them together.

Robert here is a living example of the procedure being possible. The real Robert Anderson was dying, and now they both live in the same body.

Using the same mind with Kate Olson being the most superior mind being able to retain control over Robert but, as his existing body grows weaker so does her control over the original Robert.

Where eventually the inedible will happen.

That's where the imperfection in his formula lies. One, then both will die unless another person is found, and another transfer is made.

The problem there is as James, or Robert's mind grow weaker. The possibility of the other person's minds being more powerful could result in Robert taken over.

The process is slow for that to happen but, nevertheless the threat is still there, and where still other imperfections might occur when another mind is added to the process. Three, mind but with a single thought, but who's.

Whereas Baron's mind has been perfected through preserving the pervious body in hibernation without having any deteriorating effects.

By filling the body with a special liquid and if need be preserving the original body composition before the transference took place to where it can reuse over again once it's restored back to its fill strength and its cognitive functions are restored.

Those who've came to you. Did so from out of desperation of being discovered, and from out fear being collected by James Baron, and being used themselves.

Thanks to you we have collected two, of them that still leaves several more out there for the taking. Which we were hoping would expose themselves to you but, no matter we will find them. They can't out last us, that we are sure of where we still have the means and soon the financing to go on indifferently.

However, the grin truth is. That as yet no one has achieved perfection but, by declaring are alliance we are extremely close.

Where the others are all existing on borrowed time, and the certainty that they won't come out of this alive.

Simply because we were all forced into to protecting ourselves prematurely, and in the chaos of it all. They lost the means to retain the documentation essential to their survival.

I personally don't see why anyone feels you share any importance but, someone feels that. It appears that you did somehow manage to get close to that ledger, and that there's something about you that as establish some sort of link with the professors' daughter and him.

Which establishes the means behind why she doesn't want too severe the relationship you have established with us.

That's the only reason we had no choice but, to resort to the method we have to neutralize you until it comes time to rid ourselves of you by dumping all the blame on you.

We can't afford to let you get any closer with the risk of the authorities or those others getting to you before we do what has to be done.

You should consider yourself lucky. Prison is by far a better alternative than death. We'll see to it that you get excellent legal representation out of gratitude for all you have done for us.

That means that we also have to clean up after you as well. Which we have been doing so as best as we could while having to chase you around trying to keep you out of the hand of the law.

However, there's going to be one more minor task we're going to be expecting you to do for us.

There's only one other person beside Robert here that can propose a threat to professor Baron, and that's professor William Throne. Who is in fact doctor Phillip Powell. Normans Peterson's personal physician.

It's going to be you who will have to kill him. Where Baron will have no choice but, to depend on Robert here.

Where unfortunately the police will unfortunately arrive on the scene of you doing so where Mr. Peterson will all be killed. Leaving the widow Sandy, the present Mrs. Peterson will be the recipient of his inheritance.

You asked for the truth. I'm giving it to you. We can't allow either of them to recruit any more collaborators. They possess far too great of a threat to the new order.

If you kill either of us, you are killing your only chance to come out of this alive. After all the way we see it is that you owe us at least that much.

There's no other way you are ever going to get yourself out of the predicament you've already gotten yourself in.

It's over for you no matter how you want to look at it. Where without us and this place you have no one but the electric chair for you. Where you betrayed everyone you had whoever believed in you.

Kill us and you'll have gained nothing, where we will come back and you will still be dead. Where no one is ever going to believe in anything you say unless it's your confession of admitting to all that you did for reasons unknown even to you. Refuse us and risk going to the electric chair

Meanwhile where will you go where you won't get caught. Your only hope is us.

"Do you actually expect me to believe this crock of bull-shit?!"

"Yes, I do!" Janet shouted back. "It's the truth! I didn't have to tell you a damn thing! For a supposedly intelligent detective you don't seem to have the brains to blow your own nose.

Be realistic just for one second. She's got the brains, the money, and collaborators. She can't be stopped with, or without your meddling.

What are you going to do with us? Kill us?! Takes us to the police. Turn us into the FBI. There is no way out of this for you, nor do you have any options. There is going to be no immunity for you. No one is ever going to care if you ever existed.

We are talking people in high places and authority that are going to be beckoning onto her and there's no stopping it. Least of all only one person especially such as yourself with no level of importance what so ever.

Where the professor is one, of a kind. That will never be again who's going to have governments beckoning to her every word. Who's yet been unable to even find his own daughter,

The one thing we depended on you to do, and you couldn't even do that without are help.

Not with her being a constant threat to him.

Being able to duplicate everything he's already achieve, and in position of the means to go about doing it.

His only hindrance is going to be having the lack of her genius working with him leaving him having to work out all the bugs that are presently existing, or might have overlooked, or never contemplated having to face.

Now ask yourself. What do you think he might do? If in fact she did collaborate, and with her having the means to distribute time itself. To whom he will in return be able to dictate to. Being able to regulate the amount of time?

All we were relying on you for was just to make contact with her and once you find out simply inform me. After which her identity was known to us she wouldn't be able to inflict any threat upon him.

Where with you still being free and being sought after it was going to be Janet that she would be coming to thinking that I could be the only one whom she could trust. Where by the time she discovers her mistake it will be too late.

Where she'll be stuck in her present form totally dependent on us for her survival, and with us controlling her knowing her every move.

There would be no way for her to rejuvenate herself, and she'll be forced to come to her father, and eventually reveal her hidden location.

Baron's genius is valuable too valuable to waste. All that's been happening is due to him obtaining his independence.

Your continuous involvement will be no longer needed." She looked at her watch then turn her head to look at me saying. "Daryl you really shouldn't drink so much?

By now your fingers should be too mum to squeeze that tiger. You see I took the liberty of assuring that you would be rendered harmless.

Like I said before we mean you no harm but, we need you where we know you can do no harm until you're called upon to do us the good you were intended to due. Now just let it happen."

"Shit!" I irately blurted out! "Not again!" As I faintly drifted into a state of weakness no longer being able to hold up my hand. Let alone the gun I was holding in it.

"Sorry Daryl but, you're far too unstable to be allowed to disturb all are plans. That drug that's now taking effect on you will only render you passively weak.

You propose far too great of a threat to the purpose of are mission. You think you know it all but you haven't begun to discover the real facts yet."

"He's harmless Robert. Professor Page Canon another scientist linked to professor Baron who was now occupying Janet's body." I can handle things from here you best be going."

Robert left as Kate dragged Daryl over to the sofa, and plopped him down into a sitting position. Taking the gun from his hand, and sat down beside me.

I couldn't even feel my fingers on the trigger, or anything else for that matter but, yet I was fully conscious about what was being said, and going on around me.

"Now tell me Daryl how did you figure out that I wasn't your real true love Janet?"

"You're not sensitive where she is. Your legs." I found myself answering her questions without hesitating to think about what I was going to say.

"You mean, and what you were doing at the stadium?"

"Yes, so you see you're not perfect. If I can find a flaw so can someone else.

"It would do that person no good. The real Janet is where no one can find her. I'm the one and only Janet now but that won't matter to you much longer.

It's only going to be a matter of time before your usefulness isn't necessary anymore. Them I won't need to concern myself with anyone finding out about whether I'm real, or not. The one at her club isn't the real Janet, either."

"You mean there's more of you?"

"I guess you could say that. Replicas are easy to duplicate. However, the initiations don't last very long. That's why they're implanted with a memory chip.

Sorry Daryl dearest but, for the past couple of years you've been sharing you love, and devotion with her other me.

What amazes me that it taken you so long to suddenly discover that I'm not perfect, or was it that it didn't matter seeing how.

I was allowing you to share me with all my other girls and you really interested in noticing any difference?

Whether you realize it or not I'm still very much in love with you myself. That why for your efforts I convinced the professor not to let you waste your life in prison or run the risk of going to the electric chair.

I promised you that we would be together when this was all over and I never break my promises you know that.

Knowing you the way I do I know that you will never survive living out your life in prison therefore I'm going to have a duplicate do it for you, and just let it die a moral death."

"I like my life just the way it was but, I'm sorry love it can't be with you as you are.

Yes, you made a lot mistakes that you later regretted but, you have to admit you did make a shambles out of your life.

One, being that you are only in thirty and you already look ten, years older, and your body is even worse. That being of a fifty years old man all scared up, and nearly crippled up while abusing yourself physically to the point where you are only half a man.

That doesn't mean that she still didn't hold you in my arms. Knowing why you were doing what you were doing to yourself.

I don't know how she could ever love a loser like yourself. It's deplorable how you turned out just because you wanted to do things your way.

Where I'm as real as one can get to being her where I can't forget whom she was and the way she loved you."

"Whoever the hell you are! I rebelliously channeling her sentimentality towards me rejecting her concerns for me.

" I might have made a mess out of my life, but at least it was mine too live. Why do you think that I didn't jump at the chance for the one you were offering me?

Your right anyone would jump at the chance to live it over again but, it wouldn't be my life but, someone else.

Immortality is every person's dream but, we all must face the grim reality of are many mistakes. What mistakes have you made that were of your own doing, Not Janet's but, yours?

Now that's what make your life so pathetic. Not having your own life to reflect back on. Making you just what you are. Some sort of genetic creep! Because you had no life to speak of, of your own to live.

You'll never be anything like Janet was! I knew for years that you weren't the same Janet I grew up with and loved. I just didn't know why, how what made you change.

The mind might be able to generate new life but, what about your soul? Without one's soul you're not living.

You're only existing without meaning, or purpose. Just to be screwed, and fucked over like I was doing to you!

It's in gods, powers to give life. No one has the right to play god. Such power is beyond the reach of a mere mortal person.

Whoever you are you weren't meant to be that's why you'll never be anything, or mean anything to anyone.

Living not knowing who you are, or were. For someone else making you the used, not the user where your mind, or your will never be your own but, someone else.

Who's going to threaten your existence by robbing you from anything that made you once human, and denied you from what you might have become just so you can maintain the shallow existence of having to live someone else life.

For what? Just so that you can live longer and hating yourself every moment you have to look in the mirror at someone else face staring back at you."

"How do you know if there's even been such an entity as God?! I'm a scientist with enough intelligence to realize that no such enmity could have ever existed that could have created the human race least of all this earth we all live on.

Where you most of all one of his worst sinner. You never acknowledged him before. All you've ever acknowledged him for was your contempt for what he represented!

Knowing you as well as I do. Knowing that you would sell your soul to the devil for a peace of ass! You've no respect, or concern for anyone but yourself.

Sex, and moneys that's your life, and fuck the rest of the human race! So who are you to criticize me? What are you grinning about?!"

"Nothing, it just feels good to see you back to your old self again. Knowing that, and that we understand each other. How are you going to get me out of this mess, you got me into?"

"Me?!"

"Yes, you. You were the victim I wasn't. It was you that got me mixed up in all this. If you would have come to me to begin with. Maybe I could have prevented you form going to this extreme.

Hell! I could have married you, and given you three, or four kids by now. I was told twines ran in my family. You always had to be the one, knowing what was best for me.

You never gave me the chance to prove to you that I could care for you. You always had to be the superior one making me dependent on you.

Knowing what you did wouldn't have changed my feelings for you. Nothing you could ever say, or do can ever make me stop loving you.

I would die for you without hesitation but, this is asking a hell of a lot of me to accept. You have to at least give me a chance to become accustomed to the new you.

Especially seeing how you are in a league with an insane scientist wanting to take control over the entire human race. That's a lot to take in if you don't mind me saying so.

You never know I might not have given you doing such an asinine thing a second thought. Seeing how I always knew that you were so much smarter than I.

"You marry me?! That's a laugh. As for coming to you. Knowing you. You would have started more trouble than you've already, and really botched things up.

As it is, it took less than a week for you to screw things up before you screwed things up like you have. I had to be insane to even be sitting here listening to you attempting to manipulate me. Trying to prey on sympathy and compassion for you. I'm no fool I would have to be a total idiot to trust in anything you say!"

"Speaking of trust. You best trust in your intuition. This drug you gave me leaves me with no feeling. What if I've to go how would I get to the bathroom? Do you have any dippers in the house?"

"Your futile attempts at being humorous are becoming annoying but, don't concern yourself. The drug will wear off shortly but, I'm glad you reminded me."

She rose up and walked into the bedroom and came back out carrying a strait jacket and ankle shackles.

"You can't be serous?"

"Sorry love but, you can't be trusted." She slides the straights jacket on me saying. Then shoved me face down onto the sofa, and secured the linking straps, and tied the arms straps behind my back. She then connected the ankle shackles, and sat me upright.

"There now. Now I feel more relaxed. Be good and in a few days I might release you."

"A few days? Come on. No one can hold out that long. That inhumane treatment. Where is that compassion all women are supposed to have? Beside how do you know I'll do what you are expecting me to."

"You'll do it all right. Now make yourself comfortable while I go get the car."

Chapter 11

"Well it's about time you got back. Ginger greeted Robert as he entered the living room of the Morehouse's' home.

As she nervously paced impatiently wait on his return listening to the radio. "Have you heard about that damn detective escaping from jail?!"

"Yes, I heard. It's all over the radio. I was busy taking care of that Alice bitch just like you ask but, I guess I didn't do a good enough job.

However, I'll fix that. Her and Sandy are at County General hospital right now both under guard by the FBI no less."

"Robert someone attempted to kill Sandy. I figured that it was you going after her as well. I received a phone call from a friend of mine at security that placed you at the cottage. If it wasn't you that could only mean that someone is really out there screwing thing up for us.

If it wasn't for me getting that tape of you standing out front of the cottage. You would have royally screwed yourself up good.

Now we both have to move fast. That Alice? can't be allowed to live. Not with that detective running around loose."

"Relax sweetheart I'll handle it." He walked over picking up the receiver of the phone. Dialing a secret number in Vegas, and waited for someone to answer. Speaking into the receiver.

"It's time for the Morehouse's daughter to return back home to the nest."

"Yes, alright I hear you. By the way who is this I'm speaking to?" Jerry another one of the scientists that managed to escape after the Baron disappeared. Replied back asking.

"It's me dammit! Kate Olson that's who it is! It's time for you to come back yourself, and don't stop to pack. Leave everything behind you it will be picked up." Robert hung up the phone, walking over to the bar pouring himself a drink of brandy.

"Robert dear I don't like these turn of events. We might have to go into hiding until the heat dies down. If that was Jerry, you were talking to. I'll have Jerry take care of that Alice. All you've to do is keep Sandy and yourself from getting caught.

Mr. Peterson is bond to make contact with you for you to inform him about what's going on with his wife. Make him think that she is just now taken you into her confidence.

We need you to keep on doing the dirty work of keeping the cops away from meddling. What concerns me is who got to Alice before we did to get her to turn on us.

It was she always a damn FBI agent?! It's also to convenient of that neighbor taking a shot at Sandy.

I need you to find out for sure if it was intentional. Just who the hell it was. We need him alive and healthy until we located that damn daughter of his."

"Come on Mary that damn family of yours has made a hell of a lot of enemies. Of which the Peterson's were one of. We have no idea just how much that damn Norman has let seep out to his other associates and partners about what was going on before professor disappeared. It could be coming from anyone.

All I can do where he's concerned is to follow the money for right now. I don't want you to concern yourself about it, that's my problem and I'm working on it. I need you to concentrate on finding out where that damn daughter of his is at."

"Don't quote me but I think I have a possible good lead. I'm not certain as yet. But I'm of the notion that she transformed herself and became one of that Janet Johnson's call girls. I'm checking them all out now to make sure.

I'm going to need you to make sure that your professor Baron doesn't also come upon the same information I did and finds out her whereabouts before we due".

"Those incompetent Bill and Gus never should have let her escape. They left me no choice but to dispose of them. Which left me with fewer to help me locate those others we need to eliminate.

Even though their numbers are getting fewer now after I eliminated those three, so far and there can't be but only a few left that's still a few to many that's causing me to devote all my time and effort to locate.

As for that lamebrain detective, we still have been hold on him so will still be able to continue to control him.

Page has him under her control he's not going anywhere until we want to use him again. Can you at least tell me who it is you believe that daughter of his could be?"

"Again don't quote me on this but, I was informed that might be one of Janet's card dealer by the name of Doris at Janet's place called the High Hat Card Club.

It's the same place that professor Baron was patronizing by taking her into his confidence by letting that loyal colleague Page and her go through that exchange because Page developed that overlarge brain tumor.

I still can't believe Baron actually was able to complete it successfully especially after that major failure that developed during the process.

Where he wasn't able until recently to duplicate it again by accident, and being stupid enough to leave his damn note book as to how he achieves it to where someone else could get at it.

I still strongly believe that, that someone was Miss. Perking's. She's the one who's been collaborating with his daughter all along.

She's the only who could have gotten her hand on that ledger and allowed his daughter to get at it just before she escaped."

"Now that isn't the way I heard about the two of them getting together. The way I heard it. Was that the two, of them had a thing for each.

Where the reason he did the transfer was because he continuously lost heavily and he owed her as well as Page and they both agreed to attempt it because they both had their own personal reasons for doing so. Everyone know why Page agreed to go through with it.

I still don't understand why Baron just didn't have her eliminate and have done with her? Even though he was giving her some old outdated notes.

That weren't going to do anyone any damn good but, she's one of us now so we all are just going to have to live with it like it, or not.

Your still not tell me what makes you think that his daughter is connected with Janet and her card room?"

"Call it a hunch mostly. However thus far the one I'm personally suspecting appears to have all the characteristics of being Baron's daughter.

She looks and acts like a Twenty-Two-year-old women but, extremely far to intelligent for settling for being a prostitute and a card dealer.

I'm having her watch very closely. I don't want to be making any mistakes where she's concern if she suspects that we suspect her she'll up and disappear again where we might never be able to find her again.

It's hard to be sure. That's what makes it so damn aggravating when she could be anyone just like the rest of us.

I'm having that Doris history checked out, and so far she appears as herself. That's the only reason why I haven't made a move on her just yet.

Even though it's just a coincidence that she's been working for that damn detective since Alice left to supposedly go on vacation

What I need to make sure is just one of those who assisted in the transformation. Now that person will be able to tell me for sure who she looks like.

For all I know you could have killed the only ones who could have identified her already because of what Baron is having you doing for him.

This killing should stop until we find out what we need to know before there's no one left to be able to identify her.

This is totally ridiculous on are part. I think you need to speak to Baron and try to convince him to just having you capture the rest of them so that we can question them. Hell you can always kill them after they talk. Now that would be the sensible thing to do.

There's another thought that just occurred to me. One that might have already left us all to rot. Just suppose she's already dead. What are the odds on that?

Then there's that other one. That's been closely associating with Mr. Peterson by the name of Donna Hampton. Where no one can even get close to her except for him.

Seeing how she's so heavily guarded all the time just because she's some sort of a nuclear scientist working for the government."

"What if he hell...?! Phillip Powell, entered the living room of the Peterson's home. Being over came with shock seeing Ginger standing in the living room talking to Robert. Being caught unaware that she wasn't wear she was supposed to me.

"What in the hell is she doing here...?! Why isn't she over in England with Mary where she's supposed to be? Just what's going on here anyway...? Where's Sandy Jesus...! I can't believe what's going on here."

"Well, well, now isn't this a picture to behold..." Sandy came walking into her living room catching all of them together.

Doesn't anyone ever do what they are supposed to do? What are you doing here Ginger Aren't you supposed to be in England with Mary? Dammit! You could be ruining everything for all of us. Shit!

As for you Robert. Thanks for coming back to pick me up. I had to take a damn cab to get here...

Do you've any idea how filthy those cesspools the call a cab is...?!

They ought to be condemn as hazardous containers, and burnt. "

She walked passed them heading straight for the bar pouring herself a brandy. While standing behind it looking over at the three, of then all standing together. Knowing who was who even Ginger.

"So what in the hell are you three, up too? Come on I want to hear something from one of you."

"Sandy, you're alright... Ginger was the first to speak up walking towards the bar. "I heard that someone took a shot at you... I'm glad to see that you're alright... Did they catch the one who did it?"

"No, not yet, but they will. They damn will better before I get to him! that's all I've to say. So what if anything has the three, of you been doing? As for you Robert you damn well better have a good reason for standing here.

As for you Ginger what are you doing showing up here in my living room. I want to hear something good out of someone. It's getting so that I can't depend on anyone anymore to do what's expected of them.

Robert, Phillip we need to talk, Now...! Ginger why don't you go tend to something at the Morehouse's home instead of hanging around here upsetting the hell out of everything. You forget I know who the hell you are.

You damn well better have a damn good excuse for not being where you are supposed to be now get the hell out of my house!"

"Well I never...!" Ginger angrily snapped back. "For your information I thought it better to stay here to keep an eye on my daughter, and let Mary go to England on her own. Where she could up and die just like she's suppose too. Seeing that I'm without a husband now, and my daughter is going to be without her mother.

Someone had to be here to help her through the hard times ahead." She picked up her things to go storming out of the living room.

"I'll discus her being here with her later. Right now I want to hear from the two of you telling me something good. Like that you got that quicken detective where I can get at him...! Well do you Robert?!"

Baron annoyingly started shouting at him wanting to hear some good results after being put through the fiasco of the night's events.

"Damn you Robert! Can't I count on you to do a simple thing like killing that bitch Alice?! How could you fuck up something so damn simple...?

That damn detective almost caught me inside the cottage with her. I was lucky to have made it out of the damn place.

If it wasn't for him shot at I could have gotten the hell away from the cottage, and I wouldn't have had to come up with an excuse for being at my own costal cottage.

I told the cops that Alice called me claiming the she was going to commit suicide, and when I found out that she was at my cottage I went there to stop her.

That while I was there trying to talk her out of killing herself. That while talking to her I dropped something over the railing of the deck and when I went out to get it.

That I heard commotion going on up above me them someone came crashing out through a window of my cottage. Then a shot rang out, and all I felt was a life threatening terrible pain in my fore arm.

As someone crowded up the slop beside me cottage. With the security guards chasing after him. Not having any idea who he was.

I know damn well who it was Robert. So you damn well better tell me that you have that son-of-a-bitch! I mean we knew what he was going to do before he did didn't we?! There's no way you could have let him escape us... I'm not hearing anything, say something dammit...!"

"What's there to say other than now that everything is back on track back to where we were when this all began.

I'm still not able to find that damn Steven Morehouse. I know damn well that he isn't dead, and Paul is still missing as well.

Those two, have been conspiring against you from the very beginning, and there's just so much I can do for you.

Having to play up to Mary for your sake is one thing when I was collaborating with you to find out what her husband was up to when I was myself but, having me continue to fraternize her when I'm like this. Is getting to be far too much for anyone to sacrifice for any cause. Why don't you let me get rid of her?

At least it will put an end to what her husband and her are planning on doing to you one you get rid of that husband of yours using that stupid detective."

"I need her and that damn Steven to find Paul for one thing. Besides their attempts to get something on me didn't work. They have nothing to use against me with Norman now that Miss Perking's is out of the picture.

You just continue to appease her until I tell you to do differently. Besides you might even find Ginger even more enjoyable than you did Mary. While you are concentrating on what finding those few that are left.

I want total exclusive control over everything so that after we do finally locate that allusive daughter of me and I get back what's mind.

I can end any and all threats that will stand in my way from preventing me from achieving my greatest achievement. Total domination.

I want to be myself again but with it what it took away from me back. My youth, and the power and independence to do whatever wherever I damn will please with you of course.

I know Paul betrayed you, and even through you denied my love for you because you wanted more than I was offering you sexually, and emotionally. I still never stopped loving you. That hasn't, nor will it ever change.

I knew about everything that everyone was planning on doing to betray me, and up to now eliminated all but a few of them from ever following through with their devious plans of betrayal.

The Morehouse's' plan of trying to regain control over my research hoping to use Peterson's

wife to blackmail him and every exposing him as a homosexual. Then using their own daughter Sally too support them.

I even learned about that condescending spy Alice who was colluding with the FBI to obtain my ledger thanks to my foresight of bringing Janet in with me.

I can't stand betrayal and I won't tolerate it! Anyone who even contemplates thinking about is going to end up like all the rest of them are. One way or another. That goes for everyone including you as well Phillip.

I know what it took for you to see things my way but, I met your demands. You most of all shouldn't mistrust, or believe me not to do as I agreed when I say. You will have nothing to fear from me as long as you continue to stay loyal to are agreement.

I place Alice in my cottage hoping that the two of you would handle getting rid of her saliently but you sure screw that up royally.

I mean what was so damn hard about shooting her up on heroin, and letting her OD. So that I could find her, and report her as transient who broke into my cottage, and blame security for it. How simple could I have made it for the two of you?"

"Sandy." Robert spoke up breaking the silence. "I just left cottage because I was informed that the two bodies I place at the construction site weren't there.

I went back with those security guards to check just to make sure they were looking in the right place.

Something told me that I was being followed. It had to hand be that detective. So I snuck out the back door and worked my way down the beach.

I couldn't do both so I left Phillip here to get rid of that Alice. I had no idea that she called you before I get to her, and that Phillip already shot her up with heroin before I left, and shoved her in the closet after I left.

Just before that idiot came busting into the place. You had to had arrived just after I left, and also already left yourself.

If it wasn't for those security guard calling me telling me that those two, I dumped there was gong I would have been caught up in everything that went on. As for Phillip here I have no idea how he didn't. He has to tell you his side of what went on.

By the time the three, of us got back all hell was breaking loose outside your cottage. So I decided to hang back while the two, security guards raced up to check on what was happening, and gave chase to someone.

Hell they didn't even catch sight of you lying on the ground until they came back down to look around your place and spotted you lying under the deck.

Shortly afterwards more security guards shown up and started going through your place and spotted Alice. There was no way I could get to her without getting involving myself. "

" Alright so let's hear from you Phillip. Where in the hell were you?" Sandy authoritatively asked.

"That's none of you damn business! So the bastard got away again big deal you have him now. I was there and did what you ask that's all that's important!" He blatantly snapped back answering her.

"Is that all you're telling me?! Do I understand the both of you telling me that this whole fucking evening was a total wasted effort on are part?

Where once again we've to put off everything just for us to get more involved in what that detective has been spouting off about what's been going on involving us. Is that it?! That's just quicken great!"

She angrily tossed her drink. Smashing the glass against the wall behind them shouting out at them. "Your damn intelligence never ceases to amaze the hell out of me!

All this intelligence at my disposal and I still can't find that quicken daughter of mine! When I get my hands on that deceitful brat!

I'll make her wish she was never born...! and neither of you are any damn better! Sandy irately shouted out from enraged anger.

"When I think how she been deceiving me for all these years. Knowing all the time what I was struggling to achieve...! Now could I've been so stupid to let her get anywhere near what was in those leaders of mine. I still can't figure out how she did it...

Lucky for me that I thought ahead far enough to separate some of the pages. At least I know those are safe. Now all I 've to do is to figure out how to put them back in the proper order so that I can make sense out of all my notes. I never was much good at organizing things my specialties were inventing not categorizing.

Dammit! We need someone we can trust to insure are ability to continuously repeat everything correctly.

Up to now I have been relying one what's in the system not really knowing for sure of anything or any of the side efforts or consequences we might be having to deal with.

Everything going to hell ...! I need to regain control, and get my revenge on all those who're making my life miscible.

If I didn't know better, I would think that it's my own daughter who's behind trying to destroy my attempts of achieving my goals.

I don't believe that she ever did love me, and all I did was for her so that we could be together once and for all. I truly do love her...

Well I'm here now and she's not going to allure me, and her tail leads straight to that modeling agency that the Morehouse's' owned.

I didn't run the risk of breaking free if I wasn't sure where to find her. I need that damn ledger dammit! I must have that knowledge that my daughter possesses in that damn head of hers. Once I find my daughter I'll be having you get rid of that Janet as well."

"You mean us don't you?'" Phillip ask.

"Yes, of course us... Are research is nearing the end we can't fail now. I'll have the money as well as the means to role the world for as long as I want. All those others are expendable... Along with all that other crap I unloaded on Janet is worthless.

Any scientist with any brains would know that the second they started to read anything I gave her as not having any logical merit what-so-ever."

"Suppose she's already given it to someone else to take care of. She knows that you knew she got it from you." Robert spoke up adding in his negative opinion.

"No way! She's not stupid! Once she did that her usefulness would be over. Only I know how to obtain the knowledge my daughter possesses... Now get out there and find that daughter of mine dammit!

As for that fool detective nothing must befall him, yet! When I'm through with him he will do anything I'll tell him.

Maybe on second thought maybe we should leave him out there where he's out there not being able to trust in no one or having any place to go without exposing himself out in the open.

I mean him being totally lost with no means of escaping the inedible. What choice would he have but come running to me?

If he knows anything that could be could be a sure way to get him to tell me, wouldn't you think? Let me think about this... Just make sure he stays put

"Not necessarily Phillip spoke up answering her question. You are forgetting about Janet She's always been the closest ling to him and if he's not telling her it's not very likely that he'll tell anyone, even unknowingly.

I don't honestly believe that he's very much good for anything but what you have intended to be for.

After all you were giving her all those pages from that ledger. One would think that if anyone would approach her it would be your daughter.

She is linked to you what better way to keep herself posted on what's going on where you're concern. Just maybe your trust in her has been compromise, or misguided in regards to her loyalty for you?

She's also a close friend to that cop Randy and between the two of you he's already gone to the one he trusts in the most."

"I'm not forgetting about her. All we have to do is to keep Janet advantageous towards him by convincing her that he's the one doing all the killing,"

"You do have a good point there, but there again he's struggling for his own survival. The last thing he's going to be thinking about is getting involved physically. "Phillip interjected his opinion.

However, on the other hand you could be right. He wouldn't be that stupid to draw attention to that Janet of his.

Not when he's so protective of her. Where he's not you, and wouldn't mind putting you in jeopardy."

"Phillip could be right Sandy. If it wasn't for the fact that he's not endowed with the above average intelligence, I honestly think you're right. He should come straight to you.

If nothing else but, to keep Janet as inconspicuous as possible but, still where he could observe what's going on around her.

I'm inclined to go along with you Sandy. Your daughter could very well be hiding out there right under everyone noses.

Where better to hide something but, where all the attention is concentrated around those they associate the closest. If my sense of reasoning is right.

That should also put her right under Janet's noses as well and not at that modeling agency you have been concentrating your efforts on.

If she is like I think she is, close to Janet. What better place to be but, right directly under everyone knows having all the attention drawn straight to her? Say maybe one of the card dealers, or even one of her special call girls even?

That detective possibly could have hit on something but, doesn't even know himself what it his. It's the only explanation for him still being alive where he doesn't even know what he latched onto.

I know Janet and all her girl and all those Janet has been sending to her pride and joy Robert. Where not even he knows who he could have working with him. It's worthwhile checking out?"

"You might be right Robert but, I don't need to be dealing with her right now I'll leave it in your trustworthy hands.

Where I want to know as soon as possible. We need to resolve having to apply all are efforts on locating her.

I'll give you two days and that's all. If you have any doubts at all put the snatch on her and we'll deal with her in due course.

I don't want her running scare destroying any of those pages of the ledger. A lot of those pages still are very crucial to duplicate the formals, and procedures that are presently being used. That still aren't perfected to the point where they could be relied on."

"Have it your way." Robert agree." If I'm right she's out there leaving herself totally vulnerable to get at.

Where it doesn't make any sense that she would be doing such a ludicrous thing. Look at the life she would be leading.

She'll be living recklessly, and would be exposing herself to constant danger. Where anything could happen to her at any given time.

Now that I hear myself talking about. I can't see her going to that extreme. She would be totally out of her environment A genius amongst simpletons.

Forget it Sandy there's no way. By the way here's that watch." He handed it to Sandy. "At least now he won't be able to detect any of us."

"At least this is something. By the way I feel that you're right. She's too vital to place herself out in the open like that.

However, I still want that place watched. If your right that daughter of mine could be larking about there I want her out of harm's way and here with me where she belongs.

I hate myself for not being more assertive, and just settling for speaking to her over the phone for the last four years however things became so involved and I didn't know who I could trust anymore.

I was lucky to be able to keep the few supporters I now have now. I want to thank each and every one of you for sticking with me. I don't know what I would have done without all of you staying loyal to me.

Everything I promise each and every one of you. I will deliver. I hope that all of you have found a safe place to keep your equipment. You can't allow anything to fall into the wrong hands at this point.

We're going to have to move quickly but, very carefully. None of us can afford to lose any more so be extremely careful not to draw any attention to yourselves.

As for that detective. We have to keep him alive, and appearing that he's out killing others, or making sure that he's at least seen, or noticed in the proximity until we finish what we started. We are all in this too damn deep now we have no choice but, to move forwards.

I'll continue to handle my end. Now the rest of all you do what's expected of you.

It's accentual that all of you compete the tasks assigned to you. There be no getting another chance like this again. If you lose it now we will all stand to lose it all.

Nothing of what been accomplished must ever be discovered I hope that you have prepare for the contingency like I have.

I'm not going to be living the rest of my life in a cage being experimented on like a rat in a cage. I rather die as I am. It will be their fault that the human race will be denied the discovery of the century."

"You don't need to tell us Baron. We all knew what we were letting ourselves in for, and what it meant if we failed!" Robert reiterated the vow they all took.

"I'm quite prepared to honor my end as I'm sure Phillip here is willing to do the same. There's no need to have to remind us.

However, you must admit even though we knew some killing was going to be accentual I didn't except it having to resort to having to come to killing each other.

You have to admit that it was a bad bringing him into things just complicated things that much worse.

This was mostly all your fault because you didn't do what you should have let me do when I had the chance when we could have used anyone to take the blame.

Doing things, the way you did jeopardized all of us but, things are back in under are control again now.

I have to tell you that you were causing me a lot of concern over the thought that you might have fallen for that two-bit detective. You did let it slip to me that you almost let him find out your secret.

He might be stupid, but he's still a man. You let him get to you once when you were the most susceptible, and unfamiliar with yourself as a women unstable, and emotional unbalanced!"

"Why Robert I do believe that you are jealous... That's why you don't like the idea of keeping him alive... You want to have done with him so you could have me all for yourself..."

"What if I am?! He's wasn't worthy of you! All he wants was your body. He knows, nor could care less about your mind.

You made yourself venerable to him by letting him get close to you. I have every right to become concerned knowing it's possible that he might be able to do it again where he could ruin everything because you made yourself susceptible to his advances.

Look what happen to you the other night. He might not be any damn good as a detective but, it's obvious that he's damn good as a manipulator where women are concerned!

Where I love you as the man you were and still are too uncertain of the emotional instabilities of the gender you placed yourself in."

"Robert I'm not a woman I'm still the man I always was, and I'm not gay. Robert this isn't the time for us to be quarreling amongst ourselves.

I can't help the way you feel. Things are all mixed up for all of us now don't compound it by starting to mistrust each other.

I assure you what happen between that detective and myself isn't effecting my judgment or common reasoning.

I can assure you that you've no cause to be jealous. Let's not argue because you are letting you're feeling for me physically come between us. Where all he is a means to an end and that's all he is.

Your right I did make a mistake but I'm not going to let it deter me from doing what needs to be done. "

"Sandy we know what we have to do. We just had to be sure about you. Robert rebutted.

"Are you sure now?!"

"Yes, come on Phillip let's get busy cleaning up this mess she's gotten us into...."

'Have fun you bastards!' Sandy said to herself watching them leaving. 'I long for the day I'll finally be rid of you as well... How I loathe, and detest that women she's been a pain in my ass since the day we had sex together.

If I didn't need her right now I would rid myself of her...' She sat saying to herself wondering where Ginger went off to. Contemplating going to look for her.

Chapter 12

Doctor Phillip left driving to the hospital. Carrying with him two, large hypodermic syringes. Having the intentions of just using one of them to store the crucial brain cell that was need to regenerate life cells that dealt with sustaining lasting memory in one's brain.

With the other one dealing with rendering the victims' unconscious by inducing a comatose state making it appears as if their heart stopped beating.

To be used on Alice in order to have her declared dead. Where he could take her back to Sandy's place, and let Robert deal with her.

As he drove, Phillip couldn't stop from contemplating about how he was going to compete the task he set out for himself. That was to kill professor Baron himself.

Not being able to think of anything else as he went nostalgically back too how it first started for him becoming involved with professor Baron.

Have him reevaluating his propose as well as his position of loyalty? Knowing by killing him that he would be killing himself as well.

Trying to project the outcome, and how much time he would have left if he pulled off actually killing Baron.

Phillips reasons for wanting to kill Baron was strictly personal. Where his first attempt to kill, Alice was also personal. Because she was using what she found out about him for her own selfish reason.

It all stemmed around Alice and her love for Norman Peterson chef Carl, who was the one Phillip was in love with. Where Carl didn't love her, nor Phillip but, with Norman Peterson himself.

Where it was extremely important for Phillip to keep his relationship going with Carl. While he was having relations with the two, of them playing one against the other. Until Alice came upon him and Carl making love together down in the pool house.

Using what she discovered threatening to tell Norman. Out of resentment for being betrayed by Carl lying to her.

Discovering that he was a homosexual, finding herself despising him for the revoltingly disgusting things he had her do, while believing that he was in love with her during having sex with her after having sex with other man.

Where Phillip financially depended on Norman for maintaining his elaborate life style, and was being blackmailed by Alice. Unknowing that she was an FBI informant until he discovered while at the hospital overhearing two, other FBI agents talking.

Where he also knowingly discovered that Alice also discovered that he wasn't even a real doctor, and was also threatening to go to the police to tell them. That he was practicing medicine illegally. Where Phillip couldn't permit any attention drawn to him.

Phillip learned about Sandy. Where he took it upon himself to lure Alice to Sandys' cottage under the pretext that she was going to allow her to stay there for a few days. Because she was having personal problems and agreed to do it as a favor for Janet.

When Sandy told him of her intentions of wanting to get rid of her. Because she was going to make a lot of trouble for everyone if she got herself in any serious trouble, and was arrested by the police.

Sandy felt certain that she wouldn't hesitate to inform the police of anything she might be suspicious about what was going on about her.

Seeing that she was involved with Phillip, Normans' personal doctor and he would be the best one to help getting rid of her. Especially where she couldn't ignore the threat she might propose to disrupt her plans.

When Robert arrived Alice was already under the overdose Phillip already injected her with. After he left Sandy arrived, then left herself. Leaving Phillip there to make sure that she was going die.

That's when Daryl came busting in. Causing Phillip to run upstairs to hide. Where he heard breaking of glass, and then a gun shot.

Which caused him to escape out the busted open front door to ran across the street to hide behind his car parked across the street. Out of curiosity to see what was going on about the cottage

When he saw Daryl escaping dashing across the street running from security guards chasing after him. Shooting at him as he sped off on a motorcycle.

After waiting until everyone left. He couldn't help but, to notice that no one found Alice. He went back inside to check on Alice to make sure she was dead.

When more security guards came in. Causing him to hide again. Watching as Alice was taken away.

Where he then took his car that was parked across the street and took off. Without being noticed that he was ever there.

Where Sandy was concerned, she opposed even a getter threat against him. Knowing that he actually killed for her and that he couldn't afford to be discovered because he was also warranted for murdering several other people.

Assisting Robert in disposing of two, other scientists who weren't loyal to Baron, but to that of Steven Morehouse.

Even though it was though Steven Morehouse that he became involved prior to baron becoming Mrs. Peterson in what was going on.

Where he betrayed Morehouse by using what, he leaned about his deception to approached James Baron to inform him about what Steven Morehouse was up too. That's how he came to become an active participant in his actual transfer.

Where with them he used his relationship with her husband Norman to manage to manipulated Sandy into going with him to Barons private location. Where he and serval other assisted in the transferring process.

Then shortly afterward also aided Baron in transferring Baron's most trustworthy scientist one Kate Olson by drugging Robert the chauffeur so that she could occupy his body.

Where for his loyalty he himself went through the transfer using Phillips, Normans' actual doctor body to occupy for himself

Where unknown to everyone. Phillip was also planning on ridding himself of both Sandy as well Robert. Knowing the threat that they proposed to his keeping his new identity a secret.   Knowing somewhat how the procedure worked but. Was going to need Baron's daughter along with that ledger to be able to repeat it, and learn how to do it himself so he wouldn't have to depend on professor Baron again.

Thinking on using Daryl to blame for their deaths. Knowing now where he was being held and who they now expected to be his daughter.

Phillip was in it for himself. He wanted to be rid of James control over him, and gain control over the experiments. Whereas being Normans' doctor, he would be in the prefect position to gain control of Normans assets.

To where he could virtually take over the financial aspect that his enterprise was funding the research on.

He was going to take over Sandy's body while disposing of his and the body he was using to use Sandy's laving everyone to believe that she was still James Baron.

Feeling certain that his mind was more advanced than James. Due to the fact that James was draining his own existing cells extremely fast.

By having to comfort all the challenges he's been forced to comfort. While having to deal with the unstable factors that went along with becoming a woman

Where on the other hand, while Phillip was contemplating his own take over. Unknown to him as well as James Baron himself. Was that there was another who also aligned themselves to him, who were also plotting to betray him.

Which was creating a vicious circle of deception that was being generated for the sole purpose of eliminating each other, and wanting to be the one to take control over what they already achieved.

Whereas due to no fault of James ignorance, he disrupted everyone else's plans of deception by dissecting the ledger.

Forcing them to take up James plans to find his daughter, so that he could regain control of the entire ledger.

Where now Phillip himself felt sure he could continue seeking her out now that he basically knew where to start looking.

Where all in all little did anyone know that everyone was plotting against each other for themselves. All waiting to get their hands on Barons daughter, so that they themselves could take over control for themselves.

Thinking that professor Baron was totally unaware that everything he was trying to achieve was falling apart around him. And all he achieved was doomed for failure.

Whereas still unknown to everyone was that the FBI became fully aware of what was going on through Mary Morehouse who was accidentally found but, discovered not to have existed.

When she accidentally was caught thinking that she was still Mary, but was in fact. Ginger attempting to cash some government bonds using the name of Mrs. Mary Morehouse.

While not knowing the password code that Steven set up attached to the serial number of the bonds she was trying to cash.

Solely in order to retain them under another name before Norman caught him embezzling millions from him.

Where she was turned down from cashing them due too not being able to verify her husband's signature.

Because Steven cut off all avenues of doing so and he was no longer believed to be alive, and her memory was being affected by Gingers causing her to have memory relapse.

Where in order for her to cash the bonds she had to prove that she was in fact married to Steven Morehouse and was now his widow.

Where the only existing record that he was married was that he was married to a Donna

Morehouse, and not Mary Morehouse, least of all Ginger. Where Mrs. Morehouse was believed to be overseas. Which raise a lot of eyebrows to where the police were called.

Mary totally forgot the way they set things up prior to Stevens death. Where Steven managed to erase to whom he was really married to, and wasn't around to give his okay to anyone attempting to cash any of those bonds.

With them both knowing that was all the money he had left to support themselves with, and he had to continue to paid those he was collaborating with.

So that he could continue to take advantage of the success of the experiments as well as those he had to use to insure himself of their loyalty.

After the police were call she was taken to the police station when The FBI became involved was when she broke down, and confessed telling them everything about the experiments her and her husband went though.

Where upon further question she startlingly realized what was happening to her after shockingly regaining control of her own mantle fatalities. Emphatically denied, recanting everything she said Only too realized she said too much even though she refused to say anything else that would incriminate her she continued to emphatically stopped saying anything more.

Other than whom she was now claiming herself to be one Ginger Hasten. Stating that all she was attempting to do was a favor for Mrs. Morehouse who called her and asked her to cash several bonds for her.

Saying that she would call and inform the necessary people that I was coming. That there wouldn't be any problem.

That when the police were called, and she panicked, and became terribly frighten. Then became disorientated where she lost realization what she said, or did.

Until just a few second prior, when she suddenly realized she wasn't back at the Morehouse manner.

Where the FBI became involved. Who was already involved in investigating the Peterson enterprise. Along with the Morehouse's already.

Having Alice already infiltrated investigating professor James Baron activities at The High Hat Club.

Where he's been known to patronized and reportedly giving the owner highly classified documents concern stem cell research that was being conducted unofficially.

Where the FBI, decided to monitor her activities instead of comforting her statement with what she claimed was going on. Wanting to find out just where it was going to lead them.

Where during the weeks that followed the FBI devised a plan in how to monitor the activities that were going on.

In hopes that they could accumulate enough evidence to get everyone involved in what they were attempting to do. Still not knowing exactly for sure, what it would as the end results.

Still unaware that they could believe anything that was previously said during the interview they were having with someone claiming herself to be Mrs. Mary Morehouse whose husband was confirmed murdered.

Even though Mary's husband Steven went through the transformation. He didn't realize that he was being betrayed by one of professor Barons colleagues

Even though the transformation failed somewhat. He retained most of his same body features but, gained in youth.

While at the same time retaining some of the scientist's knowledge from all that transpired previously.

Which also increased his own but, was constantly conflicting with his own mind's train of thought. Making it difficult to maintain control of his level of intelligence.

That's when he came up with the plan to get everything he could on Sandy to use against her. Knowing her situation with Norman, and how to destroy their marriage. Hoping to separate them where he could deal with them individually.

Upon Mary returning back home. She promptly informed Steven. Telling him about her getting arrested and questioned the FBI.

Which prompted him to inform all the others he was colluding with. Which set off a panic, causing everyone to take it upon themselves to desert all their plans, and scatter. In hopes of protecting themselves as best they could.

It was prior to when this all started. That Steven used his association with Baron to establish an association with Janet.

Knowing that he was patronizing her card room, and he was losing heavily where he was becoming heavily indebted to her.

Where it wasn't until just before Steven went through the transformation that he approached Janet. Too used his association with her to ask her to recommend a reputable private detective to hire to spy on Mrs. Peterson.

Thinking that was whom professor Baron was using to conceal his true identity not being able to find out through his wife.

Where the FBI already was aware of the unusual activities that were going on through Alice but, not realizing it was anything compared to what was really going on right under their noses.

Only uncovering that the card room that was owned by Janet was involved in a lot of illegal activities but, thought it to be irrelevant to warrant them becoming involved in at their level.

That what was going on was at a civil level but, decided to kept Alice on with the investigation for a while longer. While they devoted their attention to other matters.

Not realizing that Janet was already gotten to while she was over in Europe, by James Baron. Thinking to use him for her own purposes. While only keeping her involvement with professor Baron known only onto Daryl.

Not contemplating what his fate might be once everything was all over. Hoping that they still might be together but, willing to settle for living without him if need be.

Because it was due to the accident that she suffered, and her association with James Baron combined with her physical state that she was left in.

That she agreed to submitting herself to putting herself through the transformation. Providing that her existing knowledge would remain intact where it was in fact overtaken by another scientist who was in need of a receptacle because her health was failing rapidly.

Where the accident left Janet permanently cripple, and scarred for life. When Baron promised her that he could restore her back to herself again. Along with regaining her mobility of being able to walk again.

Then along with himself, Paul Murray and William Thorn his two, most loyal colleagues who added him.

They achieved the impossible, putting Janet back together again within a few short weeks. Converting Janet into his most loyal, and trusted colleague.

Whereas Robert was concern. She was too close to Baron not to be trusted. She wasn't going to let anything happen to James that she couldn't correct. Leaving her in the position of having to do James dirty work but, was working both sides.

In the hopes of coming out on top over the pile's bodies of those who didn't make it. Because for him having to protect James interests.

When in fact he wasn't the only one who was out killing. Where Phillip was also randomly killing those who propose a threat to him, because he has his own secrets to be kept hidden.

Phillip himself was out killing all those he felt he couldn't trust. Hoping to eliminate anyone who might be able to identify him for whom he was previously.

Using Sandy for the purpose so he could get at them thinking of himself only. With Robert having the knowledge of him not intervening.

To attempt to stop him knowing that he wasn't going to stop with them but, also would eventually be going after Sandy herself as well, where it will be he himself. Where she knew she would have to stop him before he got to James.

Phillips thoughts were about his involvement in the turn of events that have taken place. It all seemed somehow ironic for the professor too finally come to his editable end.

Not being recognized for what was his most incredible achievement. Due to the actual person who earned it instead himself, and not some sort of freak of mature. That he himself made himself out to be by making himself into a damn woman.

As far as Phillip was concern James exceeded the limits of human regeneration, and brought cloning into the realm of becoming a reality.

Who did so by exceeding the inhabitation of restrictive laid out to conduct his research. That actually excelled the human race far ahead of its time.

By inhumanly violating certain principles that obviously cost human lives. His monsters came into being incomprehensible human in every detail where he himself was the living proof of what he achieved.

The irony of it all is that it's all going to be lost because of the elements he couldn't control. The human elements of selfishness, personal greed, and self-preservation. As he had to overcome countless encounters of failures to prove, it was possible to play god.

Going against the law of humanity, and morals. By disregarding those he will never stop sacrificing to achieve his goals. Becoming the modern age Frankenstein.

Thinking that the human race should thank him for sparing it the onslaught of hardships that he could bring down on it, by ridding him from it.

James' obsession became so severely out of control. That he would not only use the living to perform his experiments on but, also those who would refuse to work with him. They too would become his experimental Ginny pigs.

Where Phillip himself actually witnessed with his own eyes. Him injecting some women in her 40's with an experimental serum. That failed to kill her, as she laid helplessly slowly suffering excruciating pain.

Where Phil wasn't going to allow him to do that to him. Even though it was all that was needed to create the process he was now using.

There still the serum he extracted from her still had an unknown time limit. Before it starts to dissipate within the blood stream.

That he needed from out of his ledger to reproduce the serum again that would aid him in producing a living replica of herself.

Where it didn't become, know to James that his daughter had a photographic memory from Steven secretary Miss. Perking until it was too late. After she disappeared.

That it was quite possible that she could have been taking mental pictures of his research, and with her high level of intelligence, could analyze what he was doing.

Where with the right equipment she could possibly duplicate what he has already accomplished. If she also had scientific collaborators to assist her. Using what he had written down in his ledger.

Whereas she might be able to create some chemically generated clones to aid her. Getting them from the sickly, or dying to also sustain her life span by assisting her.

Even to still maintain, or changing her original form. While she prefects the process until she eradicated all the unknown risks. Without having to murder innocent people in the process

In both cases the process was still far from being perfected, and were lethally unstable where the results deteriorated over time causing incinerating the clones from the inside out.

To prefect the process the ledger had to be verified, and complete. Even though he already had access to the pages Janet was holding.

He also needed all the portions his daughter escaped within her mind. To determined what might have been overlooked between the process procedure between what was in the ledger, and in her mind. Without having to redo all his experiments over again.

With word of others entering the cryogenic research field with government founding, where still neither side was being able to regenerate, nor duplicate the prefect process.

For over five, years where so many have been involved in it. Drew a lot of concerns about them surpassing what he has already achieved.

Where there was no way of telling just how far they could have advance in the cloning process in such a large number. Where he only had a few to get as far as he did.

His rivalry was getting to him, to where he didn't want to get robbed out of the recognition he so richly deserved.

All the while Phil was reminiscing the clock was ticking, and the FBI was getting closer as the number of death that became associated with what Ginger confessed to.

Kept piling up as the police along with the FBI started getting reports of amoralities coming back from the coroner's reports.

About how their bodies don't correspond with the actual ages were determining the cause of their death during the autopsy.

Whereas due to certain connection Norman had within the police department. He learnt about the research project he was founding was being investigated for inappropriate activity.

Along with other research facilities that were also experimenting in the same field for the same possible infractions.

Where he in return comforted Sandy. Accusing her of attempting to start trouble to gain more than they agreed upon, by attempting to try to ruin him. Before slamming the phone down in her ear.

Which cause a chain reaction from her? Where when Robert returned Sandy alarmingly confronted him. Telling him what Norman accused her of. Looking to her for answerers, she couldn't come up with.

Where the only thing James could think of. Was taking an extra-long vacation by heading to Las Vegas hopping to get the jump on the others.

Thinking only of her and Robert not evening and consideration over leaving the others to fend for themselves. Thinking of only telling them when they knew that they were out of everyone reach.

I was totally unaware of what was going on. Where I was at I was being kept so drugged up my mind was in a total daze, to where I was totally at Janet's mercy.

Knowing that I was still being wanted for murders I didn't commit. With Randy's career hanging in the balance.

While not even be able to identify where I was at, or knowing how long it's been since I'm been out of circulation.

Without having the ability to even reason clearly, or carrying about anything. Even if something did come to my mind, I was so distant from it, by watching the walls just slowly spinning around. As I strained my eyes to see though the hazy flog clouding them just to see sparkles of light blinking as the walls continued spinning sparkles of blinking flashing dots.

Only knowing that it was Janet who was holding me prisoner from going anywhere. By keeping me drugged me up, keeping me the way I was.

Thinking that she was holding me down in the cellar of the club. In an unknown compartment, hidden behind some concealing wall like she had in her office.

Knowing how good she was at making hiding places for herself. Vaguely recalling when I even seen her last where it was only to give me another shot.

Remembering her showing up to inject me with something that would render me drowsy placing me into a subconsciously state of mine.

So that she could remove the straight jacket, and that ankle shackles that was locked securely to an eye bolt to the comment floor.

Where the drug would render me helpless to resist her manipulating me. So I could go to the bathroom, maybe get cleaned up somewhat, and be given a chance of clothes.

Having no idea how long it's been that she held me helpless to defend myself. Where I don't even have the strength to attempt to break out.

I tried to talk to her, hoping to convince her that what she was doing was ridiculous. Stating that she couldn't keep me prisoner for every but, she just refused to listen to anything I attempted to say to her not caring to listen to what I had to say.

Even when I attempted to charm her, which seemed to always worked when I turned on the charm.

Especially when she was striping my down to take a shower, and did the same to herself to give me a shower while I could barely have the strength to hold myself up, my weakened legs were so weak.

I mean there I was with everything at her disposal. Just willing to be taken advantage of. With me dumbfounded over how she was able to resist the temptations I was presenting to her.

"Now I know you're not the Janet I knew. She would never pass up such a good thing that I can offer her I know I couldn't. Which I'm sure was becoming extremely noticeable I might add,

"Come on honey, be the voluptuous sinuous women you were once. I just know you can't resist to give yourself what you so richly deserve. You couldn't have forgotten how wonderful we are when we come together. "

"Forget it Daryl you're not going anywhere. Especially where you want me to let you get. Thinking that you will be able to get over on me.

Because you so egotistically think of yourself as so manly I'll become smitten by what you are attempting to entice me with. Need I remind you I have seen it as well as had it all before.

When I might add having done so. I don't want to shatter your manly ego but, you are going to be needing a lot more to get me to fall for anything you think you could offer me."

"Come on honey, don't be that way. A little bit is better than nothing at all. You best jump on the opportunity. Without some encouragement I'll start to lose my inspiration, and I'm very enthusiastic right now. What do you say? Just a quick dip I promise it won't last for too long."

"Sorry dear heart you are just going to have to wait. This is all going to blow over, as long as you say out of sight. It's you whom everyone is looking for. Where I'm in no rush I know where you are, now don't I.

Besides with you here. There's no way anyone is going to find you. For now, just relax, and make yourself comfortable, and be patient in time who knows you might get lucky.

Until them you are just going to have to settle for the washing until I'll figure out something to make your life more comfortable. Someone has to be strong for the both of us."

She stood with me leaning back again the stone wall drying me off then picked up a pair of pants to put on me. "

Now just step into your pants and let's get this over with. So that I can get back to what's going on.

Things aren't looking good. That Mrs. Morehouse has really screwed things up for all of us but, everyone is blaming professor Baron. Because she claimed to have suffered from a setback from the procedure she went through.

Whoever is at fault, she still was arrested and got the cops as well as the FBI down on everyone. With them claiming that the people, who were killed. Don't appear who they are supposed to be. Which has got everyone running for cover even the professor.

Where now because of those two, ditches stirring up so much shit. All of us have no idea just how long any of us really have, before it's all over for us.

If we don't manage to be able to go through the transition again, all I have sacrificed would have been for nothing. But, isn't that the way my luck always went for me?

Where now I have more to think, and worry about them you, and I'm not really in the mood to get screwed any more than I'm getting right now.

Which mean I'm going to have to hold you here with me longer than expected. So you are just going to have the make of best of things until things settle down and come back too somewhat moral. Where we can pick up with you again where we left off. Sorry love but that's the way it is.

Believe it, or not I'm doing you a favor by not submitting to your advances. I don't want you getting used to having things get too good for you like I have been doing for you by making it even better. Doing so is only going to fuck you over more than I ever could.

Besides you're going to have to keep your wits about you for when we do send you out there again.

That is if you have any left, at the rate things are going. Either one of us will be damn lucky if we come out of this alive. I don't want you thinking of how good you had it with me when I kick you out.

As it stands right now, the only one who's being affected by your absence his Randy where the worst they can do to him is discharge him, if that.

Where they can't prove a damn thing without you collaborating their allegations. Now after you eat, I want you to get yourself a lot of rest.

I'm having company tonight, and I need time to prepare for them, and stop looking at me as if I was some delicious desert."

She stood getting dressed as I sat on the toilet watching her annoyingly reaching out to fondle her pendulous breast fully exposed within reach of my hand.

Not giving up on attempting to get over on her. Hoping to overpower her so I could escape using all, I had going for me. Along with what was left of my alluring charm

"Come on Janet. I don't mind being your prisoner but, to torture me as well? I'm only human . . .

How could you begrudge me from being enchanted with you being the person I am? My god, but you are so ravishing beautiful . . ."

"Forget it Daryl." She stepped back out of my reach. "You're to drugged up to appreciate me allowing you to exert your manly oats.

You don't have it in you to make it worth my while. As much as I want to oblige you, it wouldn't benefit either of us.

Besides knowing you the way I do I would be an utter fool to trust you with my pants down without your hand tied together. For you not to take advantage of my vulnerability.

I'm not about to forget how devious you're.

I know why you are flaunting yourself and attempting to entice me. You are only attempting to praying on me to get me to do something stupid.

So forget it dear heart it's hopeless on your part. Thinking I'll let you seduce me only to use me so that you can attempt to escape.

Besides it wouldn't do you any good especially in the condition you're in, you wouldn't get very far in either attempt to get over on me.

Beside what would it accomplish if you did manage to escape me. Possibly other than getting yourself killed, or put in prison. Besides you're already my prisoner where it's best for you to stay right where you are.

The last thing I want is you getting yourself killed. So just knock off your bull-shit and behave yourself.

True it would resolve the mess you created but, it wouldn't accomplish a damn thing. The killings aren't going to stop, nor is everyone going to get at that ledger.

As for James daughter, she's never going to come forward. It's my guess that she's long gone never to be heard of again"

"Janet, I can' live like this. I rather be dead than to exist in a cage." I made a desperate attempt to make a lunge at her. Tackling her to the cement floor. To go rolling off her to make a desperate attempt towards the door. Crawling on my hands and knees.

Only to be yanked back by the chain attached to the shackle around my ankle. So weak I didn't have the strength to push myself up, or fight against the force pulling me back.

"You fool! I told you that you were helpless." She rose up from siting on the floor holding onto the chain.

Shoving me over onto my back with her feet against my side rolling me over. So weaken form my futile struggle against breaking from form the chain I didn't have the strength to rise up.

" Now you just lay there and think about how stupid that was to attempt such an idiotic thing. It will teach you a lesson to listen to me the next time you think to attempt of getting away.

You're not going anywhere so you might as well set your mind to that fact. "

She rose up onto her feet dragging me over towards the bed. Locking the chain to the eye bolt. To go pick up the syringe. Jabbing it into my arm then yanked it out. Stepping back from me to stand above me annoyingly saying.

"You best get your own ass up, and back into that bed before that shot takes effect. I damn sure ant going to bust my gut picking you up that's for damn sure. She buttoned her blouse up making herself look presentable.

"Now I'll be back shortly I want to see you in that bed when I get back so I can put that straight jacket back on you. If you're not, I'm going to strip you naked again and let you lie on that cement floor until morning."

She left the room leaving me lying on the damn floor, locking the door behind her. Not giving some rat's ass about whether I lived, or died. Letting that drug, she injected me with attack my brain, and my bodily functions.

Leaving me laying on the floor with the tray of food, she brought me sitting on the wooden table next to the bed. With the silverware still lying on it, and me without my straight jacket on.

Grudgingly I crawled on the floor gathering up the silverware. Thinking that I could use something to break free from out of the cage I was being locked up in.

Struggling to keep my head clear long enough before that damn drug Janet gave me overpowered my will too resist its hypnotic control over not only my senses but, my physical strength.

Feeling my fingers beginning to become mum and my arms feeling heavier than my strength was able to hold them up.

Exhausting every ounce of strength, I could muster up. Making my way over to the bed. Using it to pull myself up onto my knees so that I could reach the bench beside my bed. Thinking to pick the lock on my shackle around my ankle to break myself free.

Dizzily struggling to shake the dizziness out of my eyes, and head. Reaching for the fork on the tray becoming more faintly druggy.

Now unable to control my fingers functions. Dropping the fork as I attempted to jam it into the lock on the shackle.

The door sprang open letting blinding light filter in totally obscuring my vision. While casting a silhouette of someone standing in the open doorway

"Oh, shit!" I exhaustively gasped out. Collapsing down upon the bed upon my back to exhausted to move, or make out whom it was now approaching me. Hearing a key unlocking the lock of my shackle and woman's voice saying.

"It's I Doris I'm here to help you. It's time for you to come with me now." Before I totally passed out.

Unknown to me that drug Janet was giving me was the drug that was used to prepare someone for being transferred to put the dormer's mind in a hypnotic state. So that it can be taken control of by the more dominant mind.

* * * *

Only too once again finding my foggy, clouded eyes focusing. On where I'd no idea now, or where I was, or how I got there, or knowing how much time lapsed before I found myself opening my eyes.

Now lying in a hospital bed. Instantly finding myself feeling fantastically full of energy wanting to jump up and take on the worlds.

Only to startlingly find myself strapped to the bed by my wrists. With straps stretched across my chest and legs.

Seeing a gorgeous red-haired woman entering the room wearing a white uniform. Smiling as she entered greeting me.

"Well, I see you're feeling much better today." She walked up checking my pulse. Smiling at me with her peal white perfect teeth.

"You mustn't get to excited. Now just let yourself succumb to your new self gradually, so that you can become accustomed to all you're experiencing. I must say you went through the transition remarkably well."

"Transition . . .? Remarkably . . .?! What in the hell did you do to me?! Let me up! "I frantically struggled to break free.

Hysterically going through a paranoiac state of utter fear, shouting out panicky. Literally shaking the bed up from the floor.

Bring in several others. With one, stabling me with a twenty, foot long needle in my arm. While the others held me down, until I submissively became passive. Slumberous asking . . .

"Where am I.... What did you do to me...? You can't do this . . ."

"Honey, it's all right." Another women's voice spoke out to me saying." Relax . . . It's all over for you . . . You're free now. I'm here with you, and we are together now."

Her distant voice seeped into my ears sounding like some angles voice coming from heaven. Trying to console me, as my eyes attempted to focus on her face.

Looking down at me, blinding me with her sparkling blue glowing eyes, as her glowing blond hair created a hallow about her head.

"Who . . . Who are you . . .? Do I know you . . .?"

"Why honey, of course you know me . . . I'm Dorine honey, your wife . . . Give yourself time to adjust to you remember me. It's all going to come back to you just need time that's all.

That tumor that was in your brain is gone now. It's all over. Now you must give yourself time to recuperate . . . Now just relaxes you're going to be just fine."

'Tumor my ass!' I panicky yelled to myself.

Distraughtly recalling that there was a large void that I was missing out of my life that my brain wasn't recalling.

Feeling certain that it was the part that I was missing upon finding myself waking up not knowing what in the hell happened to me.

Knowing not what they did to me, and I wasn't going to let them get away with it. Knowing that I didn't want to be anyone else but, myself but, not knowing who I was anymore.

Not comprehending how I could just leave my whole life behind me, and become someone else I knew wasn't I. 'Asking myself, who the hell is Dorine?! When the only name I could seem to remember was Janet.

Then it all started too startlingly to come back to me. In mind shattering flashes that faded rapidly only to be bombarded with disturbing others.

Things that I started to vaguely start to recall. People's faces, places. Then recalling there was something I was wrapped up in that I couldn't get myself out of.

Nothing didn't seem to make a hell of a lot of sense. Where I then seemed to be overcome with a sense of tranquility where I found myself thinking.

That I could resign myself to giving into the benefits of becoming someone else. Having little regrets other than appearing to be agonizing over the haunting thought that I was feeling remorse over the feeling of abandonment.

That I was leaving someone without settling something first. Where I was becoming agitated by the thought there was nothing I could about it.

I was finding myself doubting that I was the person who was lying in that bed where everyone around me was looking at me like they actually know me. Where I didn't know any of them but, most of all, how in the hell I got there.

I found myself attempting to reach out to that gorgeous women standing beside my bed. Actually considering myself envious of myself for getting so damn lucky but, not knowing a single thing about her.

Emotionally being besieged with thoughts of sexual fascination of longing desire for her. Asking her if I can have a look at myself.

This woman who claimed to be my wife whose name was Dorine. Reached into her purse and pulled out a compact and opened it.

Letting me look for myself at, myself. Handing me her compact so I could look at myself in the mirror to let me see for myself who it was I was supposed to be.

I couldn't believe what I was seeing. I wasn't even able to even recognize what I thought I once looked like. All I could do was blatantly stare. Having to accept what I was seeing in that mirror.

Looking at a young guy in his middle twenties, who had light brown hair, blue eyes, with some sculptures descriptive facial structure masculine yet distinguishably cavalier looking. That was tanned, and flawless without a broken nose.

That I felt certain I had along with even facial scares that I acquired over the years from one, source or another.

Maybe from when I was young, or being active in spots but, there wasn't a single one. Not even one from shaving.

'My God.' I amazingly gasped out from disbelief. Looking at myself as the dream man of every woman's dream guy . . .

I was a guy convinced about whom he was and liking what I was seeing. Where when I lowered the mirror to egotistically looked back at Dorine saying enviously.

"I would be an utter fool to give this up . . .!" Expressing more than admiration that I couldn't have been more satisfied at being whom I was.

Not giving any more thought about anything else but, getting my ass out of that bed and back home to be alone with my gorgeously sinuous wife.

"All right I'm relaxing . . . I get it. The crisis is over. I'm I all over again . . ."

"Are you sure dear?" Dorine nervously asked. "You remembering me means' everything to me. I never would have gone through with this if

I didn't have any other choice. Without your love all this is would be meaningless.

I was so frightening that you wouldn't make it through, and that you would remember just how much you mean to me.

I just couldn't afford to lose you. You were the only one who meant anything to me, and whom I could never desert me.

I fell in love with you the first time I laid my eyes on you. Now that I know that you love me all that matters as that you are going to be all right.

Honey, so much was happening. I didn't like being forced into having to do this to you but, I just couldn't let you suffer any longer.

It would be totally wrong of me to let you do so. You are so much like me. Neither one of us had any control over anything. I just couldn't let it go on any longer.

Not when I knew, I could spare you from all you were being put through. All I could do was hope that you would make it through this if you loved me enough to want to be with me and you did, and here we are. Both alive and well and done with all of it.

Honey, there's so much I want to tell you. That's been going on while you have been here but, that can all wait. All that matters is that get better soon, and that your love for me is still intact.

'Things aren't the same any more but, you don't need to concern yourself. Time is all you need now to come to accept the changes that had to be made.

I want you to know that you can count on me to stand by you all the way as long as your love for me true.

I just want you to know that I can't undo what has been done but, you will come to understand that it needed to be done.

Thanks to you, and the results that was achieved. Miraculous breakthroughs were made possible. The risks are no longer anything like they once were but, you must take things slowly to ensure there will be no complications. I want you to be with me for a very, very long time."

I got the feeling that she was trying to tell me something but, the jest of it was going over my head.

Because I was no longer associating anything with my past to what, I was looking forward to in my future.

Seeing her, and feeling consoling hand holding onto mine assured me that I had nothing to concern myself with.

That my life with her was going to be back too moral again, were all the insensitive I needed to want to get well quick.

"Yes that's all I want too." I answered her back assuring her that I wanted the same thing.   "I guess it was the shock of finding myself back to my moral life again that disorientated me." Then suggestively speaking out king of telling her. That I still didn't quite understand all she was saying to me by evasively saying.

"Yes honey, we need to talk, so that you can bring me up to date on everything I have been missing out on."

"Yes, I know, and we will but, not right now. Later I need you to rest now. We'll leave you be, just rest now."

She waved to everyone to leave the room. Waiting to be the last person to leave. Bending down to kiss me warmly, not passionately on the forehead. While looking back towards the closed door. Whispering.

"If you know what's good for you. You will go along with me. You've a lot to thank me for. For what I'll tell you later.

For now, just go along with what I tell you to do and don't do, or say anything else to anyone unless I tell you, and not another word about what was.

That's over for a lot of people. With us being the exception besides those that were here with us, and I don't want any of them to know any more than what I tell them.

By the way you're not in any hospital but, you're well, and coherent as well as alive. That's all I'm going to say for right now.

Dorine was to say the least an extremely incredible woman. He superior intelligence over me was very obvious. So much so I often wonder how it was I even managed to land such a spectacular person.

Even though I didn't consider myself an imbecile. Her level of intelligence was so far advanced from my own, she made me feel very uncomfortably inferior at times. I had to admit it did distant me from her intellectually.

Where on the other hand. There was no more loving, or compassionate of a person I ever knew existed, and even being more admirable just being herself for she was truly all women, and raveled in flaunting her beauty.

I knew that she could do a lot better as well as go a lot further in her life without me but, she would never think of herself as above me.

In fact, all she ever did was patronize me by phrasing me for having more intelligence than I did. Where I often see her reading an extra-large book, in a matter of minutes.

Where she never forgot a single word that was written in it long afterwards but, yet never attempted to prove that she was above me by always having to compromise herself but, yet agreeing with me when I know she was right. Unless she felt it extremely important that she took the upper hand.

I knew that we were totally incomparable just by the lever of friends she associated with. When I would confront her about me feeling that I didn't belong.

That I felt out of place where they were concerned while I was involved in conversations that took place between them.

The intellectual level drastically changed while I was around so that I would feel that I was fitting in.

Knowing that it was all her doing not wanting me to feel uncomfortable. However never pressing me to be any more than who I was while not feeling that I was hindering or embarrassing her amongst her friends and colleagues.

Though I had no doubt in my mind that I was emphatically in love with her. There was always this haunting feeling that I was harboring a totally different impression of her.

Like I felt she was harboring low self-esteem of herself, and was purposely undermining herself as a person but, one who had an extremely strong sense of character, that she was inhibiting attempting to avoid letting her true self come out.

As unwavering as it was at time not knowing who I really was sharing my life with now it was the person I was totally accepting that she was truly in love with me.

It was prior to my leaving that's things seemed to even become more nerve-racking. What never dawned on me was that no one ever seemed to refer to be by my name.

It was. "How are you feeling today? Or yes dear." I knew Dourine's name but only her first name it never one accrued to me to ask her what my name was. What my last name would have to be hers as well if she was my wife.

The second she came to visit me I hit her right off saying. "Honey this might sound strange to you but, I seem to have forgotten my damn name.

I guess I'm having myself one, of those memory farts. Can you tell me?"

"Why of curse honey it's Clay Morrison. Now don't let it disturb you, things like that was bound to happen. Now let's see what else I can tell you about yourself. Just in case you might have forgotten that as well.

You are a computer technician managing your own business. Your 27 years old, married of course. No kids as yet but, we were working it that. Then there's I.

I'm your wife Dorine Morris as well. I'm a private secretary staying to become a real estate agent hoping to open my own agency.

I'm 25 but, never reveal that to anyone. Where we have been living happily up until about a year ago when you developed that tumor that brought us both here that's about it there's not very much more to tell.

Well seeing how you brought it up. I might as well tell you. That due to no fault of either of us. I had to sell the house but, I found us another place not too far from here in Las Vegas.

I also landed myself a new job because my former boss gave me an out stand recommendation. Whereas you can open a new business anywhere.

So things have worked out perfectly for the both of us. Where soon now you will be back on your feet and we'll be able to continue our lives as if nothing has happened. Isn't that great?"

She enthusiastically expressed your happiness by kissing me for the first time passionately fully on the lips.

When letting herself get close enough where I could get a complimentary reminiscent feel of what, I've been missing on for I don't know how long.

As short and familiarizing as it was. As she nervously watched the door for a brief second before stepping back. Nervously whispering out.

"That's enough. I don't want you getting yourself all worked up seeing how you are so close to coming home where I won't have to concern myself about letting you take liberties. Now just be good."

Dorine and I took time to become reacquainted. Where I learnt that we were living a moderately comfortable life style.

That Dorine was a private secretary for a stock exchange firm, while continuing her studies to become a real estate agent hoping to open her own agency.

And I was a computer technician with my own business. Who were discussing are future and not anything about are past. Where thoughts became more reminiscent about my past life

With her saying that she sold the house and that I'm just going to love the one she just brought elsewhere away from all we were going to leave behind where we once lived

That she already had us packed and ready to move ourselves as soon as I was discharged. Not even discussing any of it with me away from what friends, I briefly met and the families that I never even met.

Saying that we could establish new lives for ourselves anywhere we wanted. That we are young enough to start over again that it was the perfect time to do it.

While not taking no, for an answer or bothering to listen to any of my objections. Saying that she made up her mind and that if I loved her that I would do things her way.

While discreetly approaching me using her most persuasive method to convince me to see things her way.

So we moved to Las Vegas to start a life for ourselves but, we didn't move alone. Not far behind us came all Dorine's close friends taking up residence as well.

However, during which all I really had was my business. I came upon something that just came upon me to try. When I acquired the interests to want to start writing.

The thought of which just popped into my mind and I couldn't get it out. Which didn't seem to bother Dorine until I started to ignore her to write down the thoughts that were coming into mine.

Then when she actually started to read what I was writing she started paying more attention to what it was.

I was writing while trying everything she could to distract, or discourage me from pursuing my new founded whim, she called it.

Suddenly wanting me to spend more time with her. Whenever I would even pick up a pen to do any writing.

Where if I didn't, she would instantly discredit what I was writing by mocking my abilities to write anything worthwhile. That anyone would want to waste their time to read.

Where she would instantly become bored and want to go out, or do others things that would take my mind off my nerve-racking obsession of wanting to be a writer.

Where when I did raise the question to Dorine about something that just occurred to me. She would account for it as a case of Da-Ja-Vue, and just to forget about it. It never happened so don't make anything out of it.

As the mouths past Dorine was sharing considerable more time with her friends who joined us. To which I really shared nothing in common. Them being scientists and having careers in the field of medicine.

Where my attempts to find something in common cause me to listen to them more closely I became to hear things that I seemed to be able to associate with but, was very reluctant to bring any questions I might have up. basically not wanting to look like a total idiot.

However, the more I heard the more I wanted to find out more. Being a person with a curious mind, I got really attentively nosey.

Where I was overhearing them discussing subjects like cloning and some guy by the name of professor James Baron. Whom the government was extensively searching for.

Because he was involved is some top secret government experiment projects that was causing the government a great deal of concern,

That's when I heard someone mention the name Daryl Henderson when it caught my interest. Hearing that name caused alarms to go off in my head but I had no idea why, or who the hell he was that would cause me to have such a reaction.

Having established my own business in trouble shooting computers. I did a lot of personal house calls while.

Doing so I couldn't help to overhear as well as discover a lot of hidden secrets that people would want to keep secrets on their computers. That I became aware of while repairing, or updating their computers.

Where some of them were even personal friends of ours, whereas a favor, I would keep their computers in working condition for free.

Where they would leave me alone while I was doing it. Not paying me any mind about having access to their personal information. Having to know that they were exposing their intimated personal affairs to me.

Where I was finding myself discovering increasingly more about this professor, James Baron, and what he was really involved getting himself into.

By this time Dorine and I were both in and out of the house pretty much. So whenever time came for us to spend some time together it was important to us to get the most out of it.

Where I was becoming increasingly obsessive with writing. When the thoughts were fresh and running rapid through my mind. Especially when they were about this James Baron.

Whom I have only been hearing bits and paces of about where I had one hell of a creative imagination to fill in the blanks.

Especially when all my wife friends seem to know about, where I had nothing but a common interest.

When Dorine came walking in wearing nothing but, her sinuous smile. Enticingly motioning at with her finger that she needed some much needed attentions from me. Catching me in the process of writing away on my computer.

Only to prop both her hands on her hips annoyingly asking. "Just what are you doing beside denying your love strived wife the loving she needs." Prancing up to me, noticeably agitated saying.

"All right Clay Morrison just what are you doing? How many times have I told you your writing those ridiculous stories are nothing but, a waste of time?

That on one is ever going to believe anything you write in them. Why they are nothing but, meaningless fictional stories.

There has to be something better you can do with your time alone with me. Than wasting it on writing you fantasies about being some sort of obnoxious private detective.

Now come with me where you belong. Where you can put all that creativity to good uses. It's getting late, and both of us have to get up early tomorrow.

Beside I can give you a fantasy to really write about. That is nothing less than real in every incredible detail."

She took hold of my hands taking them off the key board. Placing them upon her hips. Turning me sideways in the chair to face her, standing beside me.

Moving herself extremely closer to me sitting before her. Making sure that I could inhale her enchanting sent hoping to hypnotically in spell me. Only to step back, pulling me with her up onto my feet.

Literally floating me out of the office. Totally erasing my mind of having any other thought but, of her using her bewitching beguiling charms on me. Mystically mesmerizing me to her will.

"With me being possessed, representing my lack of willpower to fight against her spill of enchantment by saying.

I mustered every ounce of willpower I could come up with to express my last free words saying.

"I'm going to get me an agent, and let them tell me I'm wasting my time."

"As she responded back by saying only two words. Yes, dear" Where upon I found myself, living the fantasy of fantasies in the loving arms of the most unbelievably dazzling women that god, himself had to hate himself for ever letting get away of him.

Dorine was any man's dream come true. Now ever she had this uncanny disposition when it can to certain subjects about certain improprieties that I seemed to have developed that irritated the hell out of her.

One being that I was developing this obsession of wanting to become a private detective, and then there was this craving to try my hand at writing story's no less.

Where she would try anything, she could to discourage me from. Even going so far as attempting to do anything she totally disagreed with. Using any and all means at her disposal if you know what I mean.

If, and when she ever caught me attempting to write anything that didn't pertain to my business, or her.

She would find a way to drag me away from doing anything else but thinking only of her going to any extreme she had to. "

I know what she was telling me and maybe she was trying to protect me from any embarrassment that I might inflict upon myself. By making an idiot out of myself, trying to be a writer but, it was what I wanted to do. Good, or bad, or even ridiculously terrible I wanted to know.

Where I had to admit, I was harboring a lot of doubts basically because of the story that was haunting me to write.

Whereas I felt so damn certain about being able to write a believable story, because I honestly felt as though I actually live it myself. The only drawback was the ending.

Fragments of names, places, and horrendous events I felt I could really bring to life so that it would appear too really had happened.

Until it came to the ending where everything was a blank, if that wasn't baffling enough what made the story so real to me was that name, professor James Baron.

The very one I was taking such great interest in was the one that I was hearing, and reading about. Where I never met the person but, what I know about him seemed so true. As if I did in fact have had dealing with the guy.

Names, and place became so vivid that I could describe them in detail. Along with the events that took place there.

That apparently I had to have taken an active part in. Not to have known where they could have existed, or how to find out if in fact they ever did.

One name in particular keeps popping into my mind. It was a place called The High Hat Club. I could explicitly picture it in my mind.

Where then again I couldn't focus on it what it actually looked enough like to describe what it was. It was to vaguely represented from what I could see.

I wanted to discuss it with Dorine but, something made me extremely skeptical of making her aware of why I was so obsessing with writing down what was going on in my head. When I did manage to document what came as flashed in my mind.

What I did manage to write down didn't make any damn sense. Without the places, or the people represented to fill in the blanks.

What seemed to be bothering me the most was why Dorine suddenly just upped and sold everything we supposedly worked for. Too up and move over night so to speak to Las Vegas where it was ungodly hot all the damn time.

Where she actually appears to be happy and content socializing with her few friends where I couldn't seem to be able to make any that she could feel comfortable around so I avoided bringing anyone over to introduce them to her.

Instead I just met up with them when I was out doing business. Still, not mentioning anything to any of them.

Being concern if what I said might have actually of taking place, and Dorine would find out. There was no telling just how upset she might become over me not confiding in her, or feeling that I couldn't trust her enough.

Making her feeling separated from me where the last thing I want to do was for us to break up over my obsession of wanting to write. The only story that was happening in my head.

After more than a year and a half past I secretly finally finish what I could construct of the story I was obsessed to write. Then finally found myself an agent to take a chance on it actually selling. Otherwise, you wouldn't be reading it now.

Whether you the reader want to believe it, or not, is up to you. As for the ending I got this feeling that if my wife finds out about what I did. My marriage would constitute for a part of it.

As for it ever happening I went back to where I once lived. No, I couldn't find any High Hat Club. I did however did find a lot of coastal ocean cottages.

As for where I thought the building was located that housed my detectives' office. Now that was there along with a lot of newer and taller building as well.

I was thinking of going inside and asking around if anyone recognized me but, what in the hell good would that due me.

The only thing I could feel sure of us knowing the name of professor James Baron whose name was placed all over the newspapers, who was even is in fact still wanted by the FBI.

As far as any of it being possible. If you can believe that I did manage to become someone else. Now if you believe that anything is possible, right?

However, it might have been accomplished it work better than anyone could have thought. I was informed by my wife just a couple of mouths again. That I'm about to become a father.

Now I ask you. If it's actually possible for a clone of someone else to father another actual human child?

Good luck with figuring out what could be a rational, or believable ending.

THE END

www.ingramcontent.com/pod-product-compliance
Lightning Source LLC
Chambersburg PA
CBHW071427070526
44578CB00001B/24